Rethinking Literacy Education

Rethinking
Literacy
Education

The Critical Need for
Practice-Based Change

B. Allan Quigley

Jossey-Bass Publishers • San Francisco

Substantial discounts on bulk quantities of Jossey-Bass books are available to corporations, professional associations, and other organizations. For details and discount information, contact the special sales department at Jossey-Bass Inc., Publishers (415) 433–1740; Fax (800) 605–2665.

For sales outside the United States, please contact your local Simon & Schuster International Office.

(See page 286 for copyright credits.)

 Manufactured in the United States of America on Lyons Falls Pathfinder Tradebook. This paper is acid-free and 100 percent totally chlorine-free.

Library of Congress Cataloging-in-Publication Data

Quigley, B. Allan (Benjamin Allan)
    Rethinking literacy education : The critical need for practice-based change /
    B. Allan Quigley.
        p. cm.—(The Jossey-Bass higher and adult education series)
    Includes bibliographical references and index.
    ISBN 0–7879–0287–X
    1. Literacy—United States. 2. Language arts. 3. Adult education—United States.
    I. Title. II. Series.
    LC151.Q85 1997
    302.2'244—dc20   96–21258

FIRST EDITION
HB Printing   10 9 8 7 6 5 4 3 2 1

The Jossey-Bass
Higher and Adult Education Series

Consulting Editor
Adult and Continuing Education
Alan B. Knox
University of Wisconsin, Madison

Contents

They live no longer in the faith of reason;
But still the heart doth need a language.

—COLERIDGE, "The Piccolomini"
Act II, Scene 4

Preface

In 1975, the U.S. Commissioner of Education, Terence Bell, shocked the nation with the announcement that more than half of the U.S. adult population was "functionally illiterate." According to the results of the Adult Performance Level tests, approximately 54 percent of America's adult population was unable to function proficiently because of low literacy (Dorland, 1978). For months, the press was filled with statements of outrage. How was this possible in the wealthiest nation on earth? In the subsequent two decades, politicians, educators, business leaders, and countless volunteers have been engaged in attempting to eradicate illiteracy. Yet in 1993, the comprehensive *National Adult Literacy Survey* reported that approximately 47 percent of the adult population still had low literacy skills—some 94 million adults (Kirsch, Jungeblut, Jenkins, and Kolstad, 1993). This news held the media's interest for less than two weeks. No shock. No public outcry. And no major literacy campaign followed.

As we prepare to leave the twentieth century behind, today's question is "Is it possible that the wealthiest nation on earth is simply giving up on its least educated citizens?"

Scope of This Book

If the future of adult literacy education is to be an improvement on the past, decisions need to be based on a better consideration of choices. These choices should be identified and evaluated by those in the best position to understand them, and it is the view presented in this book that that role properly belongs to literacy practitioners who have a long-term commitment to the field. It is the practitioner, not the politician and not the researcher, who will turn illiteracy around in America.

However, practitioners have great difficulty seeing themselves as much more than passive participants in a system governed by political and public initiatives. At a time when they should be asserting their leadership, most literacy practitioners fear for the very existence of their programs.

This book offers such practitioners concrete suggestions for program improvement. It also addresses wider issues that go beyond everyday literacy practice. One of its central concerns is the stereotyping of the illiterate in the media and in social policy.

The book attempts to build a new foundation for practice-based change by examining the history of two radically different views of illiteracy in America—the "political perspective" and the "popular perspective." With this understanding established, practitioners are encouraged to develop clear working philosophies that will inform future practice decisions and to bring these philosophies to bear on such major issues as hidden curricula, retention, and the recruitment of the most resistant learners. The book concludes with a discussion of ways practitioners can advocate for change at political and public levels.

Intended Audience

Rethinking Literacy Education has been written for all those concerned with the challenges posed by adult illiteracy in the United States. It speaks directly to teachers and tutors (both those who have been in the field for many years and those just entering it), administrators, researchers, and policy makers, and also has much to offer those who are interested in literacy issues without being involved with them professionally.

If you are an administrator, the book will encourage you to consider new options conducive to greater program stability and effectiveness. It will provide concrete suggestions for retaining at-risk learners and for reaching and involving reluctant ones.

If you are a teacher or tutor, the book will help you to take a fresh look at the methods and materials you are using and will provide guidance on developing a clear working philosophy for daily practice. You will learn also about a system of "action research" that can validate new ideas and build a case for new resources and approaches.

If you are a policy maker, you will find fresh perspectives on literacy issues and a model for building a statewide or multistate knowledge base to inform future policy.

If you are a researcher, you will draw useful information from several accounts of qualitative and quantitative research studies and will be provoked by a continual stream of research questions to new reflections on your work.

Overview of the Contents

The book is organized in four parts, each of which looks at literacy and literacy education through different eyes.

Part One looks at literacy through the eyes of society, with particular emphasis on the media (Chapter Two) and on political policies (Chapter Three). It shows how both the public and the political perspectives have helped create the restrictive world in which practitioners work today.

Part Two looks at literacy through the eyes of practitioners. It consists of two chapters. Chapter Four will assist practitioners in clarifying their own working philosophies so that they can make better practice choices in their classrooms and tutoring situations. This chapter suggests ways to restructure entire classrooms, programs, and institutions around learners' interests and practitioners' strengths. Chapter Five explores the rarely discussed issue of the hidden curricula found in many commercial texts used in literacy today. It also discusses possible solutions to the problem.

Part Three looks at our field through the eyes of at-risk learners and potential learners. Chapter Six discusses at-risk learners who drop out of programs in the first three weeks and suggests specific steps that can be taken to address this critical issue. Chapter Seven is concerned with those adults who resist our programs altogether; again, suggestions for action are offered.

The principal thrust of Part Four is to show how action research by practitioners can be used to test ideas, create knowledge, and advocate for change. Chapter Eight, after enumerating the practical considerations involved in such research projects, goes on to outline a multistate model for action research that could help build a better knowledge base for practice and policy change. The concluding chapter is essentially an appeal to practitioners and others who care about low-literate adults and the future of literacy in this country to rededicate themselves to the work of advancing the field.

In sum, *Rethinking Literacy Education* attempts to show how the decisions we make today are influenced by the patterns of the past and to open up new ways of understanding and practicing that are appropriate for the coming century.

Acknowledgments

This book would not have been written without the help and inspiration of many people. I would like to acknowledge the "Monroeville Center Family" for their help through the years: Joann Wilson, Anna Mae Keibler, Roxanne Daykon, Mark Vrabel, Antoinnette Capo, and Lynn Ramich. The following students and colleagues provided invaluable help with the research and preparation of the manuscript: Gary Kuhne, Roberta Uhland, Jane Deacle, Debra Doyle, James Mader, Raiana Mearns, and Mary and Gerald Cumer. I am deeply indebted to my own teachers and mentors: Alice Blakely, Marg Barclay, Dave Carton, John Niemi, Phyllis Cunningham, Sherman Stanage, and Ron Cervero. I am indebted also to my many friends in this field, including Ann Benesh, Jake Kutarna, John Biss, Bill Black, Jack Mitchell, and Terry Hansen. For their scholastic work and personal inspiration, I am particularly indebted to my colleagues Fred Schied, Hal Beder, Tom Valentine, Elizabeth Hayes, and above all, Hanna Fingeret.

This book is the result of the love given me by my wife, Linda, and my son, Patrick. They have always believed in me, and I in them. Finally, this book is dedicated to the memory of my mother and my father.

Monroeville, Pennsylvania   B. Allan Quigley
August, 1996

The Author

B. Allan Quigley is associate professor and regional director of adult education at Penn State University. He earned his B.A. in English (1967) and M.A. in English (1975) at the University of Regina, Saskatchewan, Canada. He earned his doctorate (1987) in adult and continuing education at Northern Illinois University, DeKalb.

Quigley has been working in the field of adult literacy education since 1972. Before joining Penn State, he was director of the university affairs branch of the Department of Education, Government of Saskatchewan, and prior to that was the department's coordinator of community colleges. In his earlier career, he was director of adult basic education at Regina Plains Community College in Regina—an institution he helped found—and director of further education at Keyano College in Fort McMurray, Alberta.

Quigley received the Pennsylvania Outstanding Adult Educator Award in 1994, the Award for Academic Excellence from Penn State in 1996, and the Graduate Student Research Award from the Adult Education Research conference in 1987. His main research interests have been resistance to adult literacy and ways to improve literacy programs at the teaching, administration, and policy levels. He has published articles on the history of literacy, resistance to literacy education, retention of literacy students, and social policy in adult education. He is the editor of *Fulfilling the Promise of Adult and Continuing Education* (1989).

Quigley has served on the advisory board of the GED Testing Service, the executive committee of the Commission of Professors of Adult Education, and the Adult Education Research Conference steering committee. He is also a consulting editor for several adult education journals in the United States and Canada. He works as an adviser to corporate trainers and leaders in volunteer organizations, and serves on several state government committees as well as the National GED Advisory Board.

Rethinking Literacy Education

Part One

Illiteracy Through Society's Eyes

Chapter One

Myths, Rhetoric, and Stereotypes About Literacy

To enter the world of adult low literacy is to enter a world unlike any other. Here is a world of hope, triumph, fear, and guilt. Here is an emotionally charged world of conflicting realities only partially seen. Consider the story of a man named Curtis who called a Syracuse radio station to explain what it is like to have minimal literacy skills:

> I have two kids. What do I do if one of my kids starts choking and I go running to the phone? Nine times out of ten, I can't look up the phone number of the hospital. That's if we're at home. Like if we're out on the street, nine times out of ten I can't read the street. If I should get to a pay phone, and they say, ok, tell us where you are, we'll send an ambulance. I look at the street sign. . . . I'd have to spell it letter for letter. By that time, one of my kids could be dead [Eberle and Robinson, 1980, p. 11].

Illiteracy is "20th century leprosy," according to "Mr. X," a man who refused to be identified in a report prepared by a team of literacy researchers:

> Well, right off the bat, if somebody can't read, people instamatically figure that he's stupid, or that he's dumb or that there's something wrong with him mentally. And the major reason why I don't want to be called by my regular name is, I guess you'd call it: fear. Not being able to read is 20th century leprosy is what it is, because people treat you different [Eberle and Robinson, 1980, p. 2].

Adult literacy education has a greater potential to make an immediate and dramatic impact on learners than any other field of teaching. Furthermore, no other field is so basic to a civilized society. Yet despite its value and the past century of literacy rhetoric, adult literacy education is in trouble. Though it has countless stories of inspiration and triumph to tell, it approaches the next century in urgent need of support and renewal.

As it enters the twenty-first century, adult literacy education needs to assess where it has been, consider what it has become, and address some of the conflicting realities that not only have shaped it but continue to control it.

Three Sets of Perceptions

Bourdieu has stated, "Reality is not an absolute . . . it differs with the group to which one belongs" (1971, p. 195). As we journey through the world of adult literacy education in this book, our understanding will depend on our ability to recognize whose interpretation of reality we are exploring. The suggestions and recommendations throughout are made with this in mind. The book is structured around three perceptions of literacy reality, each one having its own profound effect on practice. The three must be seen in sequence, I believe, if they are all to be clear. Even then, there will be contradictions, but at least the traveler will have a map of the territory and will know where the suggestions can be applied.

The first perception of low literacy to be examined is society's. This view includes larger-than-life literacy myths transmitted by our Western culture. One might compare these to the experience of a ship's passenger first seeing the fogbound coast of an unknown island. The passenger strains to determine what the terrain and the people there are like, and is influenced by what others on board have to say about the island. Others along the deck's railing have heard various stories while on earlier voyages and now, embellishing upon them, pass along remarkable stories that have little or nothing to do with what one would actually find if one went ashore to stay and work. This is the equivalent of the romanticized view-from-a-distance of low literacy as created and sustained by the public and political media through time. However, the myths reported are not lost on those who actually go ashore. Here are the literacy practitioners. We develop an ability to recreate the myths for other passing ships as an important part of our funding survival. In fact, it has come to be about the only way we know to keep the colony alive. As a friend of mine in literacy education has said, "We often do the wrong things for the right reasons."

The second perception is that of teachers, tutors, counselors, and administrators, already "on the island." Practitioners have evolved their own myths, which are based in part on the low-literate adults they have worked with and in part on the myths they have inherited. Of course, their perception of literacy reality is not based on the entire population of low literates or even on the majority, because no one has ever conducted a comprehensive study of the entire population at an in-depth level. The present book has been written for such professionals.

Finally, there is the multiple set of perceptions of low-literate adults themselves—some ninety-four million adults in the United States, a population more than twice that of Canada and Australia combined. So much is assumed about this group by the wider society and by literacy professionals that we need to proceed with caution. Fingeret once noted that for the literate general population, "It is difficult to conceptualize life without reading and writing as anything other than a limited, dull, dependent existence" (1983, p. 133). Few low literates would agree with this characterization, and many practitioners would personally and professionally also disagree with it (Fingeret, 1982). However, the field is so dependent on interested outsiders for its survival that practitioners have become dependent on such myths and rarely protest. The more immediate problem, however, is that fewer and fewer outsiders have been taking an interest over the past few years.

Practicing in Literacy Education

Those of us who have chosen to stay in the field will know that one does not really develop a "career path"; one typically just manages to survive. Although it is not an easy profession, nor a highly prestigious one, and far from well paid (if one is paid at all), it is a profession with enormous personal reward.

What is it like to be an adult literacy teacher, tutor, or administrator? Most conversations I have had on the subject of adult literacy seem to begin with what I have called "the amazement stage"—for example, "How could so many be illiterate in this day and age?" This is usually followed by the "name the cause stage," when the person asks, "What is wrong with our schools anyway?" or "Why wouldn't people want to learn something that important early in life?" Finally comes the "disassociation stage"—disassociation from the subject and, at times, from me: "Well, it's awful. I must go. But I wish you luck." If one introduces oneself as a college professor, school teacher, or kindergarten teacher, the response is entirely different.

Why are there such universally powerful reactions to illiteracy in the public world? No other area of adult education elicits the range of emotions that literacy does. No other carries as many stereotypes. How is it possible that such a huge group could be reduced to stereotypes in the first place? Is it possible that the stereotypes imposed on our field at the public level and the marginalization literacy education suffers at the political level are somehow linked? Could it be that we practitioners contribute to some of the program uncertainties and problems we experience? Political and public support for literacy education rises and falls, and with it goes our program destiny. Or does it? The purpose of this book is to question assumptions within our field of practice. It is to try to draw a map and explore it with a view to making suggestions for the future.

Keeping Up Appearances

Keeping up appearances before those who influence policy and make governmental funding decisions has become an obsession in our field. Traditional adult literacy education programs are extremely dependent on governmental sources for their funding; however, the funds have been dwindling and are extremely uncertain as we approach the end of the century.

In 1980, the federal government provided approximately 57 percent of the funding for basic programs within adult literacy education, but by 1991, that figure had dropped to 20 percent (National Adult Education Professional Development Consortium [NAEPDC], 1991). As an Office of Technology Assessment report concluded: "The federal literacy expenditure is small in comparison with the overall State expenditures for literacy and for other major federal education programs. . . . meager in terms of the total population in need, and low as a national priority (U.S. Congress, 1993, p. 12). Although it is true that states have been filling some of the funding gaps (Beder, 1994) and overall governmental funding for literacy education has grown over time, few in the field would agree that it has grown nearly enough.

From 1980 to 1991, the combined funding to adult literacy programs from states and the federal government rose almost four and a half times, from $174.3 million to $779 million—an increase of approximately $84.69 per student to $209.35 per student (National Adult Education Professional Development Consortium, 1991). However, compare this with U.S. public schools. The mean overall expenditure per student in U.S. elementary and high schools (in constant 1992–93 dollars) was $4,117 in 1980–81 and $5,991 in 1990–91 (National Center for Education Statistics, 1995, table 164). Beder has shown how federal funds have fallen and how states have come into the funding arena since 1980 and concludes, "No wonder we lack the capacity to do the job as it should be done" (1994, p. 18).

Through the years, many have attempted to argue that there should be some parity between child and adult literacy funding, but have failed to establish their case. Many political and public figures have contended that society should not have to spend twice on literacy—once for schoolchildren and again for adults who dropped out of school. However, others argue that literacy should be a right, not a privilege, and that the age of the learner should be irrelevant. As of 1996, the field is a long way from anything resembling parity with the public schools.

When I was an administrator of a literacy education program, I called a former adult literacy teacher and invited him to return to the field. He had left during one more "program restructuring." I offered him his old teaching job. There was a long silence. He then asked if he could have a contract that went beyond one year. I said, "Sorry, no. Our funding is on an annual basis." He asked if program funding was assured for next year. "Well, not really." His reply was: "I lived with that for eight years. I hate teaching in the school system, but I have to do it. I can't risk going back."

Not all of our problems arise from underfunding, however. Within the field of everyday practice, we deal with multiple problems.

According to some figures, funded programs in adult literacy attract only 8 percent of those eligible for them (Pugsley, 1990). Meanwhile, some 20 percent of those who say they will attend do not show up (Bean et al., 1989). Of those who do, the overall attrition rate during the 1993–94 program year was 74 percent (U.S. Department of Education, 1995). According to another study (Development Associates, 1993), the dropout rate was 18 percent before twelve hours of instruction had been completed, 20 percent at sixteen weeks, and 50 percent after sixteen weeks. What other area of education could live with such numbers? Also consider what "normal student contact" means for this field. On average, "adult literacy education students receive only 4.9 hours of instruction per week" (Beder, 1994, p. 16).

However, we need to keep up appearances. We are part of the myth-making process. Whether we want to or not, we explain and rationalize low recruitment levels and high dropout rates in terms that vastly oversimplify program realities and learners' lives. Although few practitioners want to admit it, we often stretch professional ethics to the limit with monthly and year-end reports of our "successes" (Kozol, 1985). A few years ago, I gave a presentation to a large group of state literacy administrators and talked about the issue of retaining adult students in programs. Before the presentation, I had called the state's department of education and asked for the statewide attrition rate. I wrote it on the flip chart and used it in my presentation. Afterwards, an official from the federal government came up and introduced himself. He turned back the pages of the flip chart to attrition numbers he himself had put up only the day before. The ones given him on official forms were less than half those that I, a "neutral researcher," had been given. We stared at each other, not wanting to say the obvious. Who benefits from sustaining these types of appearances? Is this what we truly want for our field?

The Training Gap

We have remarkably limited training for most literacy teachers and tutors in our traditional literacy programs. A study by the NAEPDC (Development Associates, 1992) reported that 3,696,973 learners were being served by federally funded programs in 1990. Within those programs, over 80 percent of the staff worked part-time. In fact, part-time instructors constituted 71 percent of the teaching force in 1980 but rose to 88 percent by 1991. The NAEPDC study revealed that over 95 percent of this part-time teaching workforce had college degrees and almost 88 percent were certified to teach children, but only 31 percent of the programs reporting said they had anyone with adult education qualifications. Meanwhile, approximately 75 percent of these programs used volunteers, usually as tutors. A second study in the early 1990s indicated that 45 percent of the federally funded adult literacy programs "do not have a single staff person certified in adult education [or] a single full time instructor or administrator" (U.S. Congress, Office of Technology Assessment, 1993, p. 115). Unlike in the school system, where all teachers are expected to have certification, in 1989 only "eleven states required certification in adult literacy[;] the requirements ranged from the equivalence of a master's degree in adult education to attendance at an annual workshop. Fourteen states required certification in elementary/secondary, but not adult education. Twenty-five states required no certification" (Beder, 1994, p. 16). Understandably, "This is how we do it here" often becomes the training and orientation for new teachers of adults.

"How things are done here" encompasses all sorts of assumptions and influences. I remember working in a large vocational school that had an adult literacy program—or "Vocational Preparation Program," as it was called. Like a school for children, this institution had coffee and lunch breaks that were indicated by a bell. Each instructor had his or her own designated chair in the staff room. Each had his or her own cultivated idiosyncrasies. Mine, unfortunately, was to allow learners to come into the staff room to talk to me. No one on this staff had any formal adult education training, including me. The teachers had K–12 qualifications or vocational school training. Very early on, after several "transgressions," I was informed that "students are not welcome in here." They were a nuisance, and this was the place we came to escape from them. There was no doubt that new instructors were indoctrinated early.

By contrast, I remember a teacher with a master's in social work whom I had hired in a literacy program. She considered quitting her job to devote her full-time energies to rehabilitating a student who had become addicted to drugs. I remember another with a teaching certificate who had an emotional breakdown when she read that one of her students had been murdered and his body found in a dumpster not far from our center. Neither of these teachers had adult education training. While I had hired very caring teachers for the second program and staff orientation was centered around concern for learner needs, I soon realized that, as Fingeret and Danin have stated, "Simply working with a caring individual is not enough" (1991, p. 90). I organized professional development workshops on where the responsibility of teachers should end and where that of local community agencies should begin, but there remained an ongoing debate among my staff about how much help is too much. Clearly, we need much more professional development in literacy, but professional development that prepares one for the complex emotional demands that come with many of our learners.

Whether adult low literates appear as helpless or hopeless, or both, we have stereotypes that are widely accepted in the field. These are passed along with each generation of teachers and tutors. At the program level, we need to ask why the accepted stereotypes exist, what appearances we find ourselves trying to sustain, and what the effects are of appearances on our practice.

The Need for Change

Although we can and should ask the questions posed here, it is extremely difficult to do so without a historical context. Much of what we observe and experience in our programs was not created in our time. In fact, many of today's perceptions of literacy reality are embedded in class, race, gender, and a hierarchy of educational knowledge. After a quarter-century serving in a range of capacities in this field, I have come to believe that if adult literacy education is to gain longer-term stability, a clearer sense of purpose, and a say in its own destiny, we must first obtain a clearer picture of where we have been.

However, it is one thing to be able to explain better how we have come to do what we do, why we accept our practice as it is, and why we often perpetuate appearances. It is quite another to be willing to act on these insights. In concluding this book, I will argue that the way to guide ourselves and our field is not on the basis of what researchers or our leaders of the moment tell us. Our guide must be what brought us into the field and has kept us there: our ethics as expressed in a personal working philosophy (Apps, 1973; Cervero, 1988).

Clarification of Terms

In the face of competing nomenclatures, this book adopts the one commonly used by programmers. *Adult literacy* refers to the general field of practice and study. *Basic literacy* refers to volunteer and part-time programs dedicated to teaching adults the skills of reading and writing. *Adult basic education (ABE)* denotes those programs, usually funded by state and/or federal sources, that include levels of reading above basic literacy; such programs often add other subject material, ranging from math to science to government. General equivalency diploma (GED) preparation programs are typically understood to be the senior level of what is referred to here as *adult literacy programming*. The GED exams for high school students are set by the GED Testing Service in Washington, D.C. (Quigley, 1991a).

The Question of Definitions

Few topics in literacy education have been written on more than how to define *literacy, illiteracy, numeracy,* or *basic education* (Beder, 1989a; Cervero, 1984; Clark, 1984; Cunningham, 1989; Levine, 1982).

Some years ago, I was invited to be part of a "literacy definition committee" at the state level. It was explained by a senior official that the committee's mandate was to find a way of determining how many low literates there were in the state. He said the federal government required a figure from each state "soon." We sat in a polite circle, note pads in hand. One committee member thought illiterates' individual IQs should play a part in the definition. Many of his students were just incapable of learning anything, he said. Following that comment, another member said she would quit the committee if IQ was included. After a pause, someone said the definition should be based on a school standard, maybe grade ten. Others said that would never work: there was no such uniform standard in the state and, anyway, if a person had graduated from grade ten in 1964, did that mean he or she was still reading at a grade ten level? A few members thought grade nine would be better.

After another pause, one member argued for the competency approach, reminding the committee that the Adult Performance Levels (APL) testing of the late 1960s found what adults could accomplish in specific literacy situations; this measure indicated how well adults could function in the "real world" and was therefore better than grade level. Someone else pointed out, however, that that entire study and movement were discredited in the late 1970s because the criteria used and the tasks for accomplishment were so culturally biased (Cervero, 1980); this was not a measure of low literates' real world.

My own less-than-inspired contribution was to refer to literature on the many definitions that had been concocted through history and to say that we probably did not need to do what others had been doing for decades (Clark, 1984). Why not look at the work of those who had preceded us and then try to go from there? This, however, would mean doing background reading. Moreover, the committee was expected to come up with something "brand new."

As the pauses built and the committee members began looking at their watches, someone suggested that the funds being spent on our committee might be better spent on programs. On this, everyone agreed.

Senior state officials who subsequently commented on this committee's efforts said the state was "blessed" by so many opinions and would attempt to "synthesize" a definition for itself. The result, predictably, was a school-based benchmark definition. Meanwhile, the federal government came up with its own definition in the National Literacy Act of 1991 (*Highlights*, 1991) (to be described later in this chapter), which eclipsed all others, and the momentary crisis in the state office passed.

This committee, in its complete inability to agree on what literacy was, or should be, was far from unique. Literacy and illiteracy have been defined and redefined over and over. Enormous ambiguity is tolerated, even encouraged. If one turns to the research literature and asks what would seem to be a straightforward question, "What are literacy and illiteracy?" one finds definitions abounding. In just a preliminary study of definitions in the literature, I have personally found more than 150 official and unofficial definitions used since 1880 (Beder, 1989a; Clark, 1984; Ilsley and Stahl, 1994). These have since been categorized and subdivided through time (Clark, 1984; Griffith, 1990). Beder (1991) is one of many who have recapitulated the "definitions debate" of literacy education in recent years. He distinguishes between *absolute standard* (1991, p. 2) definitions that use a grade-level set of skill criteria (Cervero, 1984) and definitions that refer to a broad base of cultural knowledge which, as E. D. Hirsch (1988) argues, all Americans must possess to be "culturally literate." Most of the census definitions of illiteracy since 1880 have been of the former, absolute grade-level type (Cook, 1977), which supports the goal of counting the total illiterate population (Cervero, 1984).

On the other hand, Beder reports how the *relativist school* disagrees with the concepts just described. For this school, the issue of literacy and illiteracy is not one of measurable skills or bulk of knowledge but one of context, environment, and the ability to handle various tasks that the adult confronts in everyday life (Cook, 1977; Hunter and Harman, 1979; Levine, 1982). Here, there is no "absolute." From this point of view, a grade nine or a grade ten is a meaningless national standard for several reasons. First, no two states necessarily have the same grade-level criteria. Second, because few adults stay at the same educational level throughout their lives, the benchmark is far from useful as a single standard. But the strongest argument made by the relativist school is that literacy must be seen in relation to the cultural setting. As Hunter and Harman concluded almost two decades ago, "All definitions of literacy or illiteracy are completely relative" (1979, p. 10). Here, the issue is not what the school system may have said but what the world of the adult low literate demands. Work on functional literacy, such as the APL studies mentioned above, has developed primarily out of the relativist school (Cook, 1977). This school appeals almost universally to adult educators, less so to government officials. It recognizes the realities of the learner's world and the necessity to make literacy education relevant to that world.

However, the approach is clearly limited by the fact that adults are mobile; they move both geographically and culturally. Contexts change. The relativist definition for one setting may not be appropriate for another.

What does it say about our field when there are such deep disagreements over definitions (Cunningham, 1989)? Cervero (1984) has discussed how the two schools described here, the absolute school and the relativist school, serve markedly different interests. The ability to "count heads" on the basis of an absolute standard or benchmark definition serves the interests of government policy makers and book publishers much more than those of learners or practitioners, he says. His point is well illustrated by two definitions of literacy that have appeared in the past few years. The 1993 *National Adult Literacy Survey* (NALS) (Kirsch, Jungeblat, Jenkins, and Kolstad, 1993) is the most recent and possibly the most significant survey of illiteracy in U.S. history. It has had few serious critics (see Sticht and Armstrong, 1996). Contained within it is what might be the essential definition of literacy: "Using printed and written information to function in society, to achieve one's goals, and to develop one's knowledge and potential" (Kirsch, Jungeblut, Jenkins, and Kolstad, 1993, p. 2). The definition has a clear relativist perspective.

It will be remembered that the U.S. Department of Education, which sponsored the NALS, had its own definition enshrined in the National Literacy Act of 1991, with an absolute standard connotation: "An individual's ability to read, write, and speak in English, and compute and solve problems at levels of proficiency necessary to function on the job and in society, to achieve one's goals, and develop one's knowledge and potential" (National Literacy Act of 1991, Section three; *Highlights,* 1991). The references to goals and potential were additions that were vigorously fought for by a small number of adult literacy educators who had been invited to advise the political decision makers on "what literacy is" (Quigley, 1993a).

Either of these new definitions might have been enough for one decade. However, the earlier "official definition" of the National Literacy Act no longer exists because the act has been rescinded. The present debate over what legislation should replace it seems to now see literacy as an ability to contribute to the workforce and to assume family values and civic responsibilities. Sadly, the *National Adult Literacy Survey* that many thought would spark a fire of public debate only sputtered in the media for a few days during fall 1993.

There is nothing inherently confusing in the skills that constitute literacy. However, the many ways our society and our profession have chosen to construct literacy is indicative of the multiple realities at work in this field. As Courtney observed, "All definitions, regardless of how abstract and wide-ranging they may appear, are crafted within a specific ideology of practice" (1989, p. 23). We are part of the reality of the groups to which we belong, and each group has its own agenda. It is not just that we in the field are "victims" of competing realities; most of us foster and function out of those realities that we believe are "normal" and "best." The basic problem is awareness—being aware of where the myths and stereotypes come from, why, and what they are doing to us when they are uncritically accepted as the only possible reality.

Winchester (1990) has observed that "faith in the powers of literacy to end discrimination, oppression, and indignity is a faith forged in the nineteenth century" (p. 21). Arnove and Graff have studied literacy campaigns and their purposes through history. They have concluded: "In the twentieth century . . . pronouncements about literacy deem it a process of critical consciousness-raising and human liberation. Just as frequently, such declarations refer to literacy, not as an end itself, but as a means to other goals—to the ends of national development and to a social order that elites, both national and international, define" (1987, p. 2). We have a long legacy of purposes and politics, definitions and ideologies.

If we are to move forward in the field of adult literacy, we must first get beneath literacy definitions and the schools they reflect. We need a clearer focus on how we have been shaped by definitions and constructs. We need to understand more about the definers, their purposes, and their orientations, and above all, about the conflicting perceptions of reality that are now our legacies (Graff, 1987).

How History Could Help

As the twenty-first century looms, it would surely make sense to look around to see what promising practices, what successful programs, what parts of campaigns should be built on for the future. However, we have great difficulty learning from the past in adult literacy. Mirroring the political world that we depend on for funding, our general attitude seems to be that the past was not particularly successful, therefore not particularly relevant. As in the definitions committee mandate given us by the state, there is a constant desire to begin "afresh." This tends to create a field without a historical context and, at the practice level, what Foucault might call "false consciousness" (1972). The "ahistorical sense" of ourselves, in combination with high levels of dependence on ever-changing political agendas, has created an unusually willing acceptance of others' perceptions of reality and appearances.

At the most basic informational level, we lack a published history of the events of adult literacy in America. Cook's thin 1977 history is now long since outdated and rarely referred to. Stubblefield and Keane include literacy in a chapter of their 1994 book *Adult Education in the American Experience,* and adult literacy is briefly discussed in texts such as Merriam and Cunningham's *The Handbook of Adult and Continuing Education* (1989) and Fingeret and Jurmo's *Participatory Literacy Education* (1989). Without more substantial histories, we have no clear memory of where we have been in adult literacy education. The enormously complex questions of what illiteracy is, why it exists, how it affects people, and what adult education and social policy makers need to do about it are typically addressed only in the context of current issues.

If we were more aware of our history, we would surely ask why we keep trying the failed and ignoring the successful. At a minimum, we would see patterns that are relevant today. Very briefly, the first literacy campaign—or "crusade," as it was called in 1924—was headed by John Finley of the *New York Times.* According to Cook, "Most likely the purpose of the crusade was to 'eradicate illiteracy,' but there is no evidence of its goals" (1977, p. 30). Although it seems to have accomplished nothing, "there was a group of people, concerned about this problem at the national level, who made some attempt to organize and work with the problem" (pp. 30–31). Many today will agree that public "consciousness raising" is a worthy cause, even if no one is taught to read a word.

By comparison with Finley's crusade, the efforts of President Hoover in 1929 were "sweeping," if less altruistic. With the goal of giving "five million adults an opportunity to learn to read and write before the 1930 census" (Cook, 1977, p. 31), a private group (again headed by Finley) was asked to raise its *own* funds for the campaign. It managed to bring in $52,001.99 (Cook, 1977)—approximately a penny per person. History shows that campaigns typically focus more on rhetoric than on funding and usually have several political agendas beyond the goal of literacy education (Arnove and Graff, 1987).

Even a casual examination of history would reveal that campaign oversell and subsequent failure have not been reserved for the United States. In 1964, UNESCO claimed that it could eliminate illiteracy worldwide, beginning with the Experimental World Literacy Program (Gillette, 1987). This quixotic and expensive effort was considered a failure even by UNESCO itself (Harman, 1977). According to the authors of the EWLP final assessment, "Literacy programs can only be fully functional . . . if they accord to social, cultural, and political change, as well as economic growth" (UNESCO and UNDP Secretariats, 1976, p. 122). The lessons of social, cultural, and political change have largely been ignored in U.S. texts and American literacy debates (Harman, 1977).

In the same heady year, 1964, the Economic Opportunity Act was passed to effect the elimination of illiteracy in America. Title II-b was aimed at "adults whose inability to speak, read, or write the English language constitutes a substantial impairment of their ability to get or retain employment," with a view to "making them less likely to become dependent on others, [improving] their ability to benefit from occupational training, and otherwise increasing their opportunities for more profitable and productive employment, and making them better able to meet their adult responsibilities" (Costa, 1988, p. 79).

The 1966 Adult Education Act expanded the promise and raised hopes even higher—miles higher. The U.S. Commissioner of Education James Allen told America that the Right to Read literacy campaign would be the "moonshot for the seventies" (Harman, 1987, p. 1).

Chapters Two and Three will take a closer look at the history and events that have helped shape our field.

The World We Believe In

One thing most can agree on is that ours has been an extremely busy field. Through the 1960s and 1970s, scholars rushed to add definitions and educational "hypotheses" for wide-scale experimentation (Anderson and Niemi, 1970). We have had no lack of models for campaigns or mechanistic programming (Cantor, 1992; Kozol, 1985; Soifer and others, 1990), no dearth of condemning appraisals (Mezirow, 1978; Mezirow, Darkenwald, and Knox, 1975), no shortage of personal position statements (Verner, 1973). However, when we turn to adult literacy research, we find mainly anecdotal and descriptive research (Fingeret, 1984; Wagner, 1991). As Fingeret found, philosophical or theoretical research in literacy education is extremely limited. Without a critical or historical context, it has been argued that much of our adult literacy research and funding have been dedicated to ultimately supporting what exists rather than seriously questioning it (Anderson and Niemi, 1970; Fingeret, 1984; Wagner, 1991).

A second point on which there has been wide agreement is that illiteracy is very expensive, both in socioeconomic terms and in terms of human dignity. The nation may be losing $20 billion annually "in direct industrial and tax expenditure" (Kozol, 1985, p. 14). The Senate Select Committee on Equal Opportunity stated that illiteracy had caused men between the ages of twenty-five and thirty-four with less than high school skills to lose $237 billion in earnings over their lifetimes (Kozol, 1985). Although the dollar figures in such estimates are rarely in the same ballpark, there is no doubt that the costs represented by business losses, reduced tax revenues, literacy program outlays, safety and health risks, and lost productivity are mammoth (Chisman, 1989, 1990).

On the level of human cost, testimonies by low-literate adults about their difficulties are legion. There is little argument that low literacy causes debilitating problems. As will be seen in Chapter Two, media stories of suffering have taken on something of a circus quality in recent years. However, adult literacy educators are daily witnesses to the real hardships imposed on many—not all—by the condition of illiteracy. They draw deep satisfaction from seeing individual lives changed through their work. As will be discussed in Part Four, it is the belief in the value of our work that needs to be our continued inspiration, our guide, and the source of our collective voice.

Attempting Change in a Time of Cynicism

After more than a century of various efforts in literacy education, perhaps there are no new ideas left. In fact, there is some evidence from art, literature, and social science that during the last ten years of a century, or *fin de siècle,* a certain despondency takes over. As noted in *A Handbook to Literature* (Thrall, Hibbard, and Holman, 1960), the end of each century is characterized by a mood of despair and anxiety. As a century winds down, it seems that everything has been tried and has failed. Society looks back, not ahead, yearning for a dimly recalled golden age. It anticipates the impending new century with a sense of gloom (Quigley, 1989). However, this is not the only response seen in the closing years of previous centuries (Thrall, Hibbard, and Holman, 1960). At the tail end of the nineteenth century, certain sea changes occurred in art, literature, politics, and social movements across North America and Europe. The 1890s also saw "radical or revolutionary social aspirations, marked by numerous 'new movements' (including the 'new woman,' who dared ride a bicycle and seek political suffrage) and by a general sense of emancipation from the traditional social and moral order" (Thrall, Hibbard, and Holman, 1960, p. 203). Historians have noted an attitude that says, "We have lost faith in the old ways, but we are going to try something radically new before the century ends."

For literacy, perhaps nothing can change. Political and public resignation may usher us into the next century. But it is equally possible to argue that the times have never been more open for radical change from the "bottom." It is a question of how our field chooses to interpret and respond to the world it is working in. A personal incident may help make the point. In the fall of 1995, I volunteered to provide "testimony" at the reauthorization hearings for the Adult Literacy Act and the Carl Perkins Vocational Act. A panel of senior officials from the U.S. Departments of Labor and Education held these meetings in several cities to gather verbal and written opinions before the two acts were to be debated in Congress. However, everyone entering the room knew that the acts—created and supported by a former Republican president and Democratic House and Senate—would probably not survive a new Democratic president and Republican Congress. The room setting was rather like that seen in newsreels of the 1948 McCarthy hearings, with a raised table draped in white from which government officials peered down on those of us who were seated in a row waiting to speak into our microphones. A full audience stood and sat in the crowded, overheated room.

The practitioners who spoke before me offered highly technical comments on language, percentages, and formulas found in
the acts. As politely as possible, they were questioned about their
testimony. But the repeated question from the panel was "And
where will these new funds come from?"

When my turn came around, I nervously made one overall
observation: we needed "a war on cynicism." I could see there was
some amusement with the notion. One or two dropped their pens
and settled back. Among other points, I said there was a time
when a report as comprehensive and respected as the recent
National Adult Literacy Survey, which found that over 90 million
adults were affected by low literacy, would have been cause for
public outcry. Instead, there was almost complete silence following its release. I asked why hearings such as these could not be
held around the country by federal and state officials to gain public input on issues of illiteracy. "Create a forum to raise the profile of illiteracy and the problems of illiteracy," I said. "This is the
tried and true method of support to our field." Panelists sat stone-
faced. I pushed on.

I argued that we could not seriously change the state of illiteracy without greater stability of programs and more full-time staff
to run them. Increased funds had been made available in the
National Literacy Act of 1991 for professional development, and
all states had been conducting much more development activity
(Pugsley, 1993). However, some literacy advisory boards were asking why such funds were not being put into the programs themselves. And in my view, universities were having great difficulty
"professionalizing" a field made up largely of volunteers and part-
time staff, especially when staff knew there were severe limits to
careers in literacy education. I said, "We have a staffing pyramid
with a huge base of volunteers and paraprofessionals, another second layer of part-time people above this, and a tiny peak of full-
time, literacy-trained staff at the top" (see Beder, 1994). I was
talking not at the micro level but about ill-defined, large-scale
needs. The panelists' eyes were glazing over. Some doodled on
their pads. I could imagine them drawing fat, topless pyramids.
Undaunted, I made my last point: we needed a longer-term commitment to the issues of illiteracy. "These two acts are the funding
lifeblood of this field," I said. "Since public debate has been a crit-

ical part of past efforts from policy makers, then perhaps you should continue with this format and build on it."

After being politely thanked, I was asked the anticipated question: "And where will new funds for all this come from?" My reply was probably not as polite as it should have been. "I can see that the idea of new funding is a point of amusement on the panel. This is too bad. There are many in the field willing to help you in any way they can, but frankly, this is a question you need to answer. You are the leadership at the governmental level." After a pause, I was asked if universities would do more. I thought they would probably do more professional development if there were a greater number of people to professionalize. The hearings ended. There were no further public hearings, no new funding. The two acts were rescinded the following year.

Recent social theorists—and in particular, postmodernists—have argued that there is a growing loss of faith in our traditions. Many will remember when "the answer" was technology—from labor-saving devices to mass investment in computer technology. People now wonder if they are slaves to systems they can neither understand nor control. There was a time when the education system, the justice system, the police system, the system of unionism, and the welfare system all inspired hope for social equity and a better life for all. Today, such systems are variously assailed as contributors to U.S. social problems. The promises of big systems for full-scale solutions carry little conviction. "Modernizing" and "development" are euphemisms for "someone else's agenda." Campaigns to eradicate illiteracy on a mass scale, which used to command a degree of public respect, are now a cue to switch channels.

Attempting Change in a Time of Opportunity

European and North American theorists in sociology, philosophy, and education have discerned a shift away from modernist naive optimism in the past two decades (Harvey, 1989; Lash, 1990; Lyotard, 1984; Foucault, 1986). Smart describes a "contemporary social, cultural and political condition" that carries a new way of seeing the world: "Postmodernity is a form of . . . reflection upon and a response to the accumulating signs of the limitations of modernity" (1993, p. 12).

The failure of many of the promises of the modern era has engendered great dissatisfaction in Western society, but there is also profound uncertainty about what should be tried next. As Chambers describes it: "We are witnesses to the ruins of previous orders of meaning that come to be re-elaborated, extended and ultimately undone. We are left turning over the traces, unwilling to succumb to their fading authority yet at the same time unsure of what lies in their abandon" (Chambers, 1990, pp. 1–2).

Postmodernity, says Smart, "is a way of living with the doubts, uncertainties and anxieties which seem increasingly to be a corollary of modernity, the inescapable price to be paid for the gains, the benefits and the pleasures associated with modernity" (1993, p. 12). According to the postmodernists, we no longer believe in modern solutions, we question almost everything. We grow cynical.

Yet some postmodernists, particularly those in North America (for example, Aronowitz and Giroux, 1991; Welch, 1990), argue against a nihilistic view of the world. They maintain that we now face exciting opportunities to envision and build more multicultural, diverse systems in society and in education that will reflect the complexity of the world we have entered. Rather than embracing singular solutions or grand narratives (Harvey, 1989), we must now foster pluralism and new forms of empowerment.

As Aronowitz and Giroux state: "Read in more positive terms, postmodernists are arguing for a plurality of voices and narratives—that is, for different narratives that present the unpresentable" (1991, p. 69). They point out that "postmodernism . . . offers educators a variety of discourses for interrogating modernism's reliance on totalizing theories based on a desire for certainty and absolutes" and creates an opportunity to expand education's "sphere of applicability to increasingly wider groups who have been excluded by virtue of their class, gender, race, age, or ethnic origin. . . . What is at stake here is the recognition that postmodernism provides educators with a more complex and insightful view of the relationships of culture, power, and knowledge" (p. 81).

In this postmodern era, I am convinced that those working within literacy education are concerned about what is not being accomplished but are even more deeply disillusioned with political promises (McLaren and Lankshear, 1993). In my experience during the 1970s and 1980s, the literacy literature and the attitudes of practitioners at professional conferences were characterized largely by hope and excitement. A positive challenge was seen in literacy education. Even in the 1980s there was (cautious) optimism with respect to federal and state government and funded literacy education programs. During that earlier halcyon and modernist time, we believed in the appearances created by ourselves and others. Illiteracy was fixable, and with governmental policies to guide us, we held "the belief that the real is rational and the system delivers the goods" (Marcuse, 1966, p. 79). However, as time passed, practitioners and administrators learned to do what was needed out of "the general necessity of things" (p. 79). Most still left in the field say the real is not as rational as we had wanted to believe. Our best efforts with the resources we possess have obviously not eradicated illiteracy, yet we are not sure what else to turn to. There is a sense that some "different" ideas need to be tried for recruitment, retention, in-classroom teaching strategies, and types of materials used (Chisman and Associates, 1990). There is a yearning to provide new forms of literacy education that might come closer to what the learner truly wants (Fingeret and Jurmo, 1989). Yet there is a pervasive feeling that the "experts" do not hold the answers any more than the governmental "leadership." There is a loss of faith in literacy leaders and in the status quo.

As Fingeret has said, the future of the field "depends only partially on policymakers. . . . If programs are going to change, people who create them must change" (Fingeret, 1984, p. 44). This, in my view, means beginning to change the way we see ourselves and our work. A practice-based perception founded in the reality of our own world, our own actions, and our own knowledge can bring us to positive change and greater ownership of our future.

The Historic Perspectives That Shape Us

Depicted in Figure 1.1 is the ambivalent relationship society has evolved with literacy and illiteracy over more than a century (Graff, 1979). If we have difficulty with definitions, goals, self-identity, or lack of voice, and if we find it hard to think differently about how to deliver literacy education, it is in large part because we are caught up in the dynamic between two perspectives of literacy reality.

Figure 1.1. Two Macro Perspectives Influencing Practitioners.

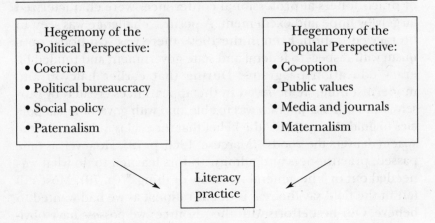

In the political perspective, we are continually provided policies and agendas to attack this "massive problem." Political checklists are dusted off with each national crisis. In the softer popular perspective that is capitalized on by the media, we find the view of the low literate as victim—often, heroic victim. Here we are given a strong sense of personal morality. We hear of "illiterates" more than "literacy." As will be seen, the two pervasive forces informing and influencing our field derive from public morality and political necessity. Both perspectives affect us in our daily decisons even as we accept both as "normal" ways of conceptualizing low literacy and low literates. It is when we can no longer see our own reality—the world of our learners and our work—that our field is truly at risk.

The Illiterate Adult in the Popular Perspective

We have seen the popular perspective in image after image through the past two decades, with the creation of the adult illiterate as heroic victim. Chapter Two discusses how recent history— coinciding roughly with the Reagan and Bush administrations— could be called the "The Decade of the Romanticized Illiterate Adult." During the campaign spearheaded by Barbara Bush, when media interest in illiteracy was at one of its highest peaks, the public display of the illiterate as heroic victim reached its twentieth-century zenith. Ubiquitous articles in magazines, posters in shopping malls, public figures giving testimony on illiteracy at Rotary meetings and alongside television evangelists all formed and helped reinforce the myth. The more cloying the story, the more tearful the response, the higher the ratings. Popular journals and news magazines such as *Newsweek, Woman's World, Better Homes and Gardens,* and *Reader's Digest,* and major newspapers from the *Washington Post* to the *New York Times* (Eringhaus, 1990), moved illiteracy onto the front pages and into the public consciousness, and the field saw a welcome acceleration of funding.

In recent years, we have turned on the television and seen "an illiterate." This person is typically middle-aged, male, and African American. In one recent television portrayal, "the illiterate" is shown with his small daughter on his knee, a homey fireplace in the background. He is struggling to read a simple child's storybook aloud. A caption appears on the screen telling us to act and "get the message out." In another television advertisement, we see an African American male (in a cardigan) turning abruptly away from his little daughter, chiding her to "go to your mother to read that. I'm busy right now." Then he turns and looks despairingly at the viewing public. The caption appears: "Get the message out. Get involved." The literature from local literacy programs is replete with such cloying sentiment, intended to stir guilt and produce both volunteer tutors and program contributions. Why do we have such an immediate response? Where did we get this singular emotional framework?

The consistent message accompanying "The Illiterate as Heroic Victim" is that he (occasionally, she) is basically an innocent large child who, with nurturing, can be saved from the grip of illiteracy and its evils. The popular perspective creates a role for a rescuer (Quigley, 1991a). Over the past two decades, there has been a definite nurturing theme at work in this perspective. After rescue comes nursing back to health. Luttrell takes this point further, persuasively arguing that the social and relational nature of literacy in the popular media is "more closely related to what has traditionally been considered 'women's work'" (1996, p. 343). In fact, there are undeniably more female than male volunteers in the literacy field, even though males make up the majority of administrators and policy makers (Beder, 1991; Chamberlain, 1988; Minnick, O'Barr, and Rosenfeld, 1988). As Luttrell points out, "Women are concentrated in literacy instruction, particularly as volunteers or as part-time instructors with little or no pay, job mobility or career advancement" (1996, p. 343). Within the low-literate student population itself, there are unquestionably more females than males nationwide (Pugsley, 1993).

As one literacy volunteer slogan puts it, "The only degree you need is a degree of caring" (cited in Luttrell, 1996, p. 343). The current rescue-and-nurture theme and the popular perspective derive from something much more pervasive, more widely accepted than the demographics of literacy. The current rescue-and-nurture theme is bolstered by media images of illiteracy. Barbara Bush helped set a maternalistic tone for these heroic victims—a tone picked up by literally dozens of governors' wives (not governors) across states. From among countless examples, Luttrell has analyzed the popular movie *Stanley and Iris* as a classic of the theme. "Iris, a white, working class, widowed single-parent who works in a bakery factory" (p. 352) meets the heroic victim, Stanley, at work. The film moves from an early sexual tryst between Iris and Stanley to a letter in which Iris asks Stanley for a "second chance"—a common phrase used in the literacy field itself. Stanley stumbles through this all-important letter. Suddenly, with no training on Iris's part and little effort on Stanley's, they "rush off to the library to confirm his amazing progress; [there] he randomly pulls books off the shelf (everything from poetry to mechanical engineering) and loudly voices his claim to the written word" (p. 352). The movie, says Luttrell, "implies that . . . nothing is impossible if you are loved by a 'good woman'" (p. 352).

The theme of this movie is not particularly new in the popular perspective and has come to constitute a genre for Hollywood and the publishing industry. Through the good efforts of literate women, males can overcome their inhibitions, their intellectual handicaps, and as seen in Chapter Two, can "get in touch with themselves." For purposes of magazine sales, females and literacy have also meant the promise of sexual adventure. A glossy Coors beer advertisement for a new romance novel, which appeared in *Better Homes and Gardens,* showed a string of pearls lying across rumpled bed sheets as captured through a gauze camera filter. Emblazoned across the advertisement are the words "Love conquers all. Even illiteracy" (Coors ad, 1993, p. 33). The advertising text for the novel claims "There's never been anything romantic about illiter-

acy, until now." The advertised book is about a woman who over-
comes illiteracy to find "love and success." A portion of the book
sales went to women's literacy organizations; therefore everyone
involved profited. Or did they?

From nurturance of the male heroic victim to sexual titillation
in the media, literacy has been sold with strong stereotypical femi-
nine overtones in the popular perspective of today. This perspective
will be examined in some depth in Chapter Two and will be picked
up again in Chapter Four as we see how this perception of literacy
reality continues to affect the decisions we make in our practice.

The Illiterate Adult in the Political Perspective

Just as history revisionists have argued that America's early common school movement was built on the backs of women prepared
to work for virtually no pay and little consideration in the workplace because they were the unquestioned "natural nurturers" of
children (Button and Provenzo, 1983), so maternalism as a theme
in the popular perspective has helped promote today's notion that
unpaid, female-dominated literacy volunteerism, as well as part-
time, underpaid, female-dominated literacy classroom teaching is
entirely appropriate (Luttrell, 1996). Adult literacy education, like
kindergarten, should be a "natural mission" for women. This is a
very cost-effective approach to a massive social problem, particularly when the total of full-time professionals has been allowed to
dwindle ("Hearings Draw," 1991). In fact, the mercy of an unpaid
or underpaid good woman is entirely welcome when funding for
programs has actually been diminishing in real dollars over the last
twenty years (Beder, 1994).

Although this is but one dimension of the popular perspective's effect on the field, virtually all feminist critiques support the
observation that to publicly locate a social problem in a traditional
female framework in this way is to immediately diminish its significance in power terms. Despite what has perhaps been the greatest "public awareness" in this century of the problems of illiteracy,
the field remains "volunteerized," and acceptably so, in the political perspective (Kozol, 1985).

As will be seen in Chapter Three, where the political perspective will be examined more closely, America has a long history of

addressing a range of social problems through the vehicle of literacy education. From illiteracy during slavery to illiteracy as the cause of crime in the 1990s, the hard-edged political perspective has created legislation, policies, and a hegemony of social responsibility that have served multiple political purposes well beyond the alleged needs of low-literate adults.

A Case Study of Two Perspectives

To bring the two perspectives closer to home, here is a familiar literacy scene. It is a minidrama repeated annually at literacy state conferences—an honored ritual of survival.

As a doctoral student and graduate assistant in adult education, I helped organize an annual statewide literacy conference. The Illinois secretary of state, Jim Snyder, was one of two guest speakers whom I helped bring to the conference. The other was Lucy Grissom, at the time the oldest student ever to have received a GED. After the master of ceremonies had welcomed the two hundred or so practitioners to the gathering, he gave a florid introduction to the secretary of state. Snyder, then new to the job, was elegant and dynamic as he strode to the microphone. After numerous thank yous and the requisite joke, he explained why literacy education was valuable and "worth doing." Moving smoothly through a carefully prepared checklist, he explained that our efforts as teachers, tutors, and administrators would

1. Improve the nation's economy (for example, reduce welfare payments, increase the number of taxpayers)
2. Prepare illiterates as responsible citizens (for example, create more voting citizens, make better use of community services, reduce the illiterate's natural vulnerability to drug/alcohol abuse, reduce numbers of illiterates in jails)
3. Enhance national security ("What would happen if illiterates got near the controls of nuclear weapons?")
4. Develop "character" (for example, break the "literacy generational cycle," improve parenting skills)

For all these reasons, the state and the nation should support literacy education, and we should keep up the good work.

This speech was like a thousand others in making illiteracy an abstraction, with an existence independent of actual human beings with faces and names. Low literates were referred to by Snyder as an abstract group, with references like "such people" and "that group." It was the kind of abstract language that helps build comfortable distance and stereotypes. "Literacy" was a complete concept attended by major responsibilities and moral rewards for those who took up "the effort." However, insinuated at the conclusion of the speech was what the seasoned practitioners were bracing themselves for. Snyder said the economy was very tight "at the moment" and that there were discussions at the federal and state levels about recruiting more volunteers into "the movement." Here, he said, was an "untapped" resource that we could call on.

He sat down to polite applause. One of the very few questions that followed was from an experienced administrator, who asked if the addition of volunteers would mean fewer funds for full- and part-time staff in our programs. Snyder skillfully answered that volunteers were needed to help the part-time people and that, "quite conceivably," the state of the economy right at that time might mean less funding for salaries. The practitioners who were new to literacy no doubt felt proud to be part of this exciting new venture. The veteran literacy practitioners were already rethinking next year's budget.

Next up was Lucy Grissom, "at ninety-one, the oldest GED graduate in America!" A bent, diminutive, white-haired lady was helped to the podium by her family. In a wavering voice, she told a story of a lifetime of personal hardship. She told how she had been born in 1893, the eldest of twelve children. She had quit school along with most of her brothers and sisters to work "in the factories." Starting in a petticoat factory at age fourteen, she moved to a millinery factory in her twenties, to a retail shop years after having her own family of five children, and had retired as a receptionist at a life insurance company after more than half a century of work. She said she was "a good worker but not an educated worker," and also that she felt she was "setting a good example" for her younger sisters and brothers throughout her life.

This brought her to something that had given her a compelling reason to obtain a GED. Recently, her great-grandson, David, had announced he was quitting school because school was "boring and of no use." It was then that she had decided to once again set an example. At age ninety-one, she enrolled in a GED preparation program. Afraid she might fail or be laughed at, she secretly attended classes by stealing out of her daughter's house at night. Her neighbor drove her to the literacy center. During the day, she hid her books under the bed until the family had gone to work or school, then she would study for her GED class in her bedroom. She was determined to show her great-grandson that anyone "can be something in life."

Grissom had graduated in the month prior to the conference. And she told us in a faltering voice that her great-grandson "has decided to stay in school." In fact, he was one of those who had helped her walk to the stage. He stood and waved back to "Gran" from the family's table at the side of the room. When Grissom was personally escorted by her grandchildren back through the audience to her seat, there was not a dry eye in the room.

The political and the popular perspectives thus came together on a single stage, but this was far from an accident of program planning. It was the basic formula for our field's funding.

Grissom did not say she took the GED "to be a better citizen" or "a better patriot." She was not worried that she might cause a nuclear war. From a personal level, she saw only her own life struggle and the part the GED played in it. The purposes and motivations of literacy education, the most fundamental notions of what literacy education is supposed to be and exist for, are worlds apart in the perspectives of Jim Snyder and Lucy Grissom. Yet we—I— helped select and invite these two people. Why not invite an experienced teacher or a researcher who could give some teaching or program advice? Why not invite more typical students to speak? Why set up this sharp dualism of perspectives?

The experienced in the audience did not care about the Snyder checklist. They wanted only to hear that the politicians were committed to literacy education. Snyder's list of archetypal purposes was heard in the hope that he would be convinced by his own rhetoric. That he found himself in a position to hear Grissom's story was carefully orchestrated. We heard Snyder indicate a move toward fewer full-time employees and "the opportunity to work with more volunteers during a difficult budget year," but all hoped he heard the indirect emotional plea of Grissom and, by extension, of thousands like her. However, the true drama was not really about Grissom. We had planned and now hoped that she would convince Jim to have mercy on us. He was the benefactor, she was the victim, we were the underfunded instruments of equity. We were the knowledgeable ones who could meet the needs of both Jim Snyder and Lucy Grissom—if funded properly.

But were we not reaching for our handkerchiefs, too? Is the field as cynical as the foregoing analysis suggests? Beyond trying to lobby through "gut-wrenching testimony," there is a deep gratification in hearing the successes of at least some of our learners. Ours is a caring field and a field of optimism and romance. Selected heroic victims fulfill a personal need in most of us who commit time and energy to this field. And in the popular sensibility, these symbols of heroism fulfill an ideal that most of us respond to and, we hope, Jim Snyder responds to. We are depending on it. But as will be seen in Chapter Two, the interest of the media has declined, and the political and legislative interest has declined as well. These annual morality plays are the staged expression of two entrenched sets of perception and two mythologies. But we are now playing to a much smaller, more skeptical audience.

Getting Beyond the Known

After nearly twenty-five years in the field of adult literacy, I am convinced that no other area of education—child or adult—is as infused as this one with political rhetoric, myth, and practitioner passivity. Yet this is a field of personal heroism on the part of teachers, administrators, and learners alike. If the field is to be made more effective and more stable, we must be able to recognize the popular perspective that helps inspire, "legitimate," and perpetuate our field even as it limits us. It is critical, too, to see the history of the political perspective, which supports and oppresses us in other ways. Understanding these two most significant influences on the field is important because they create "the known" while they lock us into it.

The dual perspectives will be explored in the next two chapters. After that, the perceptions of practitioners will be discussed. Our choices of methods, strategies, and materials are in part influenced by the popular and political perspectives. Suggestions for seeing our *own* reality will be offered. In Part Three, another set of perceptions of reality will be presented when we look at our world through the eyes of those adult students who have quit our programs early or who resist them altogether.

To survive in the political and popular world of literacy education seems to have meant a willingness to accept, not challenge, assumptions. However, renewal and the long-term survival of the field rest not with acceptance but with its exact opposite. They will depend on analysis, questioning, risk taking, and above all, the faith that literacy education is worth doing.

Chapter Two

The Popular Perspective and the Media

Most will agree that there has been a sharp rise in media interest in illiteracy over approximately the past fifteen years. Such interest heightened during the Reagan administration in the 1980s and peaked during the Bush administration, with Barbara Bush's personal campaign for literacy extending into the early 1990s. Media interest then fell sharply. From the start of the Clinton administration, the media became virtually silent on the subject of literacy, despite such newsworthy developments as the *National Adult Literacy Survey* report of 1993, which announced that almost half the nation's adults were affected by low literacy. It is apparent that illiteracy has no life in the world of media beyond what is breathed into it by politicians and supported by the reading and viewing public. In our field, it seems, politicians are the ones who identify social crises, and the media help create consensus on the "acceptable" public responses (Edelman, 1977; Herman and Chomsky, 1988).

That media and public interest in literacy rises and falls is not an original observation. In fact, after a review of literacy campaigns in U.S. history, Smith concluded, "Over the years, in times of crisis, the main body of Americans kept rediscovering the literacy problems and over the years, hastily contrived solutions to the problems were invented or reinvented. As the crisis passed, so did the concern of America's leaders" (1977, p. iv). What is not well recognized or researched in this recurring pattern of "rediscovery" is the vital link between literacy in politics and literacy in the media (Herman and Chomsky, 1988). One would look long and hard to find another field of education so dependent on this linkage.

Table 2.1 shows the number of articles on literacy carried in popular magazines and periodicals and in the *New York Times* between 1980 and 1994.

Clearly, 1984–1992 was the peak period for media interest in literacy. However, popular periodicals began losing interest in the topic in 1991. The *New York Times* stayed the course somewhat longer, but it too lost interest. In the next chapter, the media and political rediscovery of literacy is shown to be usually linked to national crises. It will be seen that the popular and political perspectives are activated depending on the amount of pressure the politicians apply to the public policy pedal. Thus, the harder polit-

Table 2.1. Articles on Literacy
(Popular Periodicals and *New York Times*), 1980–1994.

	Reader's Guide to Periodical Literature *indicating magazines and periodicals*	New York Times Index *indicating their coverage*	*Total*
1980	10	1	11
1981	4	4	8
1982	3	4	7
1983	3	7	10
1984	12	16	28
1985	10	7	17
1986	10	6	16
1987	10	14	24
1988	18	16	34
1989	14	14	28
1990	14	13	27
1991	8	14	22
1992	7	16	23
1993	6	10	16
1994 (first 5months)	0	1	1

Sources: Reader's Guide to Periodical Literature, New York Times Index.

ical perspective reappears from the top, the softer popular perspective emerges from the bottom.

Within each of these perspectives lies a fascinating set of significant assumptions, including those dealing with the question of whose explicit and implicit "responsibility" illiteracy is. In the hard political perspective, illiteracy's "cause and cure" are, in large part, the responsibility of illiterates themselves. In the softer popular perspective, responsibility is shared between an unjust society and its less than effective institutions, such as the school system. If the field is to be critically aware of these two long-established perspectives, we will be well advised to understand their roots and their implications for our field.

Ausband states: "Myths work by demonstrating order. They are true in the sense that they satisfy demonstrations or representations of a perceived order and are therefore often believed by a society to be more or less factual" (Ausband, 1983, p. 5). Let us see, then, who the "more or less factual" illiterate is in the popular press and in popular literary fiction.

"Turtles on the Beach"

Consider a number of the media's more dramatic presentations of the illiterate and illiteracy over the past decade. The *New York Times* ended a soporific account of illiteracy and its impact with the concluding statement: "To read is to be fully human" (Anderson and Dunlap, 1984, p. II-3). These "less-than-fully-human people" are often seen as being incapable of helping themselves. According to Weir, illiterates are utterly passive: "basically, they can exist. Like turtles on the beach. They are there—period" (Weir, 1986, p. 523). Illiterates are virtually without awareness of their world, according to *Good Housekeeping,* because they have "no love of learning," they are the "unteachables . . . 'those who never learned to love to learn'" (Wyse, 1989, p. 308). As Weir put it, they are "lost, just lost" (Weir, 1986, p. 523).

But the imagery goes beyond the maudlin. Besides being less than "fully human," we are told, illiterates can be so tortured by illiteracy that they may become self-destructive and may even want to kill themselves. The *New York Times* told of a man who "felt so desperate at his inability to do even the simplest reading or writing tasks that he went to the roof of the building in which he lived, ready to jump off" (Rohter, 1986, p. XII-33). Luckily, he reconsidered and, at the last minute, was "saved" by enrolling in a literacy course. Thus, illiteracy is even life-threatening.

Even if common sense fails, there is an abundance of evidence indicating that the approximately ninety-four million adults affected by low literacy can hardly all be painted with the same condemning brush (for example, Clark, 1990; Fingeret, 1982; Graff, 1979; Griffith, 1990; Manning, 1983). As for the myth that all illiterates, or even the majority of illiterate adults, are tortured and self-destructive, that is not only ridiculous on its face but has been disproven by a growing counter-literature which indicates that low literates may not only be financially successful (Clark, 1990) but entirely successful, even fulfilled, within the rich social network of their own community (Fingeret, 1983, p. 133) or their own cultural life world (Quigley, 1990a; Ziegahn, 1992). It is a vast, self-serving oversimplification to say that all ninety-four million are either "tortured" or insentient "turtles." They are simply people.

Yet the pejorative language used, the sensational images presented, the tragic and bizarre stories selected and recounted in the media reinforce popular myths and stereotypes. Although many in the field will agree that television promotions such as "Project Plus," undertaken jointly by PBS and ABC in the 1980s, raised public awareness about illiteracy, the field needs to ask what kind of "awareness" was raised and what images were reinforced. What were the networks building on? What was really achieved?

Ilsley and Stahl have discussed media imagery and its impact on "consciousness." They looked at how magazine ads such as one produced in 1989 by the Coalition of Adult Literacy portray illiterate adults—in the 1989 case, for purposes of recruiting volunteer tutors. The coalition's ad shows a crowd of people on a busy street. Underneath is the eye-catching message, "There's an epidemic with 27 million victims. And no visible symptoms" (Ilsley and Stahl, 1994, p. 29). Although the estimated numbers have virtually tripled since, the attitudes behind the images and the impressions created remain remarkably consistent over time. Ilsley and Stahl noted how terms like *victim* connote "people . . . on the receiving end of a crime or disease. . . . the word evokes images of a fool or a chump, or someone who has lost control of a situation" (p. 29). In this and in earlier articles by Ilsley (1989), classic metaphors that accompany literacy campaigns are shown to fall into identifiable categories.

The first is the school metaphor, which reduces illiterates to failed overgrown schoolchildren. They are depicted as being typically fearful, ashamed, and in need of guidance from the more mature literate community. The second prevailing metaphor, the medical/industrial, presents illiterates as suffering from a "disease" of which they can be cured by caring education systems. In this common metaphor, teachers are like doctors, complete with prescriptive curricula. Ilsley and Stahl note how Barbara Bush told the 1984 national convention of Literacy Volunteers of America that "adult illiteracy is one of the nations's most insidious diseases" (Ilsley and Stahl, 1994, p. 30). Other media examples of this category can be found from the late seventies and early eighties. Popular magazines such as *Glamour* stated that illiteracy was an "epidemic," and like sick children, millions "desperately needed reading instruction" (O'Toole, 1985, p. 369). Terms like *rampant* were extremely common in magazines such as *Essence* (Giles, 1985, p. 34), and descriptive terms such as *blight* appeared early in 1985 in *Publishers' Weekly* (Editors, 1985, p. 27). *Scourge* was the descriptor of choice in the *New York Times* in 1986 (Rohter, pp. XII-33–37).

The third metaphor identified by Ilsley and Stahl is the military, which moves the imagery from an individualistic to a collective level. In this metaphor, our nation has to "engage in battle," "declare war," "fight" the enemy of illiteracy, which is cunningly concealed in the hard-to-recognize illiterate. The punitive tone and battle cry are here connotative of seeking out and correcting those people who are unwittingly in league with "the enemy." The metaphor invokes not pity for a victim, like the first two, but concern and even fear. As will be seen in Chapter Three, sentiment changes to suspicion through these images. And the emotions evoked are very different depending on whether there is a political or a popular purpose at hand.

The final metaphor in the Ilsley and Stahl classification is that of banking. Here, the nation "needs to invest" in the poverty-stricken lives of illiterates. It is now a question of a "human capital investment." The argument is that taxpayers' money must be invested in human commodities or else the nation will go poor through the bankruptcy of knowledge.

The last two metaphors, the military and the banking, function at the societal and macro level, with the wider common good of society in mind; the first two function at the individual level, with the victim's needs as the apparent focus. All four metaphors, and the specific language they employ, connect with something already established in society. They call up collective prejudices so deep that a single image can evoke pity for an unfortunate victim or alarm at someone portrayed as a threat.

The fascinating question is how a society can both despise and pity, fear and want to help, at the same time. How can this dichotomy be so prevalent in society yet be so critically unexamined in our literacy literature? Thompson has pointed out how the literacy literature is steeped in such images. She analyzed the language used in literacy policies and promotional materials and found that "the language of 'personal deficit,' 'affliction,' and the need for 'treatment' to 'rehabilitate' the 'malfunctioning' adult into 'normal' society runs like a medical checklist through the literature" (1980, p. 87). Thompson found that terms like *disadvantaged, disenfranchised, marginalized, basic education,* and *hard-to-reach* have only helped to reinforce stigmatization.

The media attention of the past two decades has been a very mixed blessing. I cannot recall how many times practitioners at conferences have asked that the very term *literacy* no longer be used in the field or in any of the marketing for programs. I have heard literacy students make the same request in programs. As will be seen in Chapters Six and Seven, the imagery and the language used will clearly discourage some potential learners from enrolling in programs. Behind the definition committees, the legislated definitions, the changing terms, lies the fact that enduring imagery and myths are what guide many of the responses to our field and our learners. What's in a name? If it is a literacy label or metaphor, it may be a name evoking a legacy of social mythology that can shape our very existence as practitioners and researchers.

How Literacy Myths Are Made for the Popular Perspective

On December 12, 1984, at the New York Public Library, there occurred what may well have been the beginning of a new era of mythmaking. As explained in the *New York Times* by journalist Philip Dougherty (1984), media advertising, from television commercials to print, suddenly found a worthy cause in illiteracy. The nonprofit Advertising Council had decided to promote literacy. As Dougherty put it, "What greater tragedy could befall the media, advertisers and agencies than having a population that cannot read or understand what the media and advertisers are saying?" Seeing the value of "enlightened self-interest," as Dougherty explained it, the Advertising Council announced at the library that it would aim "to get 250,000 volunteers in the first year" (p. IV-29).

How did the Advertising Council set about this noble task? Not by meeting and talking to undereducated and illiterate adults. Not by interviewing adult basic education and literacy teachers or tutors. The ad campaign was mounted by media people who talked with each other, drawing from an established set of myths. As will be seen, they consciously or unconsciously drew on the tried and true images of authors such as Charles Dickens, depending on such images to evoke emotions of pity and fear.

Dougherty described the very first television ad to become part of the Advertising Council's "full-court press," as he called it: "The single TV commercial, which will be available in 30-second and 60-second lengths, highlights the problem by showing a young father trying unsuccessfully to read a bedtime story to his daughter. As he stumbles and stutters with the words, the voice of Maureen Stapleton explains that the man is functionally illiterate, one of 27 million Americans who are so handicapped" (p. IV-29).

The sad male figure, the innocent child, the maternal voice of Maureen Stapleton—these became the standard ingredients of forthcoming imagery. A nonprofessional, if not anti-intellectual, theme was chosen for the Advertising Council's project: "The only degree you need is a degree of caring" (p. IV-29).

The 1984 story explained how the harder political perspective was also represented. Dougherty wrote that *U.S. News & World Report* had chosen to take a more fear-inspiring route with the prediction that "if corrective steps are not taken, two out of three Americans could be functionally illiterate by the year 2000" (Cited in Dougherty, p. IV-29). Here is the archetypal choice of how to render illiteracy: one views low literates as victims and the other sees an abstract of illiteracy as a societal threat. Here are the two well-traveled roads of pity and fear, "good" and "evil," for public consumption.

The media group described by Dougherty set the standard for a decade of sound bites. As Dougherty admiringly reported, the volunteer coordinator for the Advertising Council's campaign, R. Lauterborn, director of marketing communications and corporate advertising at the International Paper Company, showed how simply the job could be done. "He had crafted a highly literate, though brief, speech for the occasion yesterday and during it borrowed from other writers who have described illiterates as 'dropouts from the American dream,' people who are 'discounted from the past' and 'have no future'" (p. IV-29). And so the selling of illiteracy imagery began anew.

Significantly, only four years later, the media chastised itself for the shallow coverage of literacy it had collectively created. Debra Gersh, in *Editor & Publisher*, wrote about a research paper that John Moss of *New York Newsday* had prepared for the Media Resource Project on Literacy of the Education Writers Association. Moss's paper was entitled "Soft Selling a Complex Political Story." In it, he granted that newspapers and magazines had "many . . . 'good profiles'" (Gersh, 1988, p. 20). However, he found that the vast majority of stories on illiteracy lacked all three necessary ingredients required for good reporting: immersion in the subject, fair explication of context, and "perseverance." In his research, Moss found that literacy stories "appeared to be single shots—stories that an editor or publisher ordered up one day, [and] reporters produced soon after" (p. 21).

Further, according to Moss's findings, "only the more obvious cause of illiteracy stems from the education system, just as the more obvious cause of homelessness stems in [*sic*] housing programs and in the lack of public funds or private initiative for new construction and restoration. . . . But a far more significant problem is that both illiterates and the homeless have been shoved outside the economic stream" (Moss cited in Gersh, p. 34).

Moss argued that the media could take a more challenging and thoughtful stance in relation to the statistics they had been mindlessly passing along: "If newspapers can spend huge sums taking meaningless political polls, then they can spend money doing their own surveys and sampling census taking to find out for ourselves whether the experts are right" (p. 34).

Nothing indicates that the media changed as a result of Moss's findings or Gersh's efforts to make the findings better known in the media community. But why not?

The Need for Literacy Stereotypes

Why does society evidently accept, even need, literacy stereotyping? More specifically, why single out low literates for special stereotyping? Such stereotypes and the attitudes they betray would be considered outrageously insulting to minorities such as African Americans, Hispanics, or the disabled.

Beder makes the following observation on this point: "Although it has become socially unacceptable to publically denigrate groups stigmatized by race, ethnicity, or poverty, it is completely acceptable to denigrate illiterates as being economically unproductive and incapable of making informed civic decisions. Thus for some the denigration of illiterates may be a socially acceptable form of expressing racist attitudes that are really aimed at blacks, Hispanics, and others. . . . [because] illiterates tend to be members of other stigmatized groups such as blacks, Hispanics, and the poor" (1991, pp. 67–68).

In the way illiterates are thought of, Keddie has seen a "social pathology that explains social problems as a malfunctioning of the socioeconomic system, where social ills are manifested in those individuals or groups who are most vulnerable" (1980, p. 57). Others will argue that society's need to stereotype is not grounded in the sociology of socioeconomics, but rather that it derives from a psychological need to elevate ourselves in relation to others perceived as possessing more limitations than we do.

It seems there is a process at work in stereotyping. There is a projection of our own anxieties and self-doubts onto an external person or persona—the objectified "other." This provides a sense of momentary relief and even self-congratulation. We find a parallel in the recent phenomenon of picking on Neanderthal Man.

In a 1994 *Smithsonian* article on Neanderthal Man, James Shreeve asked why this creature had been picked out for the ignominious distinction of being the 1990s epitome of something subhuman. He noted how quick columnists were to refer to "the Neanderthal who whacked [Olympic skater Nancy] Kerrigan's knee" (p.17). His research showed that Neanderthal Man was depicted as a "bash in head now, ask questions later" creature with gaping lips and pitch black fur (p. 17). An artist named Marcellin Boule had drawn Neanderthal Man this way in 1909 for the French newspaper *L'Illustration*. Only three years later, the *Illustrated London News* offered a totally different portrayal of Neanderthal Man, in an illustration by Arthur Keith. The British saw a picture of a creature who was "remarkably human, even noble, sitting quietly by a hearth surrounded by the tools of his hunting trade like a Greek hero glimpsed in a private moment at home" (p. 18).

Which of these two renderings from the early twentieth century endured? Scholars looking at the two images since have noted how "Boule's disturbingly durable version of the drooling beast was, and is, blatantly racist" (p. 20). As Shreeve put it, if we agree that Neanderthal Man embodies all the bestiality we want to have left behind us, we can "reassure ourselves" that we are beyond that creature. We "abstract this inferior animal and thrust it safely outside, where it can be seen not as part of what we are, but the definition of what we have risen above." Why choose Neanderthal Man? Shreeve made the point that his early victims "are no longer around to feel the pain" (p. 20).

Why is the illiterate singled out to be the brunt of so many jokes and "put-downs" in today's culture? Low-literate adults are typically voiceless. They are part of an amorphous group "that is powerless to defend itself" (Beder, 1991, p. 70). What is disturbing is why those who work in literacy education do not speak up on behalf of this population. This is a matter that will be discussed later in Part One.

Who is the "Illiterate"?

Although the political and popular perspectives typically ignore most of the demographic and academic research on America's adult low literates, and although we in the field quietly keep the treadmill of mythology turning, there is actually considerable literature on the subject of who low literates are (Anderson and Niemi, 1970; Hunter and Harman, 1979; Kirsch and Jungeblut, 1986). However, with no agreement on terms, measures, or definitions—

for some of the reasons mentioned earlier—the demographic and descriptive literature must be interpreted within the context of each study. No one study can be taken to stand as the final word on how the illiterate population is composed. Beder is one of many who have made this same cautionary point, adding: "Indeed the issue of definition has so frustrated scholars that Hunter and Harman . . . entitled their discussion of definitions 'Lies, Damned Lies, and Statistics' and Kozol . . . entitled his analysis 'Matters of Equivocation: Dangers of the Numbers Game'" (1991, p. 21). If the elusiveness of measurement frustrates those who want a "head count" and occasionally drives some to concoct the most bizarre, data-free "estimates," it is basically because "illiteracy" and "literacy" remain social constructs, and the measures are created in the eyes of researchers and policy makers.

In the late 1970s, I was a government employee in a Canadian province, responsible for the GED program and much of the policy input to literacy and adult basic education. In this role, it was common enough to be asked to come up with an estimate of how many illiterates there were in the province. Irrespective of how high the numbers were that we found in the literature and reported back, two things were always expected in these cases. First, the number of illiterates needed to be "reasonably high" to help build political arguments for such things as school reform or changes to program funding. In the later years of funding reductions, the numbers were to be "high enough" to help justify a volunteer literacy campaign—seen essentially as an inexpensive publicity move to help blunt the knife that would soon be making massive education cuts across the province. I sat in on discussions where it was reasoned that saving illiterates might make the government appear less heartless when we needed to cut almost everything in postsecondary education.

The second expectation when I was asked for "a count" was that our province should not look worse than our neighboring provinces. As bureaucrats, we typically turned to the census data at that time (Thomas, 1976). I remember wishing we had better relativist studies to draw on that might put more focus on the actual adults and their needs rather than the needs of the government of the day. More reliable studies have emerged in the United States (and Canada) over the past decade, even though the context, definitions, and limitations still continue to be ignored in much of the use of recent studies within the popular and political perspectives.

Beder (1991) has compiled many of the census, U.S. Department of Education, and academic findings on demographics published in the past two decades. However, much of his U.S. Department of Education data reflect those who participate in government-sponsored literacy, ABE, and GED programs. Clearly, the approximately 8 percent who participate (Pugsley, 1990) cannot be considered representative of the wider populace of low literates. Beder added census and academic study data to the narrower participation reports in an attempt to give a picture of who constitutes the "target population." However, this was not intended to be a picture of who the illiterate is.

The most respected study on that subject emerged after the publication of Beder's book. Compared with the noncensus 1975 Adult Performance Level study, which drew considerable academic criticism (Griffith and Cervero, 1977), the 1993 *National Adult Literacy Survey* (NALS) study has remarkably few critics. Conducted by the Educational Testing Service under the funding auspices of the U.S. Department of Education, it took approximately four years. The results were released in September 1993. Rather than employing the census model of gathering information door to door and basing "literacy" on some version of a benchmark standard, the NALS employed "more than 400 trained interviewers, some of whom were bilingual in English and Spanish" (Kirsch, Jungeblut, Jenkins, and Kolstad, 1993, p. 50). The definition used was in the relativist tradition, which makes it a major contribution to the field—and to policy makers.

The NALS used a nationally representative sample of 13,600 adults (p. 5). Interviewers visited "nearly 27,000 households to select and interview adults aged 16 and older, each of whom was asked to provide personal and background information and to complete a booklet of literacy tasks" (p. 5). Black and Hispanic households were oversampled "to ensure reliable estimates of literacy proficiencies and to permit analyses of the performance of these subpopulations" (p. 6). Eleven states elected to use the survey methodology to study their own low-literacy levels. Eleven hundred inmates in some eighty federal and state prisons were also included in the survey. Combining the three sources—households, individual state studies, and prisons—meant that "more than 26,000 adults gave, on average, more than an hour of their time to complete the literacy tasks and background questionnaires" (p. 6).

The NALS literacy tasks performed by this sample of adults consisted of exercises in areas termed *prose literacy, document literacy*, and *quantitative literacy*. Prose literacy was the ability to read, comprehend, and interpret prose, including editorials, news stories, and fiction. Document literacy was the capacity to find and use information in materials such as job applications, transportation schedules, maps, tables, and graphs. Finally, quantitative literacy involved the use of numbers embedded in print materials to conduct arithmetic operations—for example, balancing a checkbook or determining the amount of interest from a loan advertisement. Following the survey, the outcomes were reported in levels reflecting the proficiency in conducting the survey tasks. Five sets of levels indicated lowest to highest competency level. Placement on level one meant that the person was functioning at the lowest literacy skill level. Level five was the highest.

Only 18–21 percent of participants were found to be functioning on the upper levels, four and five. Approximately 30 percent placed on the third level. Meanwhile, approximately 23 percent, "some 44 million of the 191 million adults in this country" (Kirsch, Jungeblut, Jenkins, and Kolstad, 1993, p. xv) placed on the lowest level. When the lowest levels of one and two are combined, the total amounts to approximately ninety-four million—almost half of the nation's adult population. Worse, perhaps, the NALS executive summary adds, "The literacy proficiencies of young adults assessed in 1992 were somewhat lower, on average, than the proficiencies of young adults who participated in a 1985 literacy survey" under U.S. Department of Education auspices (p. xvi).

Given this massive picture of low literacy, we ask, "Who are the people on the two lowest levels?" Those functioning on the lowest levels are typically unemployed nonwhites with less than a high school education. More older adults demonstrated low proficiencies than did younger adults. Those on the lowest functioning levels typically had parents with lower education levels. Most participants on these levels reported that they had worked only eighteen to nineteen weeks in the year prior to the survey. This group also reported median weekly earnings of about $230–245, whereas the level-three participants reported about $350 and those on level five reported $600–680 per week. As far as race and ethnicity are concerned, "Black, American Indian/Alaskan Native, Hispanic, and Asian/Pacific Islander adults were more likely than Whites to perform on the two lowest levels" (p. xvi). In fact, "the average prose literacy of White adults is 26 to 80 points higher than that of any of the other nine racial/ethnic groups reported (p. 32).

It was further found that "the average proficiencies of the Hispanic subpopulations are not significantly different from one another. On average, Mexican and Central/South American adults were outperformed by Black adults. In contrast, Hispanic/Other adults outperformed Black adults on the prose and document scales by more than 20 points (on the quantitative scale, the difference is not significant). Their performance was, on average, similar to that of Asian/Pacific adults and American Indian/Alaskan Native adults" (p. 32).

Do lower levels of schooling mean lower levels of literacy? An attempt to find such a correlation revealed that "while adults with less than a high school education performed primarily in Level 1, those who finished secondary school performed, on average, in the high end of Level 2, those who received a college degree demonstrated average proficiencies associated with the high end of Level 3, and those who had completed some work beyond the four-year degree performed within the range of Level 4" (p. 27).

The NALS found that those older than sixty-five functioned at least one entire level lower than the forty to fifty-four age group—a finding explained, in part at least, by the fact that older generations typically had less formal schooling than did younger ones.

Although these findings are very similar to earlier studies through the years, the NALS also challenged many myths. For instance, it is often suggested that immigrants make up the bulk of the nation's low literates. In this study, "nearly all White (96 percent) and Black (95 percent) adults and most respondents of Puerto Rican origin (80 percent) said they were born in the United States" (p. 40). It is often assumed that the majority of low-literate adults suffer from some type of physical or mental handicap. In the NALS study, albeit based on self-reported data, only "12 percent of the total population said they had a physical, mental, or other health condition that kept them from participating fully in work, housework, or other activities" (p. 42). Indeed, only 3 percent reported having a learning disability, and only 2 percent reported a mental or emotional condition or speech disability.

What the NALS did not do—and was not intended to do—is give a picture of the trials, successes, or aspirations of the people it studied. This was a quantitative study of demographics. However, in seeking to comment on who the adult illiterate "is," this study and others like it leave "blind spots," to use the term of Hunter and Harman (1979, p. 55), who, after their major review of adult literacy in the U.S., noted how quantitative researchers tend to simplify complex lives into statistics and problems. We actually know little about those who were studied in the NALS or similar studies, which allows the popular and political perspectives to impute motives, attitudes, even lifestyles, to the group described.

Kirsch and Guthrie (1984), Manning, (1983), and Clark (1990) are a few who have suggested or shown that low literates have succeeded financially, even as self-made millionaires. Others such as Ziegahn (1992) and Uhland (1995) have shown the ability of low literates to succeed within their own context and to be self-directed learners. Fingeret has studied low-literate adults in their own communities and subcultures, finding that many have developed rich social networks. Low-literate individuals, she has written, "create social networks that are characterized by reciprocal exchange; networks which offer access to most of the resources individuals require, so that it is unnecessary to develop every skill personally. Therefore, many illiterate adults see themselves as interdependent; they contribute a range of skills and knowledge other than reading and writing to their networks" (1983, p. 134).

Singling out illiteracy as the defining characteristic in studies such as the NALS allows illiteracy to take on a life of its own. In fact, illiteracy was found by Fingeret to be of little significance when considering the actual lives and communities of low-literate adults:

> Illiterate adults manifest a range of abilities to decode the social world and to take intentional action in that world. Their strategies differ in different social locations and according to the resources available and the forces they must contend with. Some illiterate adults are successful cosmopolitan entrepreneurs. Others are local clients, dependent on family and caretakers; their potency is

observed by the culture and social structures of the dominant group in our society. . . . Illiterate adults are considered dependent and incompetent by the literate society because they are unable to perform reading and writing tasks autonomously. However, when reading is seen as one of many skills contributing to the exchange of relations in a social network, illiteracy no longer defines dependence in the social context of these adults [Fingeret, 1983, p. 145].

To gain a picture of low-literate adults, one needs a sense of the demographics. However, to temper the effect of studies that speak to deficiencies or limitations, one also needs a sense of the strengths and demonstrated abilities of many low literates that researchers such as Fingeret have revealed.

In Part Four of this book, it is argued that systematic observations by practitioners are essential to complete this portrait of who "the illiterate" is. Without adding our voice and experience, we will continue to be defined and marginalized as a field. Without our critical understanding of the generations of myths within the popular and political perspectives, and without the advocacy to change them, we will continue to be caught in the limitations of partial truth.

The Illiterate in Everyday Practice

As the discussion about definitions, ideologies, and programmatic objectives continues, it should be recognized that neither politicians nor the media, nor even practitioners, typically seek "objectively" solid ground in fact—even if such could exist (Cervero, 1984). The reality of the world that surrounds, gives voice to, and in many ways derives some benefit from literacy education is composed of overlapping and competing political, economic, and ideological interests. After the sound and fury of the political and academic debate, the definitions of the moment are typically ignored. Following the intensive focus on formulating the definition that became enshrined in the National Literacy Act, planners of state literacy conferences did not post the definition over the head table at annual state conferences. They basically ignored it, recognizing the process as a political necessity of the moment. Politicians such as Jim Snyder gave keynote speeches as always. The media recruited volunteers. Teachers in classrooms functioned as before. The imagery endures.

As Augusta Kappner, U.S. assistant secretary of vocational and adult education, said in her keynote address to the delegates of the annual 1994 American Association for Adult and Continuing Education conference, there is a rich set of stories around people's needs and successes in literacy. But, she said, "stories are not enough at the policy or macro level." The degree of their insufficiency depends on which audience one is addressing and which familiar set of literacy emotions one is trying to arouse. If one is functioning in the "hard" world of policy and wishes to conjure up the darker version of Illiterate Man, the absolute school of grade levels is the first step to a "head count." On the other hand, if one is communicating within the popular perspective—the "soft" world of emotion and subjectivity—for purposes of teaching, recruiting, or fund raising, one will present Illiterate Man as heroic victim. We may say we seek "objectivity," but we shape "objectivity" to suit the image of the world we choose to address. A personal anecdote may help complete this curious picture.

At a state conference, well out of earshot of the governmental representatives, a literacy teacher described to me how she raised funds in her region with the help of an adult student I will call "Winston." The two of them made the rounds of the evening church groups and the social club luncheons in the city to raise donations and recruit volunteers. She said Winston, who had rehearsed his victim performance assiduously, took it as a personal challenge to bring every last member of the audience to tears before dessert was served. Before heading up to the podium, he would ask in whispered tones, "Do you want to go for 'partial' or 'total breakdown'"? Winston and my friend would be doubled over with laughter driving back to the center after a successful performance. The situation was farcical, and they knew it.

Once, according to my friend, Winston was going for "total breakdown" but could not get to one church elder sitting at the back of the room. He focused on the hard-hearted listener and threw every tale of hardship at him. Nothing worked. Finally, in a moment of inspiration, Winston yelled: "Look at what illiteracy has done to me! Here are the scars of my attempt at suicide!" He pulled his sleeves back and stood, wrists exposed, eyes cast up to the ceiling, in an attitude of crucifixion. There was stunned silence. Then the checkbooks started hitting the table tops—beginning with the elder. It was at this point that my friend decided that perhaps it was time for Winston to return to his academic studies and her to grant writing.

Although the definitions in our literature and the stereotypes in the media are usually presented with far fewer histrionics, their references to well-understood political and popular themes are no less recognizable. And they are no less part of a tragicomedy written out of multiple motives. As Arnove and Graff put it: "Reformers and idealists, shakers and movers of societies and historic periods, have viewed literacy as a means to other ends—whether a more moral society or a more stable political order. No less today than four hundred years ago, individuals have sought and used literacy to attain their own goals" (1987, p. 2).

Despite the quest for an objective definition, the field, the policy makers, and our public are informed by the popular and political perspectives and the myths they perpetuate. Let us take a closer look at the popular perception and the heroic victim.

The Romance of Illiteracy

There is an inescapable connection between the variations on today's popular themes of illiteracy and certain enduring romantic themes in America's history. The romantic movement in nineteenth-century England found fertile ground in contemporary idealistic America. This was the age of the "common man." No longer subject to Britain's direct political influence or the rigidity of the British class system, American society lived by the dream of populist democracy. Partly in reaction to the pervasive American Protestant ethic of the early and mid-eighteenth century, partly in reaction to the disruptive effects of urbanization in the Midwest, and largely as a response to the social injustices of the industrial revolution, the early nineteenth century, "more than before or most times since," had an enduring interest in romantic concepts (Button and Provenzo, 1983, p. 48).

For children, the common school movement established under Horace Mann was for the full, "classless" participation of America's youth (Cremin, 1964). For adults, institutions such as the Chautauqua Institute and Josiah Holbrook's Lyceum bloomed (Stubblefield and Keane, 1989). It was a time when larger-than-life

American heroes emerged in literary fiction. Sir Walter Scott's novels were common fare. During this period, "grown men and women read Johann Goethe's *Sorrows of Young Werther* and wept." Edgar Allen Poe "not only wrote as a romantic but seemed to live as one" (Button and Provenzo, 1983, p. 48).

To see the origins of today's sentimental image of the illiterate, I believe we need to go to the enduring image of the Byronic Hero. In 1818, Macaulay succinctly described him as "a man, proud, moody, cynical, with defiance on his brow, and misery in his heart . . . yet capable of deep and strong affection" (cited in Jump, 1967, p. 240). This melancholy figure, an outcast by circumstance and choice but harboring a deeper wisdom, became the embodiment of male romantic heroism in the late nineteenth century. The image created by Lord Byron has since been simplified for countless novels, movies, and journalistic essays.

Today's illiterate man (rarely woman) as heroic victim has been reduced in complexity by stereotyping (Forster, 1927) but still carries all the ascribed characteristics of innate honesty, injured innocence, and above all, potential for greater good. He is presented as an inspirational figure "capable of deep and strong affection" (cited in Jump, 1967, p. 240). The cynical side of the Byronic Hero is found in a second low-literate figure that first appears in late-nineteenth-century popular literature. The more cynical figure is only a minor theme, and is actually the illiterate as a "natural man," living by his wits and scoffing at the trappings of a foolish, corrupt society. Thus, from the nineteenth-century romantic movement and images such as that of the Byronic Hero spring two types for our popular perspective: the illiterate heroic victim, a wounded but unvanquished figure; and the natural man, a feisty, self-sufficient student from the school of hard knocks. The two differ in their reactions to their worlds and in their responses to the society.

The Illiterate as Heroic Victim

Today's low-literate heroic victim is typically a male found in the popular literature and media. He is always struggling to survive. Sometimes he is depicted as tragic in his struggle, sometimes as pathetic. A story about illiterates in the *Saturday Evening Post* stated, "They suffer in silence and try to hide their problem in shame"

(Harr, 1988, p. 46). Peter Jennings, the anchor for ABC News, portrayed illiterates as the most hopeless of victims: "I have worked in wars and revolutions, interviewed people rendered homeless by nature and by man-made tragedies, but I have never encountered people as hopeless, as sad and as full of loss as those who cannot read or write" (L. Smith, 1989, p. 71).

But more typically, illiterate heroic victims are portrayed as strong men injured by an unjust society and tragic vicissitudes, yet struggling on. They are painted as being good at heart and perpetually optimistic, always sure the American Dream is attainable.

The heroic victim appears much earlier in popular fiction than does the natural man and, as will be seen, he figures much more often in today's media. The type is found as far back as the seventeenth-century religious writings and socially motivated imagery. One of the most enduring examples from the early nineteenth century is a young girl who appears in Charles Dickens's *Bleak House:* "It must be a strange state to be like Jo! To shuffle through the streets, unfamiliar with the shapes, and in utter darkness as to meaning, of those mysterious symbols so abundant over the shops, and at the corners of streets, and on the doors, and in the windows! To see people read, and to see people write, and to see postmen deliver letters, and to not have the least idea of all that language—to be, to every scrap of it, stone-blind and dumb" ([1853] 1953, p. 138).

One of the purposes of Dickens's writing was to bring attention to social injustice under the industrial revolution—in this case, the lack of schooling in Britain. Other images of illiterates in nineteenth-century England were not unlike this one.

Thomas Pole, who wrote the first history of adult education in 1814 (reprinted in Verner, 1967), argued for an adult school system, his objective being to enable adults to read Scripture. He sought to "moralize and Christianize the minds of men—Instead of idleness, profaneness, and vice—They inculcate diligence, sobriety, frugality, piety, and heavenly mindedness" (p. 18). The point of teaching adults to read (writing was not advocated until much later) was that they "will also have learned better to practice meekness, Christian fortitude, and resignation" (p. 19). The idea of literacy as a means for "empowerment" was anathema to educators of children and adults alike in this period.

With a message of careful control of the "downtrodden," stereotypes were carried to America and to education. As Graff explains, the school system of the nineteenth century was the "one central instrument and vehicle in the efforts to secure social, cultural, economic and political cohesion in the political economy of the extending capitalist order." As for literacy in the new twentieth century, it "could not be promoted or comprehended in isolation from morality" (Graff, 1979, p. 25; see also Fingeret and Danin, 1991).

The images of illiterates and the roles of educators have been ingrained in the psyche of America. Attitudes toward illiterates in American literature, even today, reflect the archetypal belief within the popular perspective that illiterates must be "saved." The illiterate as heroic victim has become a standard image in the popular literature and media, encompassing four distinct stereotypes: the simple immigrant, the simple American worker, the simple African American, and the simple white southerner.

The Simple Immigrant

The simple, hardworking immigrant man (rarely an immigrant woman) is a recurring image of the illiterate in our popular culture. He is found in novels about new immigrants, where an archetypal, passive foreigner works humbly for a piece of America's resources. Novels such as Thomas Bell's *Out of This Furnace* portray immigrants struggling with the English language and education. Bell creates an image of simple, struggling, entirely unthreatening people: "It was their good fortune, perhaps, to come unburdened with many illusions about the land of freedom, a land where all men were equal. They were glad to take whatever jobs were assigned them" ([1941] 1976, pp. 124–125).

In today's media, we still find humble immigrants struggling to acquire English and a basic education. *Reader's Digest* presented Maria Grzanka, the daughter of immigrants, as a fearful victim thanks to illiteracy: "[She] knew she had to come to grips with her fears or she would never break her family's cycle of illiteracy. . . . She missed solid schooling in her early years because her parents moved many times. When they finally settled in Detroit, seven-year-old Maria was put in parochial school, where each day the teacher called on students to stand and read. Trembling, Maria would rise, hoping the words on the page might magically make sense. But they never did" (Chazin, 1992, p. 131).

In a story in *Omni*, an immigrant adult from Jamaica explains that illiteracy is the illiterate's own fault: "You can't blame it all on other people, you are the person who is holding your own self" (Campbell, 1991, p. 33).

The constant simplifying of the immigrant illiterate in the popular literature and media is an important element in the construction of the heroic victim. Not only does it provide an inspirational example of hard work and struggle that the audience is supposed to relate to, not only does it celebrate endurance and optimism, but it presents a figure who is rarely threatening to the dominant culture. The immigrant typically "knows his place" and rarely aspires to rise above it.

Contrast this simple immigrant with the potentially more threatening simple American worker.

The Simple American Worker

The American illiterate is slightly more complex, or "rounded" (Forster, 1927). What is even more fascinating than the character himself are authors' and journalists' consistent biases and their curious cultivation of a maternalistic stance toward him. Rather than a struggle to rise to a low socioeconomic level that does not threaten the dominant culture, what is found here is a formulaic tale in which the simple American worker is presented, then humbled, then nursed back to self-composure. In the process of breaking a crude, gruff self-identity and rebuilding a new, more sensitive one, he acquires sophisticated knowledge. In a reflection of what is expected to happen in our literacy classrooms, the simple American worker "evolves" and becomes more "civilized," more in touch with his feelings, more mature and responsible. As will be seen in Part Two of this book, the catharsis presented for the simple American worker provides a model for the shift in self-image that literacy teachers and tutors are apparently expected to bring about in their learners.

One of the most famous and enduring depictions carried into American literature and today's media is Charles Dickens's quintessential simple worker, Joe Gargery of *Great Expectations.* Joe, a hard-working blacksmith, is Pip's uncle. He tries to hide his inability to read one evening when he and Pip (the narrator) are sitting in front of the fireplace. Pip is showing his uncle how well he can write on a small slate. He suspects Joe cannot read, and challenges him to read what he has written on his slate. "'The rest, eh, Pip?' said Joe, looking at it with a slowly searching eye. 'One, two, three. Why here's three Js, and three Os, and three J-O, Joes, in it, Pip!'" Pip leans over and finishes the sentence. "'Astonishing!' said Joe, when I had finished. 'You are a scholar'" ([1861] 1911, pp. 50–51). Thus, undereducated Joe is forced to reveal his shameful secret.

As seen in the previous chapter, this scene, complete with fireplace, heroic male victim, and well-meaning child has become the standard marketing image copied countless times in magazine and television advertisements for literacy campaigns. The Advertising Council's television commercial with Maureen Stapleton's overlaid voice, reported in the *New York Times* in 1984, offers but one of dozens of examples of a father figure sitting before a fireplace, child on his knee. There is a distinct pattern of the hulking male low-literate figure in today's media and movies. He is invariably being instructed by an "inferior"—a more learned child, a female, or a lower-level employee. In the "The ABC's of Courage," a story in an August 1984 issue of *Esquire,* we see a photo of a man sitting alone, somewhat slumped down, on a park bench. He is wearing a fedora, and his back is turned to the camera. A closer look reveals that the poignant photo does not match the careful descriptions of the person and the scene in the accompanying story. It obviously was just a handy photo to evoke the requisite emotions. The simple worker is pure fiction, just like Joe Gargery. He is nevertheless described as follows:

> The man is fifty-five years old. He is trying to learn how to read. He is a large man, balding and wearing thick glasses; he bears a resemblance to the actor Ernest Borgnine. His plumber's work clothes— denim overalls, a flannel shirt—are still on. Today, as he does twice a week, he has driven straight from work to Mrs. Lord's house. His hands are dirty from his day's labor; as he points to the words on the spelling list you can see that he has not had time to stop and clean up. He has been coming to Mrs. Lord's house for just over a year.

> The next word on the list is *down.*

> "Down," the man says with confidence in his voice.

> "That's right," Mrs. Lord says. "Very good" [Greene, 1984, p. 10].

This story was carried once more in December 1984 in *50 Plus* magazine, probably because the "Borgnine-like" character being romanticized is over fifty. However, why does he need to "bear a resemblance to Ernest Borgnine?" Why not say he bears a resemblance to Jimmy Stewart or Peter O'Toole, for instance? Obviously, Borgnine fits a stereotype entrenched in the popular perspective. The plumber is curiously nameless, although the teacher is "Mrs. Lord." Why not create a character who typifies the demographics of actual low literates? The reference to Borgnine is symptomatic of the close connection between the media's rendering of the heroic victim of illiteracy and the fantasy world created and fed by Hollywood and the media. Here is the fogbound island described by passersby. In the two stories just recounted, we see the world in its simplest terms, as we might like it to be, with the educated person—child or female—at the center.

The Borgnine character is from the same mold as the figure played by Dennis Weaver in the ABC made-for-TV drama *Bluffing It*. The familiar plot is about Cal (Weaver), who not only must struggle to overcome illiteracy but must first be personally humbled by having to deny his gruff, manly exterior. Unlike the immigrant stories that contain themes of passivity and acceptance, narratives about the simple American worker introduce a tension arising from "volatile ignorance" that must be turned into conforming knowledge. The theme also involves a curious denial of masculinity in what might be called the "evolution" of the prideful worker. Cal, and others who will be discussed here, must first be purged of all bravado. Like the Borgnine figure, they must be humbled, made to ask for the help of a more sophisticated, more "evolved" instructor. The result is a more passive literacy student who is now "in touch with his feelings," more aware of his former brutishness, and much more sensitive toward his family and friends. The simple American worker experiences "forced evolution."

The stages are basically as follows. First, and always a painful step, the characters must realize how their illiteracy is not only a burden on themselves but a liability to those around them. This involves accepting responsibility for family, friends, and employers. The illiterate must "get in touch with his feelings" in this phase, usually through some type of crisis. Next comes the painful admission, sometimes public, that he is in fact "an illiterate." The heroic victim must then be humbled by turning to either a child, a female, or a mild-mannered male—often of a lower socioeconomic level—for maternal help. The classic stories of the simple worker end with a "happily ever after," upbeat scene.

A description of *Bluffing It* in the *Saturday Evening Post* described Cal as "a man who has faked his way through life" (Harr, 1988, p. 48). However, "Cal's granddaughter isn't fooled when Cal stumbles over her favorite stories" (p. 48). He must swallow his pride and be tutored by his own employee. It is pointed out in the movie synopsis that "Cal went to the library three times before he had the courage to go in for the literacy program" (p. 48). Afterward, a humbler but kinder Cal becomes a proper citizen and a "better," more sensitive male.

This formula is used repeatedly. The movie *Stanley and Iris,* which was mentioned in Chapter One, "implicitly suggests that because Iris knows how to read and write she is automatically equipped to teach Stanley" (Luttrell, 1996, p. 352). She admirably succeeds in cultivating gruff Stanley, but only after Stanley is forced to see that he is indeed illiterate. There is a "forced evolution" on the part of the male illiterate: first comes the humbling, then the admission, then the saving, then the surge of sensitivity (occasionally accompanied by restored sexuality), then, assumedly, the "full life." However, the final stage is usually only suggested. We never actually see Stanley, for example, driving through the suburbs to a job at an insurance company. But we know he will now be "normal" nevertheless.

Sports figures play the role particularly well. One of the clearest cases of this is the depiction of football player Dexter Manley in a *People* magazine article, "Until he tackled his illiteracy, the Redskins' gridiron terror lived in fear of the ABC's." In this story, as in *Stanley and Iris,* there is constant reassurance that the literate population is the superior of the evolved species. Bravado and physical size are no match for brains and superior levels of evolution:

Dexter Manley, the Washington Redskins' defensive end, has been called many things in his eight-year career, like "fearsome"—the mountainous 6' 3", 257-lb. All-Pro is the Redskins' career leader in sacks. . . . Testifying before a Senate hearing on illiteracy, he struggled valiantly, and in vain, to read a statement he had prepared.

> Reduced to tears by the anxiety of reading in public, Manley sat in
> silence for almost a minute. Finally, he was able to abandon his
> script and simply tell the legislators about the learning disability
> (poor auditory memory) that left him functionally illiterate and,
> until recently, able to read only at second-grade level [Manley,
> 1989, p. 50].

Again, the humbling of the brute. One asks why Ernest Borgnine?
Why burly Dexter Manley? Why gruff Cal? The script for who the
illiterate is was written long before these figures appeared—at least
as early as Charles Dickens.

Simple African Americans and Simple Southern Whites

Our early literature is replete with racist depictions of African
Americans. A brief look at literacy during slavery is provided in
Chapter Three. What is interesting in the current popular literature is that the humbling process is still the same for these simple
African Americans, but the main characters are not always males;
that theme is largely reserved for the simple American worker.
Also, the stories do not necessarily involve the illiterate being
taught by a child, female, or teacher/tutor of a lower class status.
The simple African American and simple southern white are
already of the lower classes. They never present a threat, and their
literacy is bestowed on them only out of charity. They must first
acknowledge their ignorance and then come humbly, and directly,
to the more knowing teacher.

The highly acclaimed novel *The Color Purple,* by Alice Walker
(1982), tells how the tragic hero, Celie, must leave school when
"All us notice is I'm all the time sick and fat" (p. 11). The reader
is aware that she is in fact pregnant and does not know it. Celie
later gets a glimpse of sophisticated knowledge through the window of literacy, and she then realizes, "I was so *ignorant.*" She tells
the reader, "The little I knew about my own self wouldn't have
filled a thimble" (p. 138). Literacy and education move her a (safe)
distance up the evolutionary scale.

The popular literature is also replete with similar depictions of
white southerners as stereotypical illiterates. One such rendering
that helped entrench the stereotype of the illiterate southerner is
the powerful depiction of sharecroppers in Agee and Evans's clas-

sic, *Let Us Now Praise Famous Men* ([1939] 1966). Here, America learned of families like the Ricketts: "Mrs. Ricketts can neither read nor write. She went to school one day in her life and her mother got sick and she never went back. Another time she told me that the children laughed at her dress and the teacher whipped her for hitting back at them" (p. 276). There are images in this early classic that have added to the stereotype in the media that southern white illiterates are probably "simpleminded." George Gudger, for instance, can "spell and write his own name; beyond that he is helpless. He got as far as the second grade. By that time there was work for him and he was slow minded anyway" (p. 277).

These images of people that Agee and Evans presented have become the figure of sharecropper illiterate simplicity, even as portrayed in today's media. In "Bertha's Triumph," a 1987 story in *Reader's Digest,* we find Bertha Lee Ingram, a "stocky 63-year-old black woman" whose parents were sharecroppers. Combining African American and southern white sharecropper stereotypes, the author relates that "Bertha's father took her to school, often carrying her piggy-back on the three-mile trek. When she got older, she would take time off to help in the fields. By the time she would return to school, she'd have forgotten her lessons and would need to start all over again. Before Bertha reached her teens, she had quit school for good to work with her parents (Jordan, 1987, p. 56).

This story (also carried in other magazines, such as *People*) goes on to tell how Bertha delivers stillborn twins, how her husband dies of a heart attack, and then how she marries a man with eight children. According to Bertha, If "your parents and your grandparents couldn't read, . . . you just come up backwards with no way out" (p. 56).

The pattern established with the simple African American and the southern white is that they are right to realize their inadequacy, but they are not threatening. The portrayals of these four categories of heroic victims have much in common. They are consistently depicted as innocent, and courageous in their efforts to learn to read and be like the dominant class—however futile those efforts might be. Literacy education is presented over and over as the way to climb the ladder of sophisticated knowledge into the dominant society, but if one asks which of the stereotypes has the happiest ending in the stories we have examined, one has to note that Celie and Bertha and the African American stereotype end in a benign acceptance that offers less hope than that presented to any of the white stereotypes.

As will be seen in Chapter Three, the historic promises of adult literacy have more to do with regulation than liberation. The purpose of literacy in the political perspective is ultimately to sustain and reproduce the classes, the socioeconomics, and the politics of a world defined by, legitimated by, and controlled by the white dominant culture.

The Illiterate as Natural Man

There is an exception to the rule of the illiterate as heroic victim: a *leitmotif* in the literature and media of a romanticized "statement" hero. Unlike the heroic victim, this figure is typically presented as an anachronism, a curiosity, because he (never she) is exceptional in every normative sense. Here again, one sees the Byronic roots of the illiterate adult. This figure stands apart both by circumstance and—the key difference—by personal choice. In this stereotype, we find not passivity and humble acceptance, but a person who has evolved "naturally." This is a man who has scoffed at "sophisticated knowledge" and excelled instead in the "school of hard knocks." The natural man is a careful observer who readily adapts. He has a rare degree of common sense, and in novels shows a rebellious, cynical face to society's hypocrisies. Here is a quality often found in low literates (Quigley, 1990a)—a quality that many illiterate adults in Fingeret's research (1983) said the educated world lacks. Perhaps because of his lack of schooling, natural man is able to expose the fraudulence and injustices of the schooling system. By the author's intent, he is a "statement figure." There is an authorial purpose in the image created. The statement is not concerned with how the figure is victimized by society but presents a mirror to society itself. Through natural man and his world, we see the absurdity of our accepted knowledge systems and our revered culture.

Extremely popular at the end of the nineteenth and into the twentieth century, natural man is a theme curiously absent from our program recruiting material. He also appears only infrequently in the media. Where does this figure come from, and what does he look like?

Examples again appear to originate in British literature—for example, Mr. Doolittle, the acerbic father of Eliza Doolittle in George Bernard Shaw's play *Pygmalion*. Mr. Doolittle is the absolute opposite of the simple American worker or of Dickens's Joe Gargery. When offered a tutoring position by Messrs. Higgins and Pickering, he replies: "Not me, Governor, thank you kindly. I've heard all the preachers and the prime ministers—for I'm a thinking man and game for politics or religion or social reform same as all the other amusements—and I tell you it's a dog's life any way you look at it. Undeserving poverty is my line. Take one station in society with another it's—it's—well, it's the only one that has any ginger in it, to my taste (Shaw, [1916] 1964, p. 48).

Doolittle's contrary nature and personal capabilities are similar to those found in Somerset Maugham's character Albert Foreman in the short story *The Verger* (1957). Foreman, the title character, has successfully cared for St. Peter's Church on Neville Square, somewhere in England, for decades. When the new vicar realizes that Foreman cannot read, he calls him in and says, "I'm afraid you must go" (p. 44). The hero, as natural man, walks home after being fired and, that same afternoon, realizes a need for a tobacco shop along the very street he returns home on each day. He starts such a shop, and it succeeds admirably: "In the course of ten years he had acquired no less than ten shops and was making money hand over fist" (p. 46). One day, a bank manager who is proud to hold Foreman's accounts is amazed to learn that he is illiterate. The manager asks:

"'Good God, man, what would you be now if you had been able to [read]?'

'I can tell you that, sir,' said Mr. Foreman, a little smile on his still aristocratic features. 'I'd be verger of St. Peter's, Neville Square'" (p. 47).

In American literature, *The Adventures of Tom Sawyer* and *The Adventures of Huckleberry Finn* caught the public imagination in large part because Huck Finn and Tom Sawyer display a natural wit. Huck takes some pride in the fact that he "eventually could spell, and read, and write just a little, and could say the multiplication table up to six times seven is thirty-five" (Twain, [1884] 1958, p. 14), but schooling was like all social conventions—useless knowledge, foppish manners, and pretense concocted for the more foolish middle and upper classes.

Natural man makes an occasional appearance in the modern media. One of the few examples is in the widely circulated story of John Corcoran. In a *People* magazine version, the large-boned male appears again, but this time not as a victim:

> Success sat on Big John Corcoran like antlers on a bull elk. Six-foot-four and built like a fullback, he sported a mop of gray-blond hair, a speaking voice that played bass fiddle on a listener's bones and ice-blue eyes that lit up like headlights when he switched on the charm. With energy, presence and a flair for the dramatic, he survived college and graduate school, became a respected social-studies teacher in Oceanside, Calif., then turned a $2,500 investment into a house building business employing more than 200 people. At 48, Corcoran was a multimillionaire who owned a $600,000 villa with a slam-dunk view of the Pacific, went off on European vacations with his attractive wife, Kathy—and lived in terror that somebody might expose his unspeakable secret: He was a total illiterate [Smith, 1988, p. 199].

Versions of this story were carried in several journals. However, the four categories of heroic victim stereotypes are far more evident in today's media than the natural man.

The Impact of Stereotypes on the Adult Literacy Field

Do people such as those seen in the journalistic and fictional stories we have examined actually exist in literacy programs? In every stereotype, there is some kernel of truth. Figures described in fiction and the media are rivaled in literacy conferences across the United States. Lucy Grissom and thousands like her have told their stories, and millions have responded with pity, guilt, and money. Are there learners whose lives are as simplistic or as shallow as appear on the stage and in the media? The essence of stereotyping is to both simplify and abstract. A selected set of observations is brought together to reach a narrow, specious conclusion. Any contradictory facts must be ignored. Certain emotions are called on to drive the argument along. The media and popular literature have shown us the assumed simplicity of the illiterate through a distorted lens. As noted journalist Ben Bagdikian has explained it: "Large classes of people are ignored in the news, are reported as exotic fads, or appear only at their worst—minorities, blue-collar workers, the lower middle class, the poor. They become publicized mainly when they are in spectacular accidents, on strike, or are arrested" (1990, p. 18).

When the illiterate is so repeatedly portrayed as the "inferior other" and the victim, when he is so consistently interpreted through the biases and racist attitudes of the dominant culture, all of us are affected. The filtering out of any other "knowledges" as irrelevant gives us romanticized pictures that denigrate one group and elevate another. Thus, we have developed a public conscious-ness and a popular perspective on who the illiterate is, where he is located on the ladder of sophisticated knowledge, and what this means to us in terms of moral responsibility. And it is this latter understanding that is counted on to support our field.

If the information made available through research has become more comprehensive and more critical over time, the pop-ular imagery has unfortunately neither changed nor expanded. Why not? Researchers have made remarkably little impact on either the popular or political perspective. Thus, print copy is pub-lished, movies are sold, political careers are advanced. As will be seen, the field of literacy education is caught in the marketing of stereotypes no less than is the Hollywood film maker or the jour-nalist with a deadline.

Who is the illiterate adult in America? In this chapter, we have looked at the most recent demographic surveys and definitions. We have seen a number of examples of fictionalized and sensa-tionalized images of the illiterate adult. If, as I discuss in Part Four of this book, the ultimate responsibility for the future of this field lies not with policy makers, authors, or journalists but with practi-tioners, the following exercise, which I use in my graduate classes on adult literacy education, may prove useful to a wider audience.

I ask the graduate students to interview (1) a literacy program administrator or policy maker, or a literacy teacher or tutor; (2) a person "on the street" who they think is well informed on public events; and (3) a student currently in a literacy program. In this interview, they are to ask, among other questions,

What is illiteracy?

How would you define *literacy*?

Who is an illiterate?

How would you describe an illiterate?

The results have been remarkably consistent through the eight years I have done this. The administrators and policy makers typically describe adult illiterates in terms of a political perspective. That is, they refer to the numbers of unemployed and to individuals who have left schooling for a range of personal reasons; frequently, they discuss lack of self-esteem. There is usually more than a suggestion of poor motivation as the reason such people are undereducated. Typically, the administrator or policy maker blames lack of funding for the field's inability to do more. For teachers and tutors, the literacy student is one who has had limited opportunities, unfortunate luck, and now suffers from a poor self-image. This reflects the popular perspective with its sense of a heroic victim.

The teacher's or tutor's literacy student is typically seen as needing more help and more personal support than can be given within the parameters and restrictions of the practitioner's work hours and load. The focus of the teacher is less on people as unemployment numbers and more on the dire need for nurturing and support.

The man or woman in the street gives a very different set of opinions. For such people, illiteracy is a curious "quirk" in the normal flow of society. They search their sources of stored information and come up with what the media have fed them—fundamentally, a heroic victim perception. Illiterates are people who have quit school, probably because of drugs or wrong peer influences or poor parenting. Illiterates are tragic. They somehow got left behind. Society needs to do more and government should do more.

When the class finally interviews literacy students themselves, the views expressed are radically different. Students usually tell of schools that ignored them, families that moved too often, health problems. They are now in courses for a chance to get better employment and educational opportunities, but at least as often, they (especially females) report that they want to help their children with their homework or they want to be able to perform tasks such as obtaining a driver's license, taking other tests, or simply shopping at the sales (Fingeret, 1983; 1984). The notion of poor self-image never arises from literacy learners. The number of unemployed never arises. They do not fulfill their stereotypes—small surprise. One wonders if we are working at cross purposes. As to how to improve the numbers of literates in society, the discussion typically goes back to a poor school system that they failed or that failed them.

An examination of the stereotypes that we encounter all too frequently in our daily reading and television and movie viewing helps us to understand the influences that have formed our thinking (Bourdieu and Passeron, 1977; Bowles and Gintis, 1977). The next chapter looks at what we have been told the adult illiterate needs—for his or her own good—and how we as practitioners have been encouraged to respond to those needs over the course of this century.

The Political Perspective and Literacy Programs

A critical understanding of the political perspective is vital to those of us working in adult literacy education if we wish to respond effectively to its powerful influences.

A personal anecdote may help indicate the sharp difference between the popular and political perspectives. In 1977, I was the director of an adult basic education program at a large community college. At the time, many of our literacy students were referred to our program by an employment agency of the federal government. One of the systemic problems was that on graduation, after months of intensive work with us, many of the students still had difficulty—some great difficulty—in getting a job. Given the federal agency's job mandate, its referral process did not go far enough. Even though all of the students were advised of job openings by the governmental agency, and all were free to return to the agency for employment referrals at any point, many were fearful and could not bring themselves to take the next step. We convinced Ted, the agency counselor assigned to our college, to tell our graduates about local jobs and, for the first time, to take the most nervous students to job locations across the city in his agency car. When he did this, all those he took interviewed successfully and got a job.

At a planning meeting later with senior officials of the agency, I proposed a "bridging program" in which the agency would spend more time looking at our graduates' employment skills and interests. The designated agency counselor would then work much more closely with the graduates who were afraid to approach an employer. I brought up the success of Ted's efforts.

When I mentioned this, Ted sank in his seat at the other side of the table. He was clearly embarrassed. His body language and my own subconscious awareness of the agency culture—what I now understand as the political perspective—were signaling me to leave his personal involvement out of the discussion. There was a long pause. I shifted to the harder vocabulary of "value added" and "employment turnaround." It was too late.

"The system is basically in place," I said, trying to bolster my proposal. "We need very few resources to bridge to the employment sector. Just some adjustments."

Suddenly, the senior agency person at the head of the table slammed his pen down and burst out: "Damn it! We educate these people. If they can't take that education and get out there and find a job like anyone else, we're not going to spoon-feed them further!" Glancing frequently at Ted, he lectured all of us on the amount already spent "sending these people back to school." He informed us about other, obviously more important, funding demands from "real" employment programs, such as a new one to retrain displaced workers and several in-house vocational training projects. "Not to mention the growing demand for funding professional training in this city!" Clearly, these were steps further up the ladder of sophisticated knowledge that had funding precedence. Although I was aware that our literacy program was considered near the bottom of the training heap as a federal funding priority, I was frankly surprised at the hostility, even rage, in the manager's reply. After his brief tirade, an agency bureaucrat across the table added, "These people need to grow up and face reality eventually!"

We moved on to other business. However, the three unstated messages delivered to everyone around the table were (1) "We are not wasting more taxpayer money on illiterates who will not get out there and help themselves"; (2) "As an agent of the government and your superior, I am warning all of you not to give in to the foolish sentiments of 'bleeding heart educators'"; and (3) "The college staff needs to grow up and face reality." In that room, in the heart of the federal offices, we had all been disabused of any illusions that we were there to nurture "heroic victims."

During a later postmortem at the college, it was noted by our counselor that the manager and his assistants had never actually seen any of the students we were talking about. The bureaucrats were responding entirely out of a "knee-jerk agency attitude," as one teacher put it. Despite these in-house observations, I knew the fault was mine. If there was to be a bridging program, I was supposed to be it. As the director of the adult basic education program, I was responsible for providing shuttle diplomacy between the educators' popular perspective and the bureaucrats' political perspective—two distinctly different cultures. I should have either brought a harder case to the political table, with better quantitative data, or orchestrated a more powerful emotional case, perhaps by bringing the manager to the college and replaying a variation of the Snyder-Grissom minitragedy.

I felt especially bad because I should not have brought Ted into it. We were "winning him over," as several of the teachers put it. Their point was valid. Ted had, in fact, "gone over to the other side" to the extent that he had begun responding to the soft emotional rather than the hard policy priorities. The manager had picked this up because I had revealed his secret. Ted became distant after that and cited the rules more often. He no longer took students anywhere or arranged for bridging. A few months later, he was moved to a different government post, following which we rarely saw him.

I later moved from the college to the provincial government and was responsible for the GED program and policy aspects of adult basic education. I regularly had to defend the existence of literacy programs but knew that I could not do so out of the popular perspective or "soft sentimentality." In the political perspective and in policy settings, economics, employment figures, financial concerns, and ubiquitous politics dominate. The micro level—what benefits the individual—is not what policy is concerned with (Quigley, 1993a). For policy makers, "the true does not [necessarily] determine the good" (Brandl, 1980, p. 42); it is the society's benefit that matters most (Finch, 1984).

We would do well to remember the statement of Augusta Kappner, U.S. assistant secretary of vocational and adult education, that was quoted in Chapter Two: "Literacy stories are powerful, but stories are not enough at the policy or macro level." The shift from individual to social responsibility is a key difference between the two perspectives. It is in the political world and through the lens of the political perspective that literacy policy is ultimately shaped.

This perspective is frequently at odds with the popular one, yet each contributes to the other's legitimacy and momentum. In my experience, the political is often seriously misunderstood by teachers, tutors, and counselors within our field. There is a chasm between the popular and the political perspectives. Practitioners and policy makers live in separate worlds perceiving very different realities.

Administrators are the best bridge we have over this chasm, as they tend to live "dual lives." The survival of many funded literacy programs depends greatly on the diplomacy and "bilingual/bicultural" skills of senior program administrators. It is the literacy administrator's challenge to understand and interpret both worlds and to predict change in both. He or she also has the rather lonely role of translating and advocating across program and political boundaries.

The remainder of this chapter attempts to explain what the political perspective is, where it comes from, who benefits from it, and how those working in the field should respond to it and try to affect it.

Social Policy as a Defining Voice

Social policy is that part of public policy specifically dedicated to improving some specific aspect of the human or societal condition, typically through governmental programs. The three most common areas of social policy programs are education, social welfare, and health. As Townsend explains: "Perhaps most commonly social policy is defined as policy concerned with . . . the development and management of specific services of the State and local authorities, such as health, education, welfare and social services" (1975, p. 2). Social policy is thus the assistance side of what government does—the side that gives out in the interests of improving people's lives and rarely intends to bring back immediate revenues. It is social policy that typically tries to bring about direct or indirect development of human potential. The aim is usually to "level the playing field" or provide a "safety net" with education, welfare, or health programs.

Of all governmental policy areas, social policy is perennially contentious and among the most debated in the House and Senate because these governmental programs go to the very heart of ideological differences in democratic government. The federal and state governments try to redistribute resources for the common good, typically through taxation (see Djao, 1983; Griffin, 1987; Finch, 1984). Social policy is an instrument intended to promote the short-term good of the few and/or the long-term benefit of the many. Its objective is to adjust the perpetual inequity of resource distribution among society's various groups. To varying, contested degrees, social policy tries to create and redistribute what Griffin calls "life chances" (1987). Everyone, even citizens without offspring, pays so that all children have a right to an education. Similarly, all contribute to some form of welfare and Medicaid program, even if many never need such support themselves.

In an applied definition that will provide an organizing framework for this chapter, Finch says that social policy is "action designed by government to engineer social change" (1984, p. 4). It is used "as a mechanism for solving social problems," as "redistributive justice," and as a means for "regulating subordinate groups" (p. 4). Social policy has also been called "the attempt to use education to solve social problems, influence social structures, to improve one or more aspects of the social condition, to anticipate crisis" (Silver, 1980, p. 17). There are many definitions of social policy; however, there can be no doubt that social policy will involve degrees of governmental intervention in people's lives and levels of citizen-government debate and tension (Griffin, 1987). For literacy as social policy, history shows that literacy education (and its denial) has been used as a means for "regulating subordinate groups" more than educators or policy makers might like to recall, whereas, as seen in Chapter Two, the media often choose to reflect a "soft" view of literacy, placing the issues in the popular perspective for wide public consumption. Social policy on literacy has a history of seeing literacy education as a social responsibility and illiterates as a threat. This is the "hard" side of literacy, with punitive overtones and a variety of assertions made by the public and the government. This is where we find anger, such as was heard in the employment agency manager's lecture.

When, as discussed in Chapter Two, U.S. newspapers and magazines took up the Advertising Council's challenge to recruit literacy volunteers, most of them did so with the popular perspective and the stereotypical imagery of the heroic victim. However, some took a "warning call" approach. *U.S. News & World Report* chose to warn its readership that illiteracy could be threatening the future of America: "If corrective steps are not taken, two out of three Americans could be functionally illiterate by the year 2000" (Cited in Dougherty, 1984, p. IV-29). The decision by that magazine's editorial staff was not to sentimentalize but to warn. Such warnings went much further in the media. An editorial in *America* magazine (Broken promise, 1993) described illiterates as menacing subhumans living unchecked by any power of rationality or self-discipline. The editor began "sympathetically" by wondering what it would be like to try to live comfortably in the United States without being able to doublecheck the total at the supermarket or fill out simple forms, then answered that one would probably feel "cut off" and "angry" (p. 4), and went on to state that verbal, nonliterate people would be subject to excitability, and, when under stress, would be inclined to "go berserk in the city streets" (p. 4). According to the editor's logic, nonliterates are impulsive rather than rational and are easily susceptible to television soundbites and demagogues. It all means that "the nation is closer to Idi Amin's Uganda or the Iran of the ayatollahs than we have thought" (p. 4).

Of course, there is absolutely no evidence that low literates live on impulse, tend to go berserk, or are any more susceptible to demagoguery than any other citizens, literate or otherwise.

Whether these are hysterical fears or not, they have been heard for over a century in this country. In the engineering of social policy on literacy lie many assumptions, not the least of which is the dominant culture's assumption that its norms are the appropriate blueprint for all decent citizens. For literacy social policy, the illiterate has historically been the crude building material. Finch's three-part definition quoted earlier is particularly useful in the examination of social policy on literacy. Its component parts show how social policy on literacy education evolved from a nineteenth-century means of regulating subordinate groups to a twentieth-century quest for social engineering—with fleeting attempts to use literacy education for the redistribution of justice along the way. This also is part of our history and part of the legacy we have inherited.

A Century of Fear and Loathing

In 1871, a special report of the commissioner of education on the condition of education in the District of Columbia was submitted to the president of the Senate. The commissioner stated that the country was facing a national calamity and moral crisis because of illiteracy: "This immense evil, our weakness and our disgrace, extends among our native population as well as among those of foreign birth; in the North as well as in the East and the West; in the old States and in the new, from Maine to Georgia, as well as from Maine to California. It is a wide-spread national calamity" (Leigh, 1871, pp. 802–803).

More than a century later, the widely circulated policy report, *Jump Start: The Federal Role in Adult Literacy,* (Chisman, 1989) advised the new cabinet of President Bush that the nation was facing an economic crisis and an impending national "rendezvous" with the rise of minorities in society. Literacy education was urgently needed and those who were low literate were placing the future of the nation in jeopardy: "America must do a great many things to avoid [an] unhappy rendezvous with demographic destiny. Among the most important things it must do is ensure that the twenty million-plus adults who are seriously deficient in basic skills become fully productive workers and citizens well before the rendezvous begins. *Without their best efforts . . . there is little hope for the economic and social future of this country"* (p. 3; emphasis added).

The tone of urgency, the arguments for action, all warn of a bleak, apocalyptic future due to the illiterates among us. From Edwin Leigh in 1871 to the *New York Times* in 1982, illiteracy is an "epidemic": "We're raising a whole country of semi-illiterates" (Johnston and Anderson, 1983, p. II-3). In the same year, *U.S. News & World Report* understood the Carnegie Foundation reports on illiteracy to mean that "the nation runs the risk of drifting unwittingly into 'a new kind of dark age'" (Wellborn, 1982, p. 55). In 1987, "Newsnotes" in the *Phi Delta Kappan* told readers that "the very survival of the United States is at stake" ("Improving literacy," 1987, p. 711).

For more than a century, impending disaster has been announced and reannounced. The history of social policy on literacy reveals that society shrinks back in renewed horror as the illiterate adult is dragged into court—forever in the culprit's role, forever charged with unconscionable crimes against the welfare of the nation. Yet despite the many charges made and the exhortations to the culprit to change his or her ways before the impending disaster is upon us, the illiterate adult seems never to respond.

Because the low literate is never asked to speak, as Harman put it, "an acceptance of the recipient's world view as legitimate and a sensitivity to the dynamics of nonliterate cultures have eluded literacy programming throughout its unhappy history" (1977, p. 446).

At the social policy level, it is assumed that the low literate has no useful knowledge. In 1988, Scribner asked why the perspective of the low literate is so very absent through history and why the low literate is assumed to be so grossly inadequate: "Functional needs have not yet been assessed from the perspective of those who purportedly experience them. To what extent do adults whom tests assess as functionally illiterate perceive themselves as lacking in the necessary skills to be adequate parents, neighbors, workers?" (1988, p. 75).

In large part, the answers to Scribner's questions lie in the social policy past that we have inherited and tend to ignore, but that continues to shape the decisions affecting our field today.

Social Policy for the Regulation of Sinners

There is evidence that America may have succeeded in attaining full literacy in the northeastern colonial states during the Puritan era. This is probably as close as the country has ever come to the promise of "eradicating illiteracy." However, according to Stubblefield and Keane (1989), "full literacy" was restricted to males— and not all males. From the Jim Crow laws to this century, African Americans have been disallowed the right to vote because they could not pass literacy tests. Unfortunately, there is very little historical research on women and literacy, but as recently as the 1920s, immigrant women were denied their constitutional right to vote for the same reasons. Whereas immigrant males traditionally received Americanization literacy classes, the women did not. In New York in the 1920s, all new voters were required to "read intelligibly an excerpt of approximately 50 words from the State constitution and write legibly in English 10 words from the passage read" ("School Principals Issue Certificates," 1922, p. 71).

In fact, this country has never enjoyed a time when it has approached "full" literacy (Stevens, 1987). The notion that "neutral literacy education" has been made widely available through history without strings attached is a myth, just as the notion that literacy has been extended openly and freely for all through time is a myth (Graff, 1979).

Graff concluded that, in America, "of the panoply of reasons offered by school promoters in this period [nineteenth century], the inculcation of morality was supreme" (p. 23). The roots of literacy education in Britain and subsequently in America are located in social policies for regulation. From the beginning, literacy meant morality, and morality meant a safeguard against sin and unacceptable conduct. As Graff explained it, literacy education could bring "a mode of conduct . . . a way of life: habits, values, attitudes, which were based on the cultural necessities of progress and the requirements of society" (p. 25). Thus, in schools "in the early 1800's, education was seen as a tool for unifying the nation; the common moral lessons expressed in primers were expected to provide a basis for shared values" (Fingeret, 1989, p. 6). If adults, by dropping out of school or not attending at all, had not acquired the basics of literacy, literacy courses were provided, in large part to infuse morality for the good of the nation. This second chance was offered to certain adults by governments and educators and denied to others.

Social Policy for the Regulation of "Inferior Races"

During the eighteenth century and the period of slavery, through Reconstruction, and—some argue—up until today (see, for example, Franklin, 1967; Turner, 1994; Woodward, 1964), there has been little question that literacy education on a large scale has been for the building of consensus on social policy (Graff, 1979). The consensus to be built and guarded in early America was that literacy meant access to knowledge. However, for slaves and a great many African Americans since, the history of literacy has been a story of regulation, not education (Meier and Rudwick, 1976). Despite the Fourteenth Amendment, which gave citizenship to former slaves, the Supreme Court had to be involved repeatedly from the Jim Crow era to the 1960s civil rights movement to assure that legal equality might be realized (Woodward, 1964). Knowledge is power. Therefore, the denial of literacy meant the denial of knowledge and of power. Nowhere in America's history are this logic and the "disempowering" impact of denied literacy education more evident than in the institution of slavery. This is one of the first chapters of America's abuse of literacy, and surely the most brutal example in its history.

There is absolutely no doubt that the denial of literacy education during the period of slavery was part of state, regional, and plantation policies for the suppression and control of an "inferior race." Despite the emergence of antislavery groups and legislative efforts against slavery, state and even federal governments succumbed to wealthy slaveholders' demands (Jenkins, 1960).

The way slavery was created and maintained sheds light on how knowledge and "subordinate groups" have been controlled through our history. According to Stampp (1956), slaves were created by fostering a "slave mentality" from birth. Complete domination, including the shaping of self-concept, was the goal. According to Goodell (1968), the slave condition was composed of eleven elements, from unlimited authority of the slavemaster to the "incapacity to enjoy civil, domestic, or political rights (p. 378–379). Two of Goodell's elements reflected an attempt to control slaves' very thoughts: "the power of the master to forbid education and social religious worship at his own discretion" (p. 379) and "the power of the legislatures of slave states to prohibit education, even by masters, and to prohibit or restrict free social worship" (p. 379).

Between 1641 and 1755, every American colony enacted statutes to control the increasing presence of Africans. Contrary to the current notion that the North was always somehow a "safe haven" for blacks, Massachusetts and Connecticut recognized slavery in 1641 and 1650, respectively. Virginia gave legal recognition in 1661, Maryland in 1663–1664, New York in 1665, South Carolina in 1682, Pennsylvania in 1700. New Jersey, Rhode Island, New Hampshire, Delaware, North Carolina, and Georgia followed suit through to 1755 (Asante and Mattson, 1992).

While each was concerned with some degree of restriction for "Africans," South Carolina in 1740 was the first to pass a law restricting education for slaves (Goodell, 1968), with the following understatement: "Whereas having slaves taught to write, or suffering them to be employed in writing, may be attended with great inconveniences; Be it therefore enacted by the authority aforesaid, That all and every person or persons whatever, who shall hereafter teach, or cause a slave to be taught, to write . . . every person or persons, shall, for every offense, forfeit the sum of one hundred pounds current money" (Goodell, 1968, p. 319).

The rise of abolitionism saw a surge of more punitive laws, with the codes of South Carolina and Georgia suddenly prohibiting all forms of literacy and schooling for slaves (Klein, 1967). In 1819, South Carolina prohibited slaves from meeting for educational purposes, and in 1831, slaves were denied any assembly at a school, house, church, or meetinghouse for the purpose of reading or writing, day or night (Klein, 1967). The Nat Turner rebellion saw an increase in anti-education laws throughout the South. Following South Carolina and Georgia, North Carolina outlawed public instruction of slaves in 1835, and in 1847 Missouri made it illegal to teach African slaves (Genovese, 1972; Asante and Mattson, 1992).

W.E.B. Du Bois ([1935] 1962) estimated that by the end of the Civil War, only 5 percent of slaves had the ability to read. Because illiteracy was so widespread, records on their reading ability are few. However, the Slave Narrative Collection in the Library of Congress, compiled between 1936 and 1938, has more than two thousand interviews with ex-slaves, which include the stories of Frederick Douglass, Henry Bibb, and William Wells Brown. Here are records of amazing courage on the part of African Americans, and some whites, who dared to teach reading and writing (Genovese, 1972; Weber, 1978). A remarkable number did become literate, not just "favorite" slaves being tutored by owners but also through slaves teaching slaves in clandestine meetings. "Sabbath schools" were reported as the only other means of access to literacy education for slaves (Genovese, 1972). A "friendlier" climate often prevailed in towns and cities, where such education went on informally. However, friendliness could be a trap that could lead to severe punishment for those participating, including loss of privileges, confinement, whippings, mutilation, even death.

The struggle to read and write is told, in part, in the Slave Narrative Collection (Yetman, 1970) through slaves' stories of how they were given some literacy and numeracy education and often tried to conceal their own intelligence. Using the phonetic reporting style of the day, the exact rendering of the interviewers still stands in the collection and is quoted here. Abram Harris, age ninety-three, from Greenvillle, South Carolina, described what would happen to those

caught reading: "Dere weren't none of de white folks in dem slavery times what would let dey niggers have any learnin'. You sure better not be cotch a-tryin, to lern no readin' or writin'. Our marster
even never allowed dat. Iffen a nigger was to be found what could
write, den right straight dey would chop his forefinger offen dat
hand what he write with. Dere weren't no such a thing as no schools
for de niggers after de surrender" (Yetman, 1970, p. 161).

Ferebe Rodgers of Baldwin County, Georgia, more than one
hundred years old, told of how teaching others could mean death:
"Young marster was a fixin to marry us, but he got cold feet, and
a young nigger by name o' Enoch Golden married us. He was
what we called a 'double headed nigger'—he could read and
write, and he knowed so much. On his dyin' bed he said he been
de' death o' many a nigger 'cause he taught so many to read and
write" (p. 257).

The first national adult literacy campaign was launched in
1924, but African Americans were not included in literacy plans
until the efforts of Raymond Wilbur in the early 1930s (Cook,
1977). Well into the twentieth century, it was clearly accepted by
literacy administrators that African Americans were the least able
to learn in the field. For example, Ethel Richardson, a state administrator for adult education in California, reported in the official
organ of the federal Office of Education, *School Life,* that "it takes
a great deal longer to teach a Mexican illiterate than a Russian illiterate. . . . We have had . . . some remarkable results with Jewish illiterates," but "we had one Negro man who spent a whole year
learning to write his name" (1926, p. 136).

Forty years later, in Cook County, Illinois, an ill-fated literacy
program created by Raymond Hilliard forced low-literate welfare
recipients to either attend literacy programs or forfeit their welfare checks. The mandatory program collapsed, but not before
Hilliard received a major award for his efforts (Quigley, 1990c) or
before he made it clear in the press that many of "his boys" (referring to his African American students) came to class inebriated.
After all, what can you do if they will not give their best effort?

After almost a decade of federal policy making on literacy, Secretary Raymond Wilbur added illiterate Native Indians, along with
illiterate African Americans, as two "special groups" ("Recent Educational Conferences Held in Washington, D.C.," 1930, p. 91).

Social Policy for the Regulation
of Undesirable Immigrants

Following the Civil War, the fear that immigrant illiterates would endanger everything "real Americans" had worked for became the new American Nightmare. With the full establishment of the common school and progress made toward universal secondary schooling, the federal government moved ahead with the Discrimination Laws. By 1882, federal laws prohibited immigration by Chinese, and through lobbyists such as the Immigration Restriction League (Cook, 1977), further restrictions followed, with literacy testing used as a screening device. Henry Cabot Lodge, a strong supporter of the 1880s Discrimination Laws, proposed a bill in 1896 that would refuse immigration to those who could not read or write in any language. In his opinion, such a bill would preserve "the mental and moral qualities which make our race" and exclude "the wholesale infusion of races whose traditions and inheritances, whose thoughts and beliefs are wholly alien to ours and with whom we have never assimilated or even been associated in the past" (Cook, 1977, p. 2). These policies were to regulate those who would become "Americans." According to Lodge, literacy tests "would bear most heavily upon the Italians, Russians, Poles, Hungarians, Greeks and Asiatics, and very lightly, or not at all, upon English-speaking immigrants or Germans, Scandinavians and French" (p. 2). This bill passed Congress, as did similar ones in 1909 and 1915, but all were vetoed by the incumbent presidents (Cook, 1977).

Support for such policy was clearly expressed in public documents. Reverend A. D. Mayo did not exactly have the melting-pot image in mind when he declared, "We must stop the inflow from everywhere that, in one generation would make this Republic the mental and moral sewer of all nations" (1898, p. 34). The sense of what illiteracy meant at that time was conveyed by Mayo: "Illiteracy today in the United States means two things. First, it means the national slum, the nation's 'slough of despair'. . . in which is gathered ignorance, superstition, shiftlessness, vulgarity and vice" (p. 34). Mayo said illiterates constitute "the lowest order of every community, making it the chronic peril of the best, and the prophecy of Anarchy to the worst community in . . . every state" (p. 31). The proposed bill to restrict immigration on the basis of literacy, he said, "is a simple, sensible, American attempt to prevent the massing of the forces of Illiteracy which . . . has already become the peril of the Republic" (p. 36).

Following the Bolshevik revolution and against a background of mounting fear of communism, Immigration Restriction Legislation was passed in 1921 and again in 1924 (Cook, 1977). Literacy has always been an easily prescribed pill for the resolution of society's worst ills. Winthrop Talbot, a senior official with the census explained it this way in 1916: "Unless means are provided for reaching the illiterate and near literate, every social problem must remain needlessly complex and slow in resolution, because social and representative government rests upon an implied basis of universal ability to read and write" (Cook, 1977, p. 3).

The near doubling of Chicago's population every decade between 1850 and 1890 was one of many developments that provoked a substantial fear of "foreigners" (Schied, 1993). By 1912, the YMCA was promoting Americanization programs that would bring English and literacy education to the "foreign element." The YMCA's position was that "unless we can assimilate, develop, train and make good citizens out of them, they are certain to make ignorant, suspicious and un-American citizens out of us. Unless we Americanize them they will foreignize us" (Carlson, 1970, p. 447).

During this same period of immigrant influx, private enterprise was also using literacy to regulate immigrants. In some of America's earliest "workplace literacy" efforts, corporations dedicated themselves to measures that would Americanize their employees. Packard Motor Company and Paige-Detroit, for instance, insisted that immigrants show proficiency in literacy in their Americanization classes before they could be eligible for a job promotion (Carlson, 1970).

Prisons have found it efficacious to use literacy to regulate their inmates. In Kentucky, for example, "an added incentive to learn was given the prisoners by a resolution which was passed by the State prison board requiring that an inmate be able to read and write before his application for parole would be considered" ("For the Eradication of Illiteracy," 1923, p. 151).

An Emerging Political Perspective

There was no agreement at the turn of the century that money should be spent on illiterates. As early as 1911, M. L. Brittain, the state supervisor of schools in Georgia, requested funding from the Georgia legislature for the eradication of illiteracy in the state. However, no money was forthcoming: "These efforts were met with no success since the legislators were firmly convinced that illiterate adults could not be taught with any degree of success" (Cook, 1977, p. 15).

Whereas, at the federal level, illiterates were often regarded as latent sources of unrest and evil, regional and local adult educators more often saw them in the popular perspective—a dichotomy that remains essentially unchanged to the present day. A 1927 report of a project in North Carolina's Buncombe County by a visiting adult educator relates that "at an evening of entertainment these people, who a few years before could not be persuaded to take part in any public meeting, came upon the stage with all the zeal and enthusiasm of children, anxious to show that they were liberated from the bondage of illiteracy" (Alderman, 1927, p. 177). The same report explains that "the trained, patient teachers meant as much to them [illiterates] as does the physician to a family that has been stricken with disease" (p. 177).

What emerges from the history of social policy on literacy up through the 1920s is that legislation to regulate low-literate adults came to be passed with increasing frequency at the federal level, whereas there was a strong sense of pity at the educators' level. The first National Illiteracy Crusade arose out of a National Illiteracy Conference held in Washington in January 1924 ("National Organizations Will Combat Illiteracy," 1924, p. 128). The conference was addressed by adult educators, as well as church, philanthropic, and political leaders, with a mix of sympathy and fear. The first crusade, headed by John Finley of the *New York Times,* emerged from this emotional atmosphere. It had no goals and no resources (Cook, 1977). However, under newly elected President Hoover, another advisory committee on national illiteracy was appointed in November 1929 to advise the first national advisory committee. With advisers advising advisers, Hoover made it clear he wanted five million adults to become literate before the 1930 census was to be finished. The financial support for the campaign was $52,001.99, all to be raised through personal appeals and donations. The first true major campaign was launched on December 17, 1929, without government financial support, without mechanisms to make literacy activities possible, and with the unstated political purpose of improving the census data.

The literature documents that underfunding of literacy campaigns and successive one-year to five-year goals to eradicate illiteracy have become commonplace (Arnove and Graff, 1987). Literacy as social policy developed out of a scientific policy culture that saw a need for providing the elements of rationality, if not regulation. Just below the surface, there has always been a latent fear of those deemed "subordinate." It is a myth, therefore, that literacy education has always been promoted out of altruism. One has to ask if things have changed in today's campaigns.

Redistribution of Social Justice

The depression of the 1930s began a new era for social policy in America. Literacy was no exception. Work relief under the Civilian Conservation Corps (CCC) was initiated in 1933 to provide work for single men between the ages of eighteen and twenty-five. The CCC was designed to create employment in the preservation of the country's natural resources. Under the watchful eye of the United States Army, thousands of undereducated and illiterate young males were kept separate from urban centers in camps. However, as vocational training was being introduced among the men in the CCC camps, it was found that they had an average reading level of only 6.8—less than a seventh-grade reading capacity. It was further reported that 7,369 of the 375,000 men were unable to read a newspaper or even write a letter (Cook, 1977, p. 41). A program was therefore created in which the literate taught the illiterate. Thus, the unproductive were made productive, and there was a turn toward literacy social policy as part of wide-scale economic renewal. It could be argued that the CCC camps mark the beginning of the economic policies around literacy education that became familiar in subsequent years. Still, the camps held true to the familiar themes of morality and character development (Oxley, 1937).

One individual who courageously led social policy down the path least taken by policy makers through this period was Ambrose Caliver, an African American Ph.D. graduate of Columbia Teachers College appointed by President Hoover in 1930 to be the U.S. Office of Education's specialist in education for Negroes (Maskin, 1973; Stubblefield and Keane, 1994). Caliver led a decade of special efforts to provide literacy education to African Americans through the redistribution of social justice. He began by pointing out that African Americans were being ignored: "Although illiteracy in the states maintaining separate schools was four times greater among Negroes, the number of emergency teachers employed to teach illiterates was approximately the same as for whites" (Caliver, 1934, p. 40). He added, "Only in a few places have Negro relief teachers been employed in the same ratio as Negroes bear to the population" (p. 40).

Caliver was the designer of the now virtually forgotten set of principles then referred to as the "Magna Carta of Negro Education," printed and distributed in 1934 and 1935 (Caliver, 1934; see also Cook, 1977). This government-endorsed document asserted the rights of African Americans to an equal education. It marked one of the few moments when government, clearly influenced by one committed person, employed literacy social policy for the redistribution of social justice. Caliver, on behalf of government, argued that if African American education was to be equal, the attitudes of public school officials, of adult educators and adult education practitioners, and of African Americans themselves, needed to be seen as part of the problem. He wrote in the official U.S. journal *School Life* (1934) that public school officials needed to understand the facts and conditions of black education. They needed to reexamine "their disposition to deal fairly and justly with the Negro in providing educational opportunities." He argued that African Americans needed to see their lack of status in education and use their education "intelligently, sanely, and courageously in persistently pressing their claims for an equal educational opportunity" (p. 40). Negroes, he argued, "can do much in determining the future of their own education and in making it an instrument for personal and social betterment" (p. 41).

The lofty "Magna Carta of Negro Education" and Caliver's advocacy for African American input into the determination of their own programs slowly gave way to the familiar social policy objectives of the CCC camps: development of character, spiritual growth, citizenship, and vocational training for productivity. In fact, as time went on, it seems that Caliver became either worn down or silenced, because he later said nothing on "Negroes" and echoed the sentiments of politicians more and more (Caliver, 1951).

With the outbreak of World War II, literacy education was suddenly important for purposes of national defense. The nation's policy makers added "patriotism" to their list of objectives for this educational enterprise (Oxley, 1937). However, even if the dominance of the majority culture was left fully intact, there were moments when the possibility that literacy social policy could play a part in altering the status quo was alive. For a brief time, students and teachers were encouraged to play a larger role in social change. We now turn to the economic and patriotic purposes of literacy social policy—the extended outcomes of the CCC.

Regulation Through Social Engineering

By 1940, U.S. Commissioner of Education John Studebaker was warning that the spread of Nazism "has a special meaning for educators in this democracy—one of the 'earth's last best hopes,'" and he demanded "the eradication of illiteracy . . . Now!" (1940, p. 1). The political perspective had already developed a list of the essentials for literacy social policy—morality, good citizenship, Americanization, the building of character, and development of vocational skills—but during war, new demands were placed on low literates. By May 1942, Roosevelt reported the shocking fact that 433,000 men were ineligible for military admittance because they could not meet the military's literacy requirements (Cook, 1977, p. 49). The military ultimately became the largest "school" for literacy education in the history of the nation.

As an arm of social policy, literacy was turned toward national defense abroad and avoidance of the spread of Nazism at home. William Russell of Columbia Teachers College observed that America needed to address many shortages, including those presented by illiteracy, but "it is important that we do not follow the Nazis in the shortages that are apparent in their education and life. They have few illiterates; they have trained their bodies to be hard; they work with skill; they have apparently adjusted themselves to technology:

but somewhere . . . they have lost the . . . Christian-Jewish ideal of God and Good" (1942, p. 82).

As the war decade passed, a dual social policy purpose for literacy emerged: self-defense and productivity. As expressed by the now more passive Caliver, "The eradication of illiteracy is not only important to national defense in times of crisis, but it also has a bearing on the effective utilization of human resources in normal times" (1948, p. 17). Thus, as investment in human resources and formation of human capital grew out of the Second World War, literacy education took on the form of social engineering for a more productive economy. On January 17, 1951, President Truman asserted that the "primary aim of our manpower mobilization is to safeguard our national security through the maximum development and use of our human resources" (Caliver, 1951). Caliver echoed the president's message on literacy: "The machines required in both war and peace demand the kind of skills, understandings, and flexibility not usually found among illiterates." With no mention of "Negroes" or equality, he added, "Illiteracy is one of the most important problems in the mobilization of our manpower to meet the present emergency" (Caliver, 1951, p. 131).

The theme of meeting economic goals with ancillary literacy policies was carried through into the 1950s. Senator Harley Kilgore of West Virginia, for example, lobbied for federal funding to assist states in literacy education in 1952 by presenting the popular economic argument that illiteracy "retards economic growth." Kilgore added the common political perspective belief that "lack of ability to read makes the illiterate a menace to himself and his fellows in industry" (1952, pp. 90–91). After almost seventy years of political perspective formation, Kilgore was unopposed in his contention that illiteracy was one of the forces that could indeed "endanger democracy" (p. 91).

During the 1950s and the Korean War period, literacy was once again enlisted in the struggle against communism. According to Cook: "The expanding sphere of Communism also motivated interest in educating citizens. In order [for illiterates] to evaluate propaganda, it was necessary to have an intelligent populace" (1977, p. 63). As one writer expressed it in *The Nation's Business:* "Yesterday, illiteracy was merely a national disgrace. Today, in the face of the Communist threat, illiteracy is a grave national problem.

Tomorrow, if our states and communities do not take steps to abolish it, illiteracy can be a national disaster" (Stavisky, 1954, p. 23).

The themes common to the history of literacy as social policy have continued into the present era. However, the emphasis has turned to the promotion of literacy for economic purposes.

Regulation Through Human Capital Development

As America entered the space race in the late 1950s, social policy engineering became the nation's motor while economic growth and national security became its policy fuel. As Cook expressed it: "Perhaps the most outstanding event to influence education during the fifties was the launching of the Russian satellite in October 1957. . . . With a single event, the importance of educating American citizens became abundantly clear" (1977, p. 63). Adult educator Burton Clark stated education's role in this time as follows: "Our age demands army upon army of skilled technicians and professional experts, and to the tasks of preparing these men the educational system is increasingly dedicated (Karabel and Halsey, 1977, p. 9). The New Frontier and the New Society under Kennedy and Johnson saw a host of new legislation and funding programs in the field of literacy education. As Cook described it, "At no other period in the history of adult literacy education has the federal government taken such an active interest in the problem of illiteracy as it did in the sixties" (1977, p. 82). However, it would be a mistake to assume that the social policies of the 1960s were disconnected from America's social policy history on literacy.

A careful examination of literacy education in this period shows that the "active interest" described by Cook was actually the active formation of human capital through social policy. The undereducated adult population was encouraged to join a massive effort to develop a better-trained, more fully employed, more economically productive workforce as America entered the 1960s. It is in this period that we begin to see the establishment of "adult basic education" (ABE) and the devaluing of mere reading and writing.

The need to provide literacy education was acknowledged in Congress in 1962 with a literacy bill introduced in the House of Representatives. This appears to be the first attempt in U.S. history to craft a piece of legislation devoted specifically to literacy.

However, the bill never got beyond the Rules Committee (Cook, 1977). The failure represents an important moment in the history of literacy education. The vague term "literacy" now assumed a new, diminished meaning, and low literates were encouraged to become better producers under the construct "basic education." The Manpower Development and Training Act (MDTA) the same year succeeded where the literacy bill failed. The new thrust under this act was to have regional stakeholders conduct a survey of "the industrial needs of the area, [then] a curriculum was designed, and an educational program was set up" (Cook, 1977, p. 83). Within a year, it was realized that the ability to read and write was prerequisite to employment. The issue of illiteracy was discovered anew. However, it was not literacy but adult basic education that was now prescribed for those who fell below requisite training levels. A set of programs was created under an amendment to the MDTA that would ostensibly lead to employment and economic renewal. A new term and a new rung on the ladder of sophisticated knowledge were added above "literacy." ABE came to mean a level of literacy beyond basic reading and writing—in brief, a set of "useful" skills. The MDTA amendment was expanded in 1965 to create the Manpower Act, and a full social policy took form that linked adult basic education to the workforce.

In a historical first, the Economic Opportunity Act of 1964 provided funding for adult basic education programming through state education offices. It is important to note that the funding was made available for adults with eight grades of schooling or less, and always with the expectation that "an adult would be able to deal with occupational training" (Cook, 1977, p. 84; see also Neff, 1965). Title IA of this landmark act created Job Corps Training Centers. Title V, together with Title XI of the Social Security Act, created a Work Experience and Training Program. ABE now appeared fully developed as a type of programming that had departed from the old, stigmatized notion of "literacy education."

In 1965, yet another rung was added—the third if one is counting from the bottom. The Office of Economic Opportunity asked Cornelius (Frank) Turner, director of the American Council on Education (ACE), if the GED testing service would allow Job Corps trainees to be included among those who took the GED high school equivalency test (Quigley, 1991a). Turner agreed and personally wrote every state in 1966 asking their GED officials to now include Job Corps trainees in the GED testing so that these adults might: "obtain jobs, [be encouraged] to continue their education, or . . . [become] eligible for service in the Armed Forces" (Quigley, 1991a, p. 36). Up to this point, the GED tests had been carefully monitored by ACE for U.S. military personnel only.

Thus, the use of the GED tests in the civilian domain and in close connection with ABE is merely thirty years old. The ABE system itself, which is now the backbone of funded mainstream literacy education, is only slightly older. Although the original purpose of the GED tests was to assist returning military personnel, and though states were initially very skeptical about its validity (Quigley, 1991a), it has become the capstone of public literacy education across America. The GED had a history unconnected with the shunned illiterates of society; it was a respected program serving honorable men and women who had fought for their country, and it measured normative knowledge in a scientific way. The program became available to the public through the requests of government and is now the uppermost of three rungs at the bottom of the ladder of sophisticated knowledge.

Despite the fact that basic literacy, ABE, and GED preparation classes now typically function under one roof in local communities across America, social policy has reproduced the schooling hierarchy. This hierarchy reflects the prestige of normative knowledge and the perceived nature and needs of adult students. The lowest rung has been the least interesting to social policy makers because, unlike adult basic education for jobs and the GED, it is not seen as having a history of "legitimate learners." One might easily argue that the shift from general literacy to ABE and the GED in recent years has precipitated for the field a loss of influence over its future. Now, despite our best efforts at state conferences, the rungs are too established and the distance between literacy and funded ABE/GED is too great. We now have more and more difficulty denting the harder political perspective with the soft popular perspective because ABE/GED funding is a function of the economy and human capital formation. To the extent that the field had a significant role in determining the future of social policy on literacy, that role is now effectively lost. ABE and the GED program are part of human capital formation, part of policies to affect the economy and unemployment. Humanistic responses to learner needs have little role in serious policy formation.

The quest for efficiency that attends human capital development has come to dominate adult basic education. ABE under Title IIB of the Economic Opportunity Act of 1964 began to become a social policy for economic development almost as soon as the programs were initiated. The Adult Basic Education Act of 1965 was actually preceded by an advisory committee to review the effectiveness of the ABE programs begun a year before. The committee's criticisms included the observation that "adult basic education programs were still scattered and had very little unity or communication." It suggested that the solution for this disunity should involve "national leadership, a national resource center, and standard reporting procedures" (Cook, 1977, p. 86). Any suggestion of personal needs or the popular perspective had long since been squeezed out of this legislated brave new world of social engineering.

There is a strong case to be made that ABE policy reviews since the 1960s have increasingly done the same thing—demand greater efficiency and accountability. What began as "literacy" in the 1924 crusade was rejected in 1962 for the more productive construct of "ABE." Through time, the social policy purpose became more narrowly focused on productivity and employment, leading to more and more accountability being required in the 1990s. As practitioners await their funding fate today, it is hard not to agree with Warren Ziegler's observation: "[t]he history of public educational policy leads to the conclusion that to support means to define, curtail, render accountable, and ultimately govern" (1977, p. 17). The widely circulated policy advisement paper by Chisman for the Bush cabinet found our field to be "intellectually, institutionally, and politically weak and fragmented" (1989, p. 5). In the established tradition of governmental centralization following review, the National Literacy Act of 1991 created yet another National Institute for Literacy, one of its goals being to "develop uniformity among reporting requirements, develop performance measures, and develop standards of program effectiveness" (Quigley, 1991c, p. 172). The lowest rung on the ladder has been left for (mainly female) volunteers. ABE was elevated to a second rung worthy of public funding and has suffered the political consequences. Beder argues that our field is not unique in this trend: "[h]uman capital theory has become the dominant rationale for all public subsidy of adult education including adult literacy" (1991, p. 107).

The most recent (and probably the last to be seen in this century) endorsement for ABE came with the National Literacy Act of 1991, which was passed under George Bush with remarkably little public fanfare (Quigley, 1991c). However, this act defines *literacy* as "an individual's ability to read, write, and speak in English, and to compute and solve problems *at levels of proficiency necessary to function on the job and in society,* [emphasis added] to achieve one's goals, and develop one's knowledge and potential" (National Literacy Act of 1991, sec. 3). The last phrase on personal development was added after hard lobbying by literacy professionals and members of the Commission on Adult Basic Education (Quigley, 1991c). The funding programs contained in the act are aimed at job acquisition. The legislation is the stepchild of the Economic Opportunity Act of 1964, but without anything resembling Title IIB. In fact, the act is the logical outcome of the desire to eclipse stigmatized "old literacy" with solid social policies on ABE. The soft popular perspective found its natural home with the maternalistic volunteer literacy campaign of First Lady Barbara Bush. Harder policies were behind the National Literacy Act, which the president signed to fund ABE.

Irrespective of how one thinks of the construction of policy and programs in our field over the past three decades, there can be little doubt that the field became "policy disenfranchised" with the move toward ABE. Over recent years, we have been singularly ineffective in presenting employment or other economic "hard data" to inform or influence the political perspective. Now, with government's interest in its own ABE programs at a low ebb and virtually no interest in literacy among the media to shore up the popular arguments, the field is in trouble. It is common today for literacy programs to apply for charity tax numbers, as they might receive funds from businesses as do the United Way, charitable community organizations, and churches. It seems that the field would be glad to turn the clock back to a time before government chose to define, curtail, and govern it.

The entire literacy enterprise is at risk in America. We have a field that has lost favor with both perspectives. What should we expect, and what is our role as practitioners, as we approach the twenty-first century?

The 1990s: Illiteracy, Crime, and the Economy

This section of the chapter will examine the linkages between illiteracy and two of our currently salient social problems: crime and failing corporations.

"More nonsense is being written about illiteracy than any other subject," said Distinguished Service Professor Emeritus Paul Woodring of Western Washington University, according to an article in the *New York Times* (Hechinger, 1987, p. III-7). The recently discovered "linkage" between crime and illiteracy certainly supports that contention. In Woodring's view, "Political candidates have got into the act because 'they have discovered that no political issue is safer than illiteracy when they want to take a firm stand against something.'" As already seen, the theme of illiterates as immoral is a very old one, and the notion that they are inclined to criminal acts is far from new. As Verner explains, the first adult literacy efforts in early nineteenth-century Britain were made "because people believed that the ability to read the Bible would strengthen the morals of the poor . . . reducing crime and other associated ills, [thus] philanthropy took the form of adult schools" (Verner, 1973, p. 9). The linkage between illiteracy and crime is still assumed today. During Barbara Bush's campaign for literacy, she continually implied a direct causal link between the two: "Eighty-eight percent of the juvenile delinquents who end up in court are disabled readers," she noted at a luncheon meeting of Women in Communications, Inc., in 1982. She added, "I hope that I'm scaring you, because I'm scared" (Gaiter, 1982, p. II-6).

Politicians have used this theme consistently in America; the linkage is one of our few "bipartisan" political issues. In 1980, Senator George McGovern was quoted in *USA Today* as asserting, "Many adult illiterates who are locked out of the job market, or locked into entry-level jobs due to functional illiteracy, turn to crime." He also speculated that "the rising generation of lawbreakers seems to suggest that the correlation between crime and illiteracy is certainly more than coincidence" (McGovern, 1980, p. 26). At least one Supreme Court justice seemed to agree. Chief Justice Warren Burger and Senator Edward Kennedy asserted that illiteracy leads inevitably to "dead-end lives of crime and drugs" ("America needs," 1987, p. 27). The notion crosses color lines in the media. The black magazine *Jet* reported in 1986 that District Judge Alcee Hastings of the southern district of Florida announced his own "strategy to stem the tide" of black illiterate youth with the opening assertion that "increased illiteracy will lead to increased crime" ("Judge announces," 1986, p. 22).

There are no empirical data that illiteracy causes crime. It could just as easily be argued that illiterates have worse legal representation than the educated. Despite the observations of Barbara Bush, George McGovern, Edward Kennedy, and Warren Burger, scholars such as Griffith have noted that anyone remotely familiar with research or statistics agrees that "correlation is not proof of causation" (Griffith, 1990, p. 59).

The political perspective has fostered and maintained a series of stereotypes based on public distrust and fear of low literates. And as awareness of crime has increased over the past two decades, so has scapegoating of the low literate.

In the 1980s and 1990s, there has been a second obsession, which sees the illiterate as a menace to business and the economy. Business magazines often begin articles with scenes of incompetence: "Imagine an auto mechanic who cannot read a repair manual. A nuclear power station technician who can read but not well enough to understand safety precautions. A machinist who cannot read his equipment's operating instructions. An insurance employee who pays a policyholder $2,200 on a $100 dental claim instead of the $22 authorized" (Wantuck, 1984, p. 34).

That low literacy can affect safety and profits is common sense. To say that low literates "cause" poor profits or poor safety records is often simply a convenient form of scapegoating. Some of the allegations take absurdity to its limit. Harvey Jacobs, editor of the *Indianapolis News,* actually told an audience at Indiana-Purdue University in 1980 that illiterates were responsible for the near-meltdown at the Three Mile Island nuclear facility in Pennsylvania. He agreed with Richard Mitchell, a college professor whom he cited at length, that "if English had been taught well and learned in the schools, the accident at Three Mile Island could have been prevented. An inbred inattention to detail found its inevitable climax at Three Mile Island and will be repeated again and again" (Jacobs, 1980, p. 563). The comment, of course, had no foundation in fact. The Kemeny Report of 1979 clearly stated that a design flaw caused a relief valve to stay open (The Media Institute, 1980).

Illiterates as the Nation's Scapegoats

After a century of social policy on literacy, it is illuminating to compare a speech by President Calvin Coolidge in 1924 with an excerpt from the 1987 article by Chief Justice Warren Burger and Senator Edward Kennedy previously cited.

Coolidge, after referring to the "shame of adult illiteracy" (1924, p. 1), went on to extol the benefits of literacy: it stimulated "the power of the people to produce"; cultivated "a taste for literature, history, and the fine arts"; served as "the handmaid of citizenship"; strengthened patriotism; and promoted "morality, character, and religious convictions" (p. 2). Without the foundations of literacy, Coolidge saw the abyss looming: "There are likewise 3,000,000 native [that is, nonforeign] illiterates . . . [W]hen it is remembered that ignorance is the most fruitful source of poverty, vice, and crime, it is easy to realize the necessity for removing what is a menace [that is, illiteracy], not only to our social well-being, but to the very existence of the Republic" (p. 2).

Sixty-three years later, Burger and Kennedy argued that "illiteracy costs the nation heavily in reduced international competitiveness, increased poverty, higher welfare and unemployment benefits, lesser skills in the armed forces, industrial accidents, lost productivity and dead-end lives of crime and drugs" ("America needs," 1987, p. III-27).

Though the rhetorical emphasis may have shifted to some extent, the essential objectives of literacy education have been consistent throughout the past century. The list of the nation's demands on illiterates remains remarkably unchanged. Despite the accumulation of "objective" data from census reports, literacy surveys, and scholarly studies, the perspective of reality carried in the media remains at the level described by Stechert in 1985. Illiterates are "those who cannot function fully, don't pay their share of taxes, can't maintain basic health and nutrition standards, can't understand governmental processes, and can't share civic responsibilities" (p. 27).

After a lifetime of paying taxes and raising children, people such as ninety-three-year-old Lucy Grissom, whom we met in Chapter Two, would have reason to protest at such characterizations. Apart from the desire to get better employment, no adult learner I have encountered in more than twenty years of literacy work, and none I have ever heard of, has come to a program asking to be made "a better patriot," a "more moral person," "a more complete citizen," or a more "productive human being." This, however, is the historical and political context our field works in.

Reshaping Images of Our Learners and Our Field

Our society lives with differing ways of seeing, relating to, and defining literacy. The effects of the deeper ideological assumptions that social perspectives are founded on are inescapable for those of us who teach, tutor, research, or formulate policy in this field. As Blakely put it, "We can—and usually do—refrain from asking philosophical questions, but we cannot avoid acting according to philosophical assumptions" (1957, p. 93). The ultimate question that arises for our future is, Can we reshape and improve the world of practice? I believe we can.

Future change of any substantial degree will not depend on funding levels or professionalization of practitioners or increased accountability. Real change will be dependent on our assumptions about this field and how we choose to act on them.

Though our field has developed a "voluminous" stock of descriptive research, experiential anecdotes, and "how-to-manuals" (Fingeret, 1984, p. 3), we have an extremely limited body of theoretical and philosophical articles "exploring some of the underlying assumptions, values, beliefs about adult literacy and illiteracy, [and] the relationship between illiteracy and other 'social problems'" (p. 4). Partly as a consequence of this, the field has not regularly subjected its practice to critical examination and has lacked the ability to support theoretical discussion (Wagner, 1991).

At the macro level, it is fair to say that the reality of literacy education is to be found not in the pronouncements of alleged "political saviors" or "single solution research experts" but in the world we know best—the one in which we teach and tutor our learners. Further discussion will be presented on how we can increase the practical field-based knowledge of who participating low literates are, what they seek and fear, and what seems to work best with this

complex group. It is at the practice level where we need to seriously ask if we can envision a more "honestly understood" and
more adequately supported field of practice based on our own
knowledge. As Chisman has stated: "They [practice leaders] should
not await political action. There is no good reason why literacy
leaders should not begin at once to tackle the key issues of the field
head on with the resources available to them" (Chisman and Associates, 1990. p. 22).

On a policy level, it is apparent that the political and popular perspectives have helped develop a field that functions in relative isolation from other services or parallel agencies. Perhaps it is because the
illiterate adult in the United States has been treated as a sorrowfully
separate "species" in the popular media, or because the political perception so often sees "illiterates" as a volatile segment of society that
needs to be regulated for its own good and the good of society, that
we have today a fragmented and highly vulnerable field of funded
ABE and volunteer programs with remarkably weak linkages to the
rest of the educational, corporate, and social service communities.

Waiting for "political action" is the traditional way our field has
tried to survive. We have been buoyed up in the turbulent seas of
politics only to sink when the turbulence abates. Can we take internal leadership? I believe we not only can, but must. The alternative, of waiting for help to come out of the status quo, involves
much greater risk for our field. Following are a number of broad
recommendations for action at the macro levels of policy and perception. They are based on two major beliefs: first, that our field
needs to understand its sources of strength and build on them at
the policy and public levels; and second, that the field must be prepared to challenge the worst aspects of the two perspectives that
shape us. These may be simple principles to give "moral support"
to, but they are not simple challenges to meet in practice.

Recommendations at the Level
of the Political Perspective

Following is a pictorial overview (Figure 3.1) to help summarize
the two perspectives discussed to this point in the previous two
chapters. It points us to the strength of our student base as the true
source for our reality, to be discussed in the next chapters.

Figure 3.1. Influencing the Macro Perspectives.

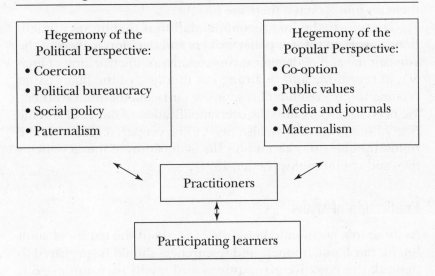

In the broadest terms, practitioners, researchers, and policy makers need to open the conventional and unquestioned world views, or hegemonies, created by the two historical perspectives to greater field-based, learner-based, and classroom-based knowledge. This needs to happen in several areas.

Education of Policy Makers

If literacy education is based solely on "scientific," modernist constructs and lacks a humanistic, culturally informed foundation that takes the complexities of society and the learner into account, it becomes severely diminished as a field of practice. Theoretical concerns are often ignored in our field along with history. Issues of class and of socioeconomic status, of race and ethnicity, of gender and social role, are suppressed. Further, with a singular quasiscientific, modernist set of assumptions informing the political perspective, the purposes of literacy education become extremely narrow. Opportunities to foster critical thinking are labeled "frivolous," attempts to encourage self-empowerment are deemed "radical," and efforts to improve quality of life are dismissed as "purposeless" (Aronowitz and Giroux, 1985). Serious preparation for entry or reentry into the world of work is reduced to human capital formation—"prepare them for jobs" (even if there are no jobs).

Therefore, the first recommendation is that literacy practitioners work to inform policy makers and decision makers of the educational and pedagogical complexities of the teaching of literacy, of recruiting and retaining low literates, of the many issues relating to the creation of responsive curricula for adult learners. We need to work against the oversimplification of our field and the lives of our learners. We also need to be prepared to answer the follow-up questions about how the acquisition of literacy affects lives and communities (Beder, 1994).

Eradication of Myths

As those in a position to know the most about the nature of adult low literates, practitioners and researchers should be prepared to debunk the negative assumptions and myths surrounding our learners. One of the very practical reasons why such myths are often accepted is the belief within the profession that funding may be jeopardized if the political perspective is challenged. Such beliefs give rise to professional ethical concerns, but the practice of leaving the political perspective unchallenged has proven in recent years to be shortsighted. Moreover, allowing assumptions to oversimplify one's work does not contribute to long-term survival and is destructive of professional respect.

Therefore, the second recommendation is that we should not accept paternalistic statements by policy makers that characterize our learners as inherently misguided, easily misled, latently dangerous, in need of self-discipline, or afflicted with any of the other negative traits discussed earlier.

Research and Evaluation

The field needs to put more energy into research and carefully controlled evaluations so that sound empirical data inform the policy formation process. As the director of the GED Testing Service has stated, if we are to have a meaningful influence on the crucial issues concerning the future of adult literacy—for example, Will adult education programs as we know them survive? Will [federal] block grants remake the delivery systems now in place?—we must "not only tell stories, but also provide facts supporting our claims" (Lowe, 1995, p. 2). Where we need better research, we should insist that it be provided by researchers. Where we lack accuracy in our demographic frameworks or analyses, we should be prepared to challenge those who base their assumptions on such misinformation.

On the program funding level, since the early 1960s, the highest political priority has been to make ABE and GED graduates more "economically productive." As Chisman notes, "an estimated 80 to 90 percent of the people who sign up for adult literacy instruction in the United States are served by government-supported programs" (Chisman and Associates, 1990, p. 11). The policies that govern these programs will be affected much more by data on learner successes, on economic gains in communities, on quality-of-life improvements, on cost-effective ways to reach and teach low-literate adults, than on popular perspective "stories" or requests for more resources (Alamprese, 1990). If we believe in the value of knowledge for our learners, we must believe in the value of knowledge for our own practice.

Funding and Support

The field must work toward a greater diversification of its funding base and resource support. Chisman has recommended that literacy leaders "join their limited resources for more investments in research, technology and staff" (Chisman and Associates, 1990, p. 22). Why have they not done so in the past?

As mentioned earlier, one of our inherited limitations is that literacy education has come to be the domain of a governmentally funded system concerned solely with literacy and ABE in relative isolation from other social issues. The field of practice has become isolated from most educational, business, and community agencies and is not well linked to programs seeking to address other or even parallel societal issues.

In the daily delivery of literacy education, the quasi-institutional system carries the bulk of the responsibility for addressing illiteracy. If literacy education is understood as being absolutely needed for all work skills, coping skills, and self-esteem, then illiteracy becomes an entity unto itself. Illiteracy should not be isolated and "fixed," isolated and "cured," isolated and stamped out. We end up with a set of programs removed from the mainstream of society, when in fact literacy is part of the fabric of society. As will be seen in Part Two, there are several ways to interpret literacy education in the classroom. Most of these interpretations assume that literacy should not be understood as an end goal; rather, it should be seen as a secondary goal, an enabling vehicle for achieving other aspirations for oneself, for one's family, and for one's community.

Imagine for a moment what literacy would be like if it had not been singled out by the political and popular perspective for "special consideration." It is likely that we would have today a much more diversely supported field, as well as a more stable one. The Department of Labor and labor unions, the corporate sector and their employees, community-based organizations and individuals working to improve their communities, social service agencies, professional interest groups concerned about those in their work sectors—these are our natural allies. We must work to convince them that illiteracy is a wide-ranging societal issue deserving of their funding and support. It does not "belong" to anyone—least of all to the political perspective.

Professional Advocacy

The field must develop a stronger voice at the social policy level (Quigley, 1989). There are a number of national professional associations in the field of adult literacy, and virtually every state has an adult education professional organization with a mandate for literacy. As Beder put it so succinctly: "If only half of the 206,352 . . . personnel who work in adult literacy education joined the Commission of Adult Basic Education and paid fifteen dollars in dues, we would have a locus of professional advocacy of over 100,000 members and a war chest of over a million dollars." He goes on to make a second good point: "If, as part of the curriculum, each adult literacy education student wrote a letter of support to his or her congressional representative, that would amount to 3.8 million letters a year" (1994, p. 23).

We are accustomed to professional passivity, but it has not always served us well. When policies on literacy are formulated, it is rare for professional associations or actual practitioners to be called in to advise (Koloski, 1989; Quigley, 1989). My personal experience from working in government is that many officials at both the state and federal levels truly want to help us build a better field, but we ourselves do not stand up to be counted. And when we do, we have few compelling data to offer. At conferences, we speak out of the soft popular perspective, hoping that people like Lucy Grissom will make our case for us. Is this the best we can do?

Recommendation at the Level of the Popular Perspective

Although our field has traditionally depended on public concern and sympathy for its broad base of support, the media and popular literature have not always been our friends. The literacy acquisition process is not a mechanical or rote activity, and our learners are not caricatures. However, we rarely challenge the stereotypes. Rather, we often endorse them, even manipulate them, for funding advantage. Aside from the ethical dilemmas involved here (to be discussed in Part Two), as our learners and our work are trivialized, so are we trivialized. When policy makers and the public accept simplistic images of literacy education, we too become simplified and marginalized. The stories of the popular perspective can inspire all of us. However, stereotypes of illiteracy and the illiterate adult have developed lives of their own in the popular media and literature.

The recommendation here, therefore, is that the field accept the daily responsibility of presenting documented facts about our adult learners and of confronting literacy stereotypes. As a friend of mine once put it, "Low literates act a lot like people."

Playing the Popular Against the Political Perspective

Although Lucy Grissom's story is an inspiring one, I believe we need to reexamine the ethics, the assumptions, and the sheer practical usefulness of playing the popular perspective against the political in an attempt to secure public sympathy and political support. As was mentioned earlier, support for programs at the policy level is elicited primarily by the presentation of factual data. "Stories" are considered only later, if at all. Finch has found that it is the "society's benefit rationale" that informs policy, not the "individual's benefit rationale" (1984, p. 91), which is emphasized in the popular perspective. In my own experience in government, the conventional response to expression of need was "Get in line." If a politician responds more favorably, the benefit lasts only as long as he or she is in office. The popular perspective is probably best left for personal inspiration. We cannot hang our future on a set of perspectives such as these.

For the Future

For decades, the American public has been told about illiteracy in terms that have helped ingrain in its consciousness certain concepts, images, and expectations that often bear little relation to the reality experienced by practitioners or undereducated adults. Staffing and career development in literacy are tenuous and utterly dependent on next year's political decisions. We have evolved a field that lives for political approval, a field that has learned to be passive, a field that anxiously watches political trends and struggles to interpret the political rhetoric at every turn. We constantly labor to keep the flame of the popular perspective alive. Without a permanent infrastructure or long-term commitment at the policy level, even after a century of rhetoric and fifty years of campaigning, we have a field that is not really a field—more a legacy of "goodwill." If we act like a major field of practice and study, we have a chance of being treated as one. The decision to challenge assumptions, for our sake and for the sake of those we serve, is one *we* need to make. I believe our strength lies in our commitment to helping others. If we choose to build on this, and to be informed by our learners, our field will be able to draw the respect and the support it deserves.

Part Two

How Teachers and Administrators View Illiteracy

Chapter Four

Rethinking Educational Approaches

The literacy teaching-learning process is many things, but in the final analysis, it is an interpersonal relationship charged with emotion (Brookfield, 1990; Daloz, 1986; Wlodkowski, 1985). Compassion, anxiety, periods of guilt mixed with moments of pure joy—these are the elements that make up the adult literacy educator's journey. On this journey, we are continually called on to make choices thrust on us by the tensions inherent in teaching and learning. Over 2,500 years ago, Aristotle saw education as being a contested territory: "As things are . . . mankind [is] by no means agreed about the things to be taught. . . . The existing practice is perplexing; no one knowing on what principle we should proceed—should the useful in life, or should virtue, or should the higher knowledge be the aim of our training, all three options have been entertained. Again about the means there is no agreement; for different persons, starting with different ideas about the nature of virtue, naturally disagree about the practice of it" (Brubacher, 1969, p. 1).

In adult literacy, the conflicting pressures are threefold, and the functioning of our programs is greatly affected by them and by the way we choose to understand them. Niemi and Nagle (1979) have pointed out that the teaching-learning process has three sets of expectations. As seen in Figure 4.1, the first comes from society and its various agencies. This is an extremely powerful set of pressures in the field of adult literacy education, as was seen in the discussion of the political and popular perspectives in Chapters Two and Three. Next are the expectations and norms that our colleagues, our institutions, and our profession impose. These give

Figure 4.1. Three Influences on Literacy Teaching and Learning.

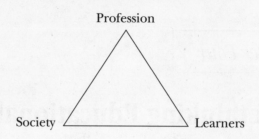

rise to demands for program standards, measured progress, acceptable criteria. Finally, there are the demands, hopes, wants, and needs of our learners.

The society-teacher-learner dynamic is an inescapable part of our job. Making sound decisions in the face of the three sets of demands is a serious challenge because every educator is constantly forced to choose among them. Which of the three is most important? Do the demands and funding expectations of policy makers outweigh all else? What of our profession's expectations? What if following policy means ignoring or compromising what we know to be good standards of professional conduct? And what of the learners? Are they not the reason for our existence? Should we be prepared to challenge the other two sets of pressures if learners need our personal intervention?

If the teaching-learning process is to bring more rewards than regrets, I believe it is vital that we be able to recognize, understand, and find the right balance among these three competing pressures. Let us begin by considering what might be seen during a typical three-week period in the life of an ABE center.

Three Weeks at an Adult Basic Education Center

A woman comes to the door of an evening adult basic education class. She is African American, between the ages of twenty-five and thirty. She holds a manila folder in her hand. She spots the teacher, who is bent over talking with a student. The other students look up and stare at the woman. She keeps her eyes on the floor. A student says, "Somebody's at the door." The teacher, a female Caucasian in the same age range as the woman, smiles and says, "This must be our new student." She approaches the woman, who keeps her eyes down. In lowered tones, the teacher asks her name and takes the file folder from her. She then introduces her to the other students, one by one. Some wave, some sit and just look back at her. The teacher says this is like a family. She adds, "We all hope you will feel at home with us." The teacher takes the woman's arm and shows her to her wooden school desk.

The newcomer looks around. Students are seated in rows, writing. Some are African American, some Caucasian. Most are female. The one next to her is chewing gum. The teacher is explaining something on the blackboard to a student. The woman watches intently. She understands almost nothing of what they are saying.

The teacher comes over to her, opens the manila folder she brought, and studies the contents. She then says, "I've got your reading test results here."

Hoping no one can hear, the student ventures, "How do they look?"

"Oh, you've got a ways to go, but we know where to start you."

The student waits. The teacher brings over two reading books—both thin, soft-covered, with pictures of smiling white people on the cover. The teacher asks her to start with these, and flipping to the end of the chapter, she tells her to try to answer the questions at the end in her exercise book. She will be back later to check on her. The student slowly reads the first page and realizes this is essentially a child's book. It is a book not unlike those she would sit and try to help her children read.

She wonders if her children are safe with their grandmother. Looking around, she is struggling with the realization that she, too, is a child. Part of her, the fearful part, is comforted by this realization. Another part of her, the part that is a middle-aged mother, who has succeeded in several jobs, who has made thousands of adult decisions, reminds her there is small comfort in the fact that she has obviously failed in her life and it has all come to this. Staring at her child-level reader, she realizes that she is, after all, what others have told her throughout her life—stupid.

As the rest of the first week goes by, she finishes two of the readers and makes some progress on math. She still has no idea what grade level she is in or how long it will be before she can take her

GED equivalency test. However, she has begun to reevaluate her first impressions of the program. She has now come to realize that the teacher and the others in the class assume she will be there for at least a year. She has noticed that two of those who were present the first night are not there now. She was startled to learn that at least two students were "sentenced" to be there by court order. She has begun to see that although she may be "stupid," she is less so than many around her. Maybe her situation is not so bad. She has no ill-feeling toward the teacher, but still, she is generally made uncomfortable by the teacher's deferential treatment. "After all," she thinks, "here is a woman younger than myself, white, not from my background, who is basically showing me the same sort of motherly attitude I show to my own children." She feels as if she is regressing to being a schoolgirl again. She desperately wants to move forward and take her GED exams. But she is told politely that "the GED is a ways off yet."

Ironically, when she asks for help, she dreads the attention that is focused on her. She quietly begins to skip sections in the books that she finds too hard to understand. She just wants to get through this stuff. "It really has nothing to do with my life," she thinks to herself. She is repeating her earlier pattern of school, and she knows it.

At home, her friends ask her what she is learning. She is embarrassed to tell them how basic the material is and refuses to show them her child-level books. Her children do not like being at their grandmother's place. Money is getting tighter. Moreover, after the second week of evening classes, she finds she is getting bored. She sits in class wondering what the point of it all is. The teacher is fine. The students are fine. But her children need her. Maybe she can get her old job back and try this again when they are grown.

As when she was back in grade school, she experiences mounting guilt as she moves closer to her decision. She rationalizes: "Maybe this wasn't such a great idea." She tells no one what she has decided—certainly not her teacher. She attends one last class meeting in week three to look at the situation again. What was so fearful a short time before seems distant and irrelevant now. She looks at the other students around her as being rather childish. She quietly drops out.

After a few days, the teacher sends a report to the administrator saying that the student appears to have quit. Her notes on the form state: "Showed progress. Very low self-esteem." The administrator phones the former student. Embarrassed, she tells the administrator that her babysitter wasn't working out. "No, nothing was wrong with the program. . . . Yes, I'll try to come back when things settle down." The administrator is annoyed because this will only push the attrition rate up even further in the month-end government reports.

So concludes "Three Weeks in an ABE Program."

Literacy for What?

What went wrong in this not-so-fictitious story? In a sense, "nothing went wrong," because this was business as usual for thousands of programs that experience attrition rates of 65–80 percent (Bean, Partanen, Wright and Aaronson, 1989; Cain and Whalen, 1979; U.S. Department of Education, 1995). In another sense, "everything went wrong." Despite a dedicated literacy teacher, a caring support staff, a hard-working administrator, and program materials that are used by most other programs across the region, the learner found the program so impractical—if not irrelevant—that she did not make it past three weeks. Why?

Why was this student so ill at ease? What did the teacher actually know about her, beyond the scores in the manila envelope? Why was this learner even participating in the program? Was she hoping for a job? What type of job? Was she perhaps thinking of going on in her education? Was she there so that she could help her children with their school work? Was her decision to enroll "triggered" by a particular problem or transition she was facing in her community or her job? Was her self-esteem so low that she was in need of much greater assistance and attention? How much self-esteem did she have outside of this classroom?

Although all in the room were adults, the fact is that the teacher had succeeded in school and the learners had not. The two radically different sets of experiences, together with a host of social, cultural, and learning issues, create two perceptions of reality connected by the unspoken awareness that teachers have an "authoritative" role and students have a passive, ignorant role. Very often, we fall into our respective roles as if the situation were scripted like a school play. Why?

Many students in traditional literacy programs seem to lose self-esteem from the first day (Beder, 1991). Although some new adult teachers enter literacy classrooms wondering if they will find it hard to gain respect or "keep discipline" because their students will be as old or older than themselves, they need not worry. Like it or not, most literacy teachers find themselves in a position of "instant authority" on virtually every topic. It is as if they were teaching in elementary school, but without the bonus of children's spontaneity.

However, the assumed teacher-student schooling roles have further ramifications. Research shows that if literacy learners are considering dropping out, very few turn to their teacher for support or guidance (Quigley, 1993b). This is a learned behavior. However, so is the widespread teacher/tutor practice of keeping information on the learner's background to the absolute minimum. In my experience, many teachers (and administrators) become uncomfortable when the more "sordid" details of the learner's past or present life are revealed. It is unclear how much we should know, or need to know, about our learners. However, it seems obvious that many teachers and tutors subscribe to various abstractions drawn from the popular perspective to keep a certain distance from the learners' reality. Perceived needs are often taken to be much more important by practitioners than the felt needs learners might actually express (Mezirow, Darkenwald, and Knox, 1975). For example, one of the teachers interviewed by Fingeret in a study of ABE in North Carolina explained, "I really feel like they are little lost sheep and they've just got to get all the help they can get." (Fingeret, 1985, p. 82). This statement is based on perceived, not felt, needs.

Whose needs are we to act upon? Should we see the learners as victims—as the media-promoted popular perspective suggests? Are we to serve the needs of society, as policy makers suggest? Should we be much more involved with the learners? How much more? Let us look at the nature of the programs we offer and some of the assumptions they are built on.

The Unseen Philosophies Behind Our Actions

The field of adult literacy education is so varied in its problems, the influences of the social context so dominating, and the overall training of practitioners so limited that our practice tends to be something of a repository for our personal belief systems and the ideas we have absorbed from the popular and political perspectives. This uncritical approach gives rise to many ethical dilemmas. However, there are options.

Several authors in mainstream adult education, such as Apps (1973), Elias and Merriam (1980), Cunningham (1989), McKenzie (1985), and McDonald and Wood (1993), have discussed the ways adult education practitioners look at their own profession and what they believe that profession is supposed to be achieving. However, no such research has been conducted within adult literacy education. The range of working philosophies that inform our actions is not clear. Some twenty years ago, Mezirow, Darkenwald, and Knox presented a summative discussion of the literacy philosophies they observed, concluding that the field was essentially composed of four competing philosophies that were pulling the field in different directions:

> There are many who want to change the rules of the ABE game to give the players better odds. There are plenty of suggestions. Persuasive theorists would *politicize* adult basic education to create a *Pedagogy of the Oppressed* designed to motivate learners by making them more fully aware of the political, economic, and social forces structuring their disadvantaged situation. Some educators want to *vocationalize* ABE by making it the handmaiden of job training. Others would *socialize* it by integration into a comprehensive program of social services. Still others would *academize* it by giving the whole program to the community colleges that already operate in several states. [1975, p. 141; emphases added].

Unfortunately, the four operational philosophies were never discussed at any length in the book. This is unfortunate, because as Fingeret (1984) found and as was mentioned earlier, we have a lack of understanding of the philosophical assumptions that guide our perceptions and decisions.

As seen in Table 4.1, there are still four basic philosophical approaches to literacy teaching and administering, each of which points to different choices about how we function in the field.

The vocational philosophy argues that literacy education should be, above all, a preparation for the job market. This is the philosophy and purpose found in most of the social policy initiatives since the Second World War, with roots in the CCC camps of

Table 4.1. Four Working Philosophies
Underlying Literacy Practice.

Political Perspective		Popular Perspective	
Vocational	Liberal	Humanist	Liberatory
Literacy is mainly for job preparation and financial independence.	Literacy is mainly for acquiring cultural knowledge.	Literacy is mainly for personal growth, self-actualization, and self-esteem building.	Literacy is mainly for critical thinking and political awareness.
A. Early Advocates			
Skinner	Livingstone	Rogers	Freire
Watson	Adler	Maslow	Alinsky
B. Current Advocates			
Stitcht	Hersh	Fingeret	Heaney
C. Methodological Underpinnings			
Behaviorism	Pedagogy	Andragogy	Case studies
Competencies	Great literature	Discussion	Site visits
D. Content Applied			
Technical	Great literature	Inspiring stories	Case studies
Work-related	History	Student-authored	Conflict

the 1930s. The humanist philosophy is, in my experience, easily the dominant philosophy among literacy teachers and tutors. As will be discussed, this is the view that literacy education should provide an opportunity to nurture and build self-esteem among learners; nothing of significance can be achieved until learners have the confidence to change themselves and the ability to get their lives under control.

There are also some teachers who argue forcefully for the liberal philosophy. This is the view that literacy education should introduce low literates to the cultural knowledge base of the Western world. The emphasis here is placed on thinking and reasoning.

The fourth, liberatory, philosophy (too often named the "radical" philosophy) is essentially concerned with empowering learners to address social injustice. Because of the historic fear of empowering rather than, in some way, "regulating" low literates, many of its proponents find themselves struggling to survive financially. They rarely see government funding. In contrast to liberal or vocationally operated programs, which are almost always favored for governmental funding, liberatory programs are typically avoided by government. Curiously, liberatory literacy programs are rarely advocated or even mentioned in literacy social policies or even in much of the research literature of our field.

Literacy education is not unique in encompassing several different philosophies. As Cervero observed: "All professions have differing, if not conflicting, ethical frameworks that guide the work of practitioners. In the same way, educators' practice is embedded in a variety of philosophies and ethical frameworks. The ethical questions that are central to educational practice are why should learners have this knowledge and to what ends will this knowledge be put? And the most important judgements adult and continuing educators must make in order to answer these questions are: who should decide on the content of the educational program and by what criteria should decisions be made?" (1989, p. 110).

The four teaching philosophies discussed here present differing options for how we make our judgements, how we select our materials, how we organize our curricula, and in a real sense, how we understand our learners.

Vocational Literacy Education

The vocational philosophy is as old as the training and apprenticing of adults. According to Bloom's famous taxonomy of learning (Bloom et al., 1956), teaching involves a focus on performance skills and clearly measurable behaviors. Behaviorist methods that require learners "to recall or recognize information" (Wlodkowski, 1988, p. 163) are key here.

There are many literacy practitioners who argue forcefully that the vocational approach has the "best" purposes and disciplines of learning. Learners are often said to be prepared by this approach for the "real" world. Teachers seek out content that is technically based and job-related. Language and skills learned should be help-ful on the job, whether present or future. "The job" is the central focus here (Fowler, 1992).

There is a range of schools within vocational literacy education. Skills-oriented training with the use of phonics is one school (Pen-dered, 1991), and variations of functional context approaches (Sticht, Armstrong, Hickey, and Caylor, 1987; Philippi, 1991) are another. In both, the approach to teaching is to try to connect the learner directly to tasks to be performed in the context at hand or anticipated. As Gowen states, the "functional context not only assumes certain characteristics about knowledge, it also supports specific assessment measures. What constitutes a literacy skill and how that skill is measured are both directly tied to quantifiable measures of specific tasks" (1992, pp. 16–17). Gowen adds a third school that she terms "worker-centered" (p. 15). Here, the tasks to be learned and performed are defined by the student. The oft-stated ideal is for the student-as-worker to learn literacy skills at the job site, with most input coming from the learner (Chang, 1989; Stein and Sperazi, 1991).

Vocational literacy programs are a response to the many reports over the past decade of the demise of industrial competi-tiveness in America—for example, *The Bottom Line: Basic Skills in the Workplace* (U.S. Department of Labor and U.S. Department of Education, 1988), *Workforce 2000: Work and Workers for the 21st Cen-tury* (Johnston and Packer, 1987), and *Workplace Basics: The Essen-tial Skills Employers Want* (Carnevale, Gainer, and Meltzer, 1990)—and to ongoing promises that literacy will "rescue" the economy of the United States (for example, David, 1992).

Despite the metanarratives and periodic political and employer rhetoric claiming that vocational literacy is the "one best way" for America's economy and for literacy education in general, some researchers argue that this approach is not a panacea, either for the economy or for literacy (Gowen, 1992; Levine, 1982). As early as 1979, Hunter and Harman wondered if there really was a one-to-one relationship between literacy acquisition and employment, hav-ing found that "hiring patterns seem to be related not to reading levels needed for job performance but, rather, to years of school-ing completed." Years of schooling, they commented, "inevitably favor the dominant groups in our society" in the job market (p. 48).

Darkenwald and Valentine (1984) criticized policy emphases on individual employment, noting that the benefits of literacy education are only indirectly related to employment, at best. Blunt (1991a, 1991b) took this line of research further, in an analysis of the Canadian government's *Survey of Literacy Skills Used in Daily Activities,* which covered 9,455 cases representing more than eighteen million adult citizens. He found that "for the majority of cases . . . there is no significant financial benefit attributable to increased functional literacy" (Blunt, 1991b, p. 11). Both initial hiring and income gain while on the job have much more to do with school credentials and with racial and gender demographics than with literacy skills, according to Blunt as well as Harman and Hunter (1979). As Blunt added, if literacy skills are obtained while on the job, there is little guarantee that this will be financially rewarded: "There is evidence that the human capital investment model does not apply broadly to literacy education" (Blunt, 1991b, p. 12; 1991a).

Even though vocational literacy guarantees neither a job nor financial gain while on the job (Merrifield, 1990), there are unquestionably many who come to our programs believing that our efforts can help them in the job market. We can and should create programs for such learners that make a serious effort to help them achieve their goals.

The following is an example of a successful program that I was involved in. It had its flaws, as will be described, but it may stimulate ideas on how to direct vocational literacy to those who seek it.

In a large ABE program I worked in at a vocational college, I gave "social studies" a new name: *career and vocational studies.* I was assisted by the college counselor, who used aptitude tests, career-applicable personality tests, and indexes of occupational types to develop career profiles showing each learner's interests and aptitudes, as well as the range of jobs in their interest areas. Students also learned more about what employers usually looked for in employees. We conducted videotaped role plays of job interviews and assisted each student in developing a résumé. Often, learners discounted their own experiences and strengths, and we had to encourage them to think about the job and performance successes they had had. Local employers, chosen on the basis of students' interests and aptitudes, were invited to speak to the class. Most valuable of all, we set up placements at local businesses so that students could spend a week observing or (on an unpaid basis) working at the jobs of their choice.

We tried to point learners toward careers in which they could apply their abilities and interests. The process helped lower some obviously unrealistic learner expectations. One student suffered from a bad stutter, but wanted to be a radio disk jockey for a local rock station. After three days at the station, he discovered that he was not one of those stutterers who speak perfectly when facing a microphone. Nevertheless, he still wanted to work at the station, and decided that a production job would suit him. He did, in fact, get one.

A female student wanted to be a welder, but was intimidated by the male-oriented nature of the trade. After a few days in a local factory, she decided that she definitely wanted to pursue her ambition. She was helped to enter a vocational welding program and was one of its top graduates. She subsequently obtained a job with a large oil company.

Meanwhile, as teachers, we passed the outcomes of this course to the reading, English, math, and science teachers and asked them to try to use as much learner-specific language and as many situational problems as possible to build the vocational knowledge base of each learner for his or her chosen area of work. For example, if a student's apparent strengths were in working with people, and if she showed an interest in and aptitude for math, we might discuss with her some aspect of finance or banking and try to place her in a bank setting for two weeks. Thereafter, we would ask her math teacher to devise math problems based on banking situations and her English teacher to teach some banking terminology. The student might also write papers about her vocation of choice.

Despite the persuasiveness of the political perspective, it simply is not true that every ABE and literacy student comes to a literacy program to gain a better job—or any job. As mentioned earlier, learners come for a host of reasons, and some are not there voluntarily. However, at my vocational community college, the management and vocational teachers simply assumed that all of our basic education students would be moving into the vocational programs. They were potential numbers. Had I been more critical, I would have questioned this vocational hegemony. We put the college and perceived needs first. However, for those seeking a career, our program worked well. I still regret steering every last one into the funnel, however.

The recommendation for vocational education is that we create situations like the one just described for those who are truly seeking improved employment and career opportunities. But what if there are few resources to support activities such as these? Following are a few suggestions that may be of help in gathering the needed resources and expertise for vocationally oriented literacy programs:

• If programs do not have the benefit of a counselor who can conduct interest and aptitude tests, it may be possible to contract with or collaborate with a community agency that could take on these responsibilities. If this is not feasible, state grants are often available to develop program demonstration projects. One possibility is to develop an internal career counseling system among teachers, tutors, and administrators, with self-administered interest and aptitude tests that can suggest directions for the learner. One or two teachers in the program can take on responsibility for these tests and slowly build expertise in the area. Something is better than nothing. The effort to help learners secure employment is well worth it even if only a few are assisted.

• There are standard texts that describe job clusters in various occupations. These can be used to show learners what their options might be. In some cases, the descriptions will help to scale back learner expectations, at least in the short run, while indicating that the preferred occupational field offers more than one type of opportunity.

• A "job board" on which local, regional, and out-of-state jobs are posted can be developed with the help of learners and program graduates. Students can clip newspaper job advertisements; graduates can send in job notices from farther afield; friends and allied agencies can provide details of openings; and employers can be made aware of the program's interest in their staffing needs.

• Guest speakers from employment agencies and local companies and organizations can introduce learners to careers matching their interests and aptitudes. It is important to choose lively, nonintimidating speakers; often, learners can play a part in this process.

• Many ABE programs help learners develop a résumé and/or enhance their job interviewing skills. A video camera and playback equipment are extremely helpful if role plays are used. In the program I was involved in at the vocational college, we spent hours working on interview techniques before a video camera. Afterwards, we would analyze the taped "performance." From time to time, local employers would come in to play the interviewer role.

• Field trips to places of employment can be valuable. Beyond this, on-site internships are one of the best ways to help learners see the problems and advantages of the type of employment they are considering.

• Part Three discusses ways to build knowledge by means of practitioner "action research." As will be seen, practitioners can develop systematic information during the daily "action" of the job. Building information and data through practitioner research can be a powerful force for program change and funding growth. In many states, literacy grants are available for systematic studies that can include such research projects.

• Some programs have used state grants for demonstration projects to build community networks. In one I have seen, a group of employers, union officials, literacy and vocational educators, service agencies, and referral organizations created a communitywide action committee. They obtained an interagency grant to hire a coordinator—and later two assistants—who worked to see that the referral agencies sent appropriate learners to the ABE and literacy programs (as well as to local vocational institutions and the like). The committee met monthly to review progress, and the coordinator kept the whole operation flowing. It would be useful to build an on-site internship system with a group of employers within a network of this kind. The process would first help learners discover their interests and aptitudes, then give them an opportunity to work voluntarily in a job within their chosen occupational cluster— if not in their job of choice—and following graduation, offer a prospect of placement with the same employer, or at least a letter of reference. It is important to note that the employers who accepted our vocational college students for on-site internships hired many of the program graduates.

In a few larger cities, referral systems something like this have been developed, but unfortunately, given the limited resources in literacy, "territorialism" abounds. What Kozol calls "encrusted and competitive hegemonies" (1985, p. 49) often grow up around established programs, militating against cross-referral networks because the competition for grant money is so fierce. For example, it is common for a new literacy program of well-intentioned literacy volunteers to spring from a church group or a helping agency only to find themselves excluded from the local literacy resource pool and informal network. There is only so much room at the watering hole, whether potential drinkers are well-intentioned or not. However, it normally takes only a few committed people from a few agencies to build a referral network and make vocational literacy a more complete and successful system for at least some of the learners who are seeking better job opportunities.

When the threefold set of pressures is applied, it is not uncommon to find a teacher, program director, or policy maker stating that the vocational approach is the "only way" to build and deliver a literacy program. To assume one goal for all is to force a false homogeneity and, often, a preconceived philosophy onto the learners. Although the vocational philosophy and workplace literacy have had successes at the job site, they too have their own sets of problems and misconceptions (Gowen, 1992). Still, the various forms of vocational literacy can be a great help to those learners whose primary goal is employment. However, the vocational philosophy is not the only one.

Liberal Literacy Education

Liberal literacy education rests on the premise that literacy education should be grounded in the cultural knowledge base of the Western world. Its more intellectual curriculum embraces literature, history, philosophical and political ideas, critical thinking, and self-knowledge.

Whereas policy makers and many administrators who subscribe to the political perspective see the ability to read and write as a ticket to the job market, liberal educators view it as the means by which enlightenment and quality of life are found. In terms of Bloom's taxonomy (Bloom et al., 1956), they are attempting to enhance the cognitive reasoning area of the learner's mind.

In the school-based literacy literature, the liberal perspective has advocates such as E. D. Hirsch, whose *Cultural Literacy: What Every American Needs to Know* (1988) attempts to catalogue the requisite contents of American culture. To attack Hirsch's lists is to attack both cultural knowledge and the educational hierarchy that teaches it. Liberal literacy is open to charges of elitism since the issue is always who should decide what is "sophisticated" knowledge, and for whose "benefit" (Quigley, 1990c). However, scholars such as Aronowitz and Giroux (1985) have not been deterred from arguing that this approach is thinly masked cultural elitism defined and prescribed by the dominant class.

Despite the legitimacy of such concerns about liberal literacy, I must admit that liberal literacy seems to be a compelling approach on those occasions when, for example, one refers to the two world wars and no one in the class knows what you are talking about. In the first class of low literates I ever taught, I had to teach a unit on the role of social clubs in the community: Kiwanis, Rotary, Lions. I asked if anyone could think of any others? "Zebras?" was the only (earnest) reply.

There are real reasons to value liberal literacy education (see Vella, 1994). I once was told of a prison program in the southern states during the 1960s where, after dinner, the television was turned off and virtually every inmate sat and read a book. The literacy director noticed that several of the better readers picked up and read one particular book, so she decided to promote it as a "lead item" in the library. New readers were then introduced to other popular books she had seen inmates reading. The very first one she referred them to was Eldridge Cleaver's *Soul on Ice*.

From time to time, anecdotal stories along this line are reported in the media. In 1995, the Associated Press carried a story by Vern Anderson about selected inmates at the Utah State Prison at Point of the Mountain, Utah, who had been "reading, completing rigorous computerized study guides and attending discussions with University of Utah student volunteers about such books as 'Cheaper by the Dozen,' 'Call of the Wild,' and '1984.'" They were part of a Cognitive Restructuring Through Moral Literacy program, intended to be part of a "radical alteration of a criminal's self-concept and view of the world" (Anderson, 1995, p. 26).

One school of psychologists and medical researchers has investigated what Ireland, in 1929, termed *bibliotherapy*. This group believes that attitudes and behavior can be altered through selected reading (Lenknowsky, 1987). According to Harris and Hodges, who subscribe to this school of thought, bibliotherapy is "the use of selected writings to help the reader grow in self awareness and/or solve personal problems" (1981, p. 33). Menninger argued in the 1930s that literature can be a medical treatment (cited in Warner, 1980), and Shrodes (1955) argued literature's value in "deep" psychotherapy. However, much more research is needed to ascertain whether or not literature can bring about lasting affective changes in literacy education (McGovern, 1977). There are numerous examples of liberal literacy attempting to utilize literature for its intrinsic value quite apart from other teaching strategies or goals.

The question often asked by critics of liberal literacy and cultural literacy is, Who is to decide what books are "appropriate"? As Giroux and McLaren (1987) and others point out, cultural literacy, irrespective of intent, is an open door to the cultural and intellectual domination of others. However, the liberal philosophy does present some important opportunities for our practice. As with vocational literacy, this should not be a "one size fits all" philosophy for all low-literate learners. But liberal literacy education certainly can be an important part of our programs and can enhance learners' lives.

Other questions are raised about liberal literacy education. For example, what part should public libraries (which used to be involved) play in current literacy programs? How can personal interests be effectively discovered and related to literary works? How can literature be used as a means for enhancing critical thinking, whether in relation to issues of self-esteem or with respect to social change (Greene, 1988)?

In the final analysis, if we are to develop greater independence in our students, what better way than to instill through reading the ability to be better self-directed learners? Regrettably, the value of a liberal education in literacy and the question of how best to build it into curricula have been greatly underresearched.

Liberatory Literacy Education

For many adult educators through our history, liberatory literacy has been the prime means of empowering learners for personal and social change. However, its proponents have too often found themselves struggling to survive in the world of non-governmentally funded programs. Liberatory literacy is often considered to be "radical" (Darkenwald and Merriam, 1982)—an unfortunate label that speaks to the highly political, often highly conservative nature of mainstream literacy education in America (Stuckey, 1991).

The legendary Highlander Research and Education Center in Newmarket, Tennessee, has been a shining example of adult literacy education for social action. Highlander has actually shunned governmental funding in order to avoid the controls that so often come with the funds (Horton, 1990; Bell, Gaventa, and Peters, 1990).

Universidad Popular, which was an adult education center of City Colleges in Chicago, developed a liberatory literacy center essentially run by and for the students, most of whom were Hispanic. Project Literacy in San Francisco "developed a pedagogy of liberation" (Heaney, 1984, p. 58) for young Hispanic adults in the 1970s. The Liberacion Learning Center in South Florida was established for farm and migrant workers of the area. In Canada, the Antigonish Movement in Nova Scotia worked for the establishment of fisherman and worker cooperatives during the 1930s, and literacy was a component of this internationally recognized project in community action and change. Frontier College in Canada has, for over a century, worked successfully with low literates and the homeless on the streets of cosmopolitan cities, on remote Indian reservations, and in the Far North of Canada (Morrison, 1989). There is a substantial history of liberatory literacy in the United Kingdom (Thompson, 1980).

These programs and hundreds more like them in the United States and Canada were often inspired, if not guided, by Paulo Freire's work in Brazil and Chile (Freire, 1973) and the ongoing work of the Highlander center. Liberatory literacy has long been part of worker education (Schied, 1993), and its value for feminist liberation and feminist pedagogy has been recognized and forcefully advocated (Rockhill, 1987). It has also been advocated in the school literature for decades (Aronowitz and Giroux, 1985; Lankshear and McLaren, 1993). However, in the literacy social policies of the past several decades, such programs have not even been mentioned. Nor are they the models shared with incoming literacy teachers or tutors. Sadly, this entire dimension of our field is essentially ignored by the mainstream of adult literacy education in America.

The primary goal of liberatory literacy is to help develop a *critical awareness,* or *critical consciousness,* among learners. It argues that the more traditional philosophies of adult literacy ignore the social context of learners' lives—the world learners live in and deal with every day—and therefore that most literacy programs minimize or overlook cultural, social, economic, ethnic, and gender injustices. According to advocates of liberatory literacy, not everyone has a fair and equal chance in society. If a literacy curriculum helps learners to *problematize* their world so that they can see that their situation is not necessarily "their fault," they can begin to gain greater control over their lives.

To take one example, a literacy teacher noticed one day that when she stayed with her students during the class break, they talked about the class or about other "acceptable" topics, such as problems with their kids or things that had happened that day. However, one day when she was sitting apart from the students, she overheard them talking about the housing authority that ran the projects where many of them lived. Some were resigned to the situation, feeling that "It's always going to be this way." But two in the group believed they were being "ripped off" by a certain official of the authority, who was unilaterally raising rents and failing to observe the "lead time" regulations as they understood them. The teacher intervened and asked if they would like to make this the centerpiece of their course for the coming weeks. They agreed. They moved the situation from a "given" to a "problem." They began thinking critically about "fair" rent and "fair" pricing in general. They obtained and read the housing authority regulations, talked to legal aid workers, and wrote several letters, including some to the city council. The topic was absolutely relevant to all involved—and they won a reversal on the rent increase.

Several staff members I know at the Highlander center have said that the field will never engage more low-literate adults in traditional programs as long as the time and effort learners put into such programs do not produce a truly relevant end. In most instances, this would mean the chance to clarify and resolve a personal or community problem arising, for example, from gender, race, or economic issues.

In the liberatory philosophy, then, the goal is typically to help low literates recognize the sociological, cultural, and economic reasons behind the problems they may be struggling with, rather than simply to promote individual improvement.

Humanist Literacy Education

As mentioned earlier, of the four philosophies being discussed, the humanist has by far the greatest following among literacy teachers and tutors. In the language of the Bloom taxonomy, this approach focuses on the affective domain—values, attitudes, beliefs, and the motivations of learners. A large component of this approach is concerned with making learners feel good about themselves. Fingeret found in North Carolina (1985) that "instructors appear to feel very strongly that ABE programs must develop a 'family' feeling in order to meet students' social needs. East, for example, asserts that, 'Someone said last week that we're a family in here and that makes me feel good and I think they all feel good. *And that's really what ABE is all about. It's really making adults feel good about themselves by picking up the skills that they didn't get*" (p. 87).

In adult literacy programs, humanism typically means that teachers and tutors take as their first goal the improvement of self-esteem. This approach can be enormously beneficial to some students. However, it can create problems for others, who may avoid or quit humanistically oriented programs because they feel they are put in a child-like role. Our students enter classes with many fears and mixed feelings. Some do not want to have their self-esteem "enhanced" (Quigley, 1992a).

The field of literacy education still contains a remarkably small body of literature concerning the dynamics between the literacy teacher/tutor and the learner. Among fundamental areas that have not been researched are the most effective teacher-student relationship and the best way to achieve it; the range and depth of personal involvement that practitioners should seek; and the lasting outcomes and comparative effects of the humanist approach.

Although the approach is one of the major reasons I personally remain so dedicated to literacy education, I am convinced that it is inadequate for some of our learners, if not actually harmful. I am also convinced that the humanism embodied in many of our programs often confounds our recruitment and retention efforts and has, in many respects, helped marginalize our field in the minds of policy makers.

One sees at least two sets of detrimental effects from humanism in literacy education—one that relates to learners and one that affects many practitioners. Concerning the practitioner, Fingeret has conducted two of the few studies that have looked closely at the dynamics and differing goals of ABE teachers and learners. The first was in North Carolina (1985) and the second was with the Literacy Volunteers of New York City (Fingeret and Danin, 1991). In both of these, and in her earlier writing, Fingeret has discussed the "deficit perspective." She has written that "adult basic educators continue to define their student populations in terms of incompetence, inability, and illiteracy, even though . . . [this] 'deficit' perspective is under attack in a variety of social science disciplines" (1983, p. 133). This is certainly one of the least desirable sides of "humanistic" literacy.

Practitioners' working philosophies and perceptions come from somewhere: they are learned. In only the rarest of cases are they learned before or during employment through a comprehensive adult education program of study and training (Beder, 1994). The popular perspective has helped us evolve a form of "maternalistic," not *always* entirely selfless, humanism in many of our classrooms and much of our tutoring work. Because the popular perspective goes largely unquestioned in our society and in our practice, this approach exerts a disproportionate influence on classroom activities.

Fingeret's research in North Carolina ABE programs supports this thesis at the classroom level. In her study of eight representative case study programs at twenty-five different sites in North Carolina (a design agreed on by a statewide advisory panel), she and her associates made several important findings with respect to the teacher-student relationship. Presenting their interpretation of ABE teachers, Fingeret stated, "The prevailing view in adult basic education nationally is that ABE students have a history of failure in public schools which has undermined any confidence they may have had in their ability to learn" (1985, p. 54). The conventional response, therefore, is maternalistic humanism. The North Carolina study noted the following, for example: "*Often it is not clear that students are adults* [emphasis added]. Cozart, for example, appears to be describing young children, 'They need special attention. They get very upset if they need your attention and you are too busy—very, very upset. It's very difficult to explain to them that I can't do it right now because I'm helping someone else'. . . . And it is not clear that Schall really sees herself as working with adults when she says, 'I really feel like they are little lost sheep and they've just got to get all the help they can get'" (p. 82).

Fingeret and her research team concluded: "The tone of the theme of repeated failure and inability reflects an apparent condescension towards students—an inability to take students seriously as adults, despite their age. This can be seen clearly in the ways that many instructors describe their work" (p. 82). The team saw many actions and opinions of the teachers as indicating condescension toward their adult learners. But is what they saw actually condescension? If teachers accept the idea that low literates are victims who are to be nurtured in a family setting, then they naturally become the protecting parents. The analogy of family is a good one because it becomes as natural for the teachers to make decisions for their adult low-literate learners as for parents to do so for their children (Niemi and Nagle, 1979). If mothers typically do know what is best for their children, it is not *necessarily* condescension that Fingeret was observing. It was probably overprotectiveness, however misguided. In my experience, many literacy and ABE teachers would be appalled to think they are condescending toward those they work so hard to help.

There is a strong case to be made that maternalistic humanism in the teacher-student relationship of adult literacy has two faces. One face, reflecting the popular perspective, expresses idealistic encouragement of romanticized illiterates. But given certain situations, certain decisions, even certain students, and the passage of time, the romantic ideal can fall foul of the principle that "familiarity breeds contempt." The face of conscious or unconscious condescension then often appears. Despite the power of popular imagery, adult literacy students are not "large children." If they were our own children, maybe we could make more allowances and sustain the ideal further. But they are not, and the altruistic face of humanism can fade or even become eclipsed by the face of condescension and the deficit perspective that Fingeret has written about.

The second set of detrimental effects arising from the humanistic approach is seen in students. There appears to be a learned passivity among literacy students that maternalistic humanism seems to encourage. Considering how very rare it is to find standardization in literacy education from one state to another, and considering that there is no standardized training for teachers, no philosophical stance promoted in the infrequent training courses, and no set curricula or consistent program content, one might imagine that literacy programs would have little in common. One might expect to find a broad patchwork of highly varied, innovative programs based on all of the philosophies that have been discussed. However, I have personally made a point of asking in dozens of presentations and workshops at state, provincial, and national conferences if teachers place self-esteem as the first and primary goal of their work (the humanist priority). The answer is typically "Yes." I ask if their students seek to be part of a lively atmosphere of critical thinking within an educational institution (the liberal ideal). The answer comes back, "No" or "Rarely." I ask if there is direct job preparation and a job placement system of some kind (the vocational agenda). "No." Does your class take up issues such as housing problems (the liberatory approach)? "No."

I then ask if students play a part, or seek to play a part, in framing the course content or syllabus. The answer is typically "No." Do students play a part, or seek to play a part, in deciding the evaluation or test criteria for their own advancement? "No." As for the teaching approach or methods, this too is normally left to the teacher or tutor to decide. As Mezirow put it, andragogy (the humanist technique defined by Malcolm Knowles that puts the learner at the center of all decisions) in literacy education is treating adults as children—"except more politely" (1978, p. 185). It seems that most programs are characterized by "protective maternalistic humanism," which gives rise to the observation that we have rampant condescension toward adult learners.

What is indisputable is that in many literacy classrooms, the teacher is cast as the authority and the student as the child, repeating the pattern laid down in elementary school. This is a set of roles that is known and safe for all involved. But does it provide the best basis for approaching adult education?

Added to these observations is the question of how caring and concern for the learner should actually translate into practice. Where is the line beyond which protection and nurturing of adults become excessive? The answer is far from obvious. Is it ethical to withhold placement or test scores from learners, even though the intent is to protect them from disappointment? Within the framework of a caring humanist philosophy, is it ethical for teachers and administrators to unilaterally decide what is "necessary knowledge," especially when these decisions are based on the assumption that the learners cannot possibly know what is best for them? Or if they are asked, is it ethical to assume that they would obviously make the wrong choices? Is it ethical to work subtly toward changes in the affective domain without informing the learner at any point in the program that this is being done? (The latter question is particularly significant when teachers and administrators assume that the learner would not willingly participate if he or she knew what was going on.) Is it ethical to "clarify" learner values through ostensibly neutral classroom activities and discussions in the hope that more "appropriate" values will be substituted for the "inappropriate" ones?

I will make two final points on the efficacy of humanism as a dominant philosophy. The tone, language, and imagery of maternalistic humanism in our recruiting materials may in fact be helping build resistance to participation (Beder, 1986; Quigley, 1990b). Research on this point will be seen in the Part Three. However, I have been told by literacy administrators from the southwestern states that Hispanic men avoid literacy and ABE—"would not be caught dead in such a program"—because they are portrayed in the media as something demeaning to any "real" male. I have been told that Native American men on reservations in the United States and Canada avoid these "adult school programs" assiduously because they do not want to be "seen as if they were children" (Ziegahn, 1992).

Finally, as our discussion has shown, it is highly questionable whether the traditional strategy of using the popular perspective as an influence on the political can sustain funding in this field. This is "soft" maternalistic humanism trying to make its case to "hardheaded" policy makers. As the previously quoted Office of Education director said, we need more than stories at the macro level (Beder, 1989a; Finch, 1984).

We do not know which is the "best" working philosophy, but it is clear that there are limits to the humanistic philosophy as it is applied in our field. Fingeret concludes in the North Carolina study: "Students must be treated as 'individuals,'" but according to her, many ABE teachers "appear to find this difficult; they seem to be struggling with attitudes and values they have inherited from the larger society and from their own schooling process" (Fingeret, 1985, p. 91).

The "family atmosphere" we work to create, largely out of a humanist approach to literacy, is a facade for many learners. When they think about quitting, they do it in isolation. They do not turn to their "family" for support—least of all to the teacher-as-parent. This point will be taken up in the context of retention research in Chapter Six. It is tragically ironic that despite all of the nurturing and support and building of self-esteem, the vast majority of dropouts simply disappear quietly, without a word to the people who have tried their very best to help them (Quigley, 1990b).

The fundamental issue is not the sincerity of practitioners but our ability to see the strengths and weaknesses of various working philosophies, our capacity to examine unquestioned assumptions, our willingness to be critical of our own practice and to work to improve it with the options we have available to us. We need to ask, What is the best philosophy from which to work on a regular basis? How can we make choices from day to day? What should our working philosophy be, and how should we apply it? What is a better, more balanced future for this field?

Making Choices in Practice

If the field is to progress, it will do so with small victories rather than with grand solutions from the pens of political advisers or academic experts. Let us begin by asking where we get our "personal principles" for literacy. The practitioner will obtain little guidance from the administrative or governance level of most educational institutions. Many volunteer boards of trustees or program advisory boards will draw their views from aspects of the political perspective, a few ("oversentimental") board members will speak from the popular perspective. However, in my experience, most of the people who sit on our advisory boards could count the number of low-literate adults they have met or known on two hands. Critical reflection or guidance on working philosophy will rarely be found at this level.

One can turn to the literacy literature, but reading for personal answers on working philosophy may not be the solution either, because the body of literacy literature was highly anecdotal through the 1960s and 1970s and, as mentioned earlier, there has been a dearth of literature at the theoretical and philosophical level since (Fingeret, 1984).

Where does one turn for guidance? Where does one find first principles? They can be found within ourselves and tested against our own daily experience.

Questions We Should Ask Ourselves

Brookfield has argued that a good working philosophy helps practitioners know both what they are doing and why they are doing it. He adds that a working philosophy helps them stand up for what they believe: "You will sooner or later find yourself under pressure from powerful figures in your institution to do things (such as introduce poorly developed curricula, implement irrelevant evaluative criteria, or adopt ineffective teaching criteria) that you find inappropriate and immoral. Sometimes there is little you can do short of resigning. At other times, you can argue against the wishes of institutionally powerful figures citing in your defense your distinctive organizing vision" (1990, pp. 16–17).

As Brookfield explains it, a "philosophy of practice," or what is here called a working philosophy, may not guarantee that you will always win the argument, but "you will . . . be much more likely to communicate a sense of confident clearheadedness, a sense that your position is grounded in a well-developed and carefully considered philosophy of practice. Opposition to the wishes of superiors is less likely to be interpreted as sheer stubbornness. You are more likely to gain a measure of respect for your thoughtfulness and commitment, which is important for your self-esteem and for your political survival" (p. 17).

Despite the frequent calls in the mainstream adult education literature for practitioners to develop an "ethical framework," a "philosophy of practice," or a "working philosophy," few include specific advice on how to accomplish this (Apps, 1973), and I am aware of no such advice for adult literacy practice. Apps defines a working philosophy as a system of beliefs concerning several dimensions of a lifelong educator's practice (1973). He first discusses the need for the educator to consider what is real—in this case, the need is to distinguish literacy myth, tradition, and assumption from reality. He asks us to consider why we believe we know what is real. For literacy, answering this question must involve critical reflection. Finally, Apps challenges us to think about what is "right."

It is my experience that when specific questions arise about whose values are most important on the job, or who should prevail when the threefold set of pressures discussed earlier is brought to bear—how the budget should be allocated, for example—it can become painfully clear that we are not all working with a common set of purposes. Indeed, it becomes clear more often than not in conflict situations that people in the field are not working out of the same philosophy at all. As Apps put it, "There is obviously no agreement as to which educational philosophy should be followed" (1973, p. 24).

Developing a Frame of Reference for a Working Philosophy

To begin this process, it is often helpful to ask a number of basic questions.

Three Fundamental "Purpose Questions"

Apps (1973) has offered a useful set of principles that suggest in our field of literacy education a set of "first questions" for a working philosophy, adapted as follows:

1. *Should adult literacy be mainly for the purpose of helping learners acquire knowledge?*

If the answer is "Yes, acquiring knowledge is valuable in itself and is basically why I am involved in literacy education," there may be an affinity for a liberal or vocational working philosophy. The difference between these two will be immediately clear because the content and goals of the liberal and vocational approaches are so different.

Within the liberal philosophy, which strongly advocates content acquisition, there is an inherent belief that both knowledge and the process of acquiring it are of great value. Cultural knowledge is at the very basis of a civilized society, in the liberal view. But beyond this, the acquisition of knowledge develops mental discipline and thinking processes, as well as a range of informed perspectives. Thus, a liberally oriented education can both inform and teach specific ways to think critically about issues.

In the vocational philosophy, there is an assumption that basic workplace knowledge is essential if learners are to find and hold a job or pursue a career. Such knowledge includes math, reading, and science specifically tailored to the demands of the work setting. To the extent possible, literacy students should be exposed to workplace vocabulary and workplace concepts. Like the liberal philosophy, the vocational attaches importance to the process of knowledge acquisition. The logic and the intellectual processes built into many vocational curricula (for example, Cantor, 1992) are those believed to be fundamental to the world of work. Problem solving is thus an important part of both liberal and vocational education.

2.   *Should adult literacy be mainly for societal problem solving?*

If the answer is "Yes, I am here mainly to help learners identify and solve their own problems, enhance their problem-solving ability, and empower them to bring about social change where necessary," there is reason to think there is an affinity for liberatory education. In the literacy context, the problem is the starting point for learning. But it should be the learner's identified problem rather than the instructor's or institutions's idea of the problem or "deficit." Here, the learner's "agency" or choice takes precedence over the profession's or society's. In this philosophy, the emphasis is on "problematizing" and problem posing, with much less focus on a norm or absolute standard of knowledge (Cervero, 1988). The learner and instructor ask, "How can the combination of knowledge and our collective experience help to solve this specific problem?" The learner is assisted mainly in identifying and working to resolve problems he or she is confronted with or is likely to be confronted with in the future, literacy skills being used as tools in the process.

The argument for the liberatory philosophy is that it can be highly relevant to learners' needs. Literacy content merely serves relevance (Lankshear and McLaren, 1993). One of the arguments against this approach is that, at times, it may point to solutions that demand action outside of the classroom. Many literacy teachers or tutors are uncomfortable with this prospect. The philosophy is sometimes termed "radical adult education" (Elias and Merriam, 1980). It is sometimes called a "countercritique" view of the world (Beder, 1989a). The terms used often suggest the authors' response to empowering learners for social action. Not all are comfortable with this philosophy; others argue that it is the only way (Welton, 1995).

3.   *Should adult literacy be mainly for self-esteem building and self-actualization?*

If the answer to this question is "Yes, my main purpose is to help literacy learners feel better about themselves, learn more about themselves, develop their abilities and their potential," there is reason to think that there is an affinity for the humanist philosophy. Carl Rogers and Louis Nelson explain the philosophy this way: "It is the quality of the personal encounter which matters most . . . the quality of the personal encounter is probably, in the long run, the element which determines the extent to which this is an experience which relates or promotes development and growth" (1969, p. 297). As Apps puts it, "Content serves as a means towards self-actualization" (1973, p. 56). As stated earlier, many teachers enter the literacy field with the popular perspective as their framework. Growth, fulfillment, and the rebuilding of self-esteem are important objectives in many literacy programs. However, maternalistic humanism or the deficit perspective may be the prevailing versions of humanism new practitioners find in their literacy programs.

As seen earlier, in Bloom's terms (1956), the vocational approach looks to the psychomotor domain for measurable training outcomes, the liberal mainly to cognitive knowledge, and the humanist normally to the affective domain. Fingeret and Jurmo (1989) have made a valuable contribution to the application of the humanist philosophy with *participatory literacy*. In this approach, mutual decision making and learner input are central to teaching and learning.

Specific Practice Questions for a Working Philosophy

Having established which of the four philosophies one is most and least comfortable with, one can now begin analyzing why one may answer "Yes" to one of the above questions and hesitate over another. The following set of literacy questions helps in this inquiry. Some practitioners I have worked with find it helpful to keep a reflective journal in which they record their responses both to the three questions already posed and to the following more specific questions. Thereafter, they can examine and reexamine their orientation in light of the challenges and pressures they face every day on the job.

A.   *About the Learners in the Program*

1. What lasting outcomes do I hope learners will take away from the program and as a result of my efforts?
2. How will I recognize these outcomes? How will they be manifested?
3. What is my "minimum success" with my learners? What is my "optimum success"?
4. What should be my learners' responsibilities to this program?
5. What should be my learners' responsibilities to me as their teacher/tutor/program administrator?
6. What should be my professional responsibilities to learners?
7. What part should learners play in this program?
8. How much input, if any, should they have on such operational decisions as

   The content of the course?
   The stated goals of the course?
   The seating arrangements in the classroom?
   The overall schedule of events during the class?
   The reading materials used in class?
   The examples used for exercises to illustrate points?
   The types of tests used for diagnostic in-class student evaluation and course-end evaluation?
   The consequences for days missed or assignments not finished?
   The criteria for a successful teacher?
   The criteria for a successful student?
   The criteria for a successful program?

B.   About the Work I Do

1. The things I like best about the work I do are . . .
2. The things I like least are . . .
3. The things I worry about most are . . .
4. If I could change just three aspects of the overall program, they would be . . .
5. If I could improve just three aspects of how I actually perform my work, they would be . . .

C.   About the Future of the Program and About My Own Self-Improvement

1. What I want to be better at by next year is . . .
2. I would hope my job would change in the following three ways over the next two years:
3. The things I could do to make this happen are . . .
4. I would make a long-term commitment to this program if . . .
5. My long-term hope for the program I am part of is . . .

In working with practitioners, I have found that it is not easy to answer the initial goal questions, but it is even harder to carry what one says in the first set of questions consistently through the second set. The exercise now becomes even more challenging.

Testing What One Believes Against What Is

Now the question becomes, What do I actually do, as opposed to believe? To test the learner, content, and "what I like" sets of questions against the reality of our everyday work, I recommend using the journal to reflect on what actually happens. This process, which should extend over at least three weeks, with regular journal entries, can benefit from the involvement of a colleague. It can also be useful to note how often one is "told" to make certain decisions or take certain actions and to consider the philosophy underpinning the actions of others. An important element is to continue looking at working philosophy options. Often, "trying on" new glasses through which to look at the world can mean the difference between routine drudgery and excitement. After three weeks or so, one may well end up right where one began, in the philosophy initially identified, but this will probably mean the first reaction was authentic and that one wants to stay with it. Personal questions for a journal might include the following:

Working Philosophy Identification

- What working philosophy do I mainly exhibit? Why?
- What is the dominant working philosophy of the program? Why?
- What working philosophy is projected in our recruiting materials? Why?
- What working philosophy does the program director appear to subscribe to? Why?
- What working philosophy is implied in the policies and funding requirements for this program? Why?
- What working philosophy is used in selecting class materials? Why?

A comparison of "what is" and "what should be" can reveal things you may want to work on in your own classroom or tutoring.

Working Philosophy as the Basis for Program Change

A useful staff activity is for everyone to keep a journal in the manner described and then, using the journal entries as a basis, to conduct a review of the program with the help of a group facilitator. The following questions can help toward the development of a mission statement, a code of ethics, or a statement of "What We Believe Here":

- What working philosophy or philosophies "should" this program build on?
- How much input do learners have in decision making? Why? How much "should" they have?
- How are learners viewed by most of the staff? Why? How "should" we view them?
- How are the funding agencies viewed here? How "should" we view them?
- What are the responsibilities of teachers here? Why? What "should" they be?

- What are the responsibilities of learners here? Why? What "should" they be?

Bear in mind that it is both normal and healthy to have more than one set of working philosophies in a program. The question for everyone is not how to "bring each other around," but how to build on the dominant working philosophies and learn from each other's perspective; also how to serve learners more effectively through better "matching"—a topic to be returned to before the close of this chapter.

In one program I coordinated with thirty teachers, we had three working philosophies, reflected in three types of offering: (1) mainly humanist, focusing on life skills (and the affective domain) and usually preceding learner entry into the other areas; (2) liberal, for those who were preparing mainly to complete a high school equivalency and wanted to go on in their academic study; and (3) vocational, with community internships for those wanting to go directly to a job. Learners were streamed at intake according to their interests. Those who were "at risk" were placed in the humanist stream, in an effort to retain them longer. Since then, research has indicated how a process of this kind can be undertaken in a more sophisticated way; the details are discussed in Chapter Six.

Building Program Options and Matching Learners to Philosophies

For the administrator, the longer-term challenge can be to evolve philosophic streams within programs, or entire programs around working philosophies. This topic will be picked up again in Chapters Six and Eight. If the main working philosophies of teachers can be identified, learners can be matched with suitable teachers during the intake period. The basis for placement can include the interests of the learners as well as cognitive testing. In Chapter Six, a specific placement system is discussed, where three teachers in a rural Pennsylvania ABE program matched students and teachers to address program retention problems, and continued because it just made sense to do so.

Obviously, not every program can develop devoted philosophical "streams." Furthermore, if program streams or classrooms are constructed around the working philosophies of the teachers, and if the interests of learners carry even more weight in placement than does cognitive testing, it might be asked how the teacher manages several academic levels at once in a "vocational literacy classroom" or in a "liberal education classroom." In fact, most teachers can accommodate a wide range of academic levels in one room, and in my experience, many actually prefer it *if* they have a class that is working toward common goals. When, for example, everyone in the classroom is there because they are working toward a better job or a career, the class takes on a driving energy and purpose. Similarly, if learners are concerned about solving a problem in a housing project, and if the curriculum is built around this issue for several months, a high level of commitment can evolve. Mentoring and small group work become natural in such classes, while guest speakers and field trips take on special meaning.

How to manage such a program, however? If there are multiple academic levels in one room, it can be most helpful to share the workload by having other teachers cover certain content areas. In Chapter Six, it will be seen how three teachers in Pennsylvania restructured their program so that their respective working philosophies were matched with incoming learners' interests. Cognitive testing, considered secondary to this matching process, was delayed. Some learners now work with a teacher committed to vocational literacy and a supportive curriculum. Others study with a literacy teacher who emphasizes knowledge and thinking skills in the liberal arts tradition. Yet others—particularly those identified as "at risk"—are referred to the humanistic literacy program that is centered on self-growth. Members of the latter group are often—but not always—merged into the other classes as time goes by.

Because teachers and learners often come with such diverse purposes, experiences, and cultures, clustering people together around mutual learning purposes can close some of the many gaps that exist. Everyone is centered around the excitement of learning for common reasons. It can also bring the differing perceptions of reality closer together. Chapter Eight will show how action research can play a part in systematically collecting data on the workings of each of the four philosophies we have discussed. Such data can reveal, for example, exactly how much cognitive gain, or retention, or job acquisition a program is producing. But for the moment, it is useful to work on one's beliefs concerning what is and what "should be."

Chapter Five

What Textbooks Can Communicate to Learners

In a graduate class I was teaching about two years ago, the discussion turned to literacy and the texts used. One of the students, a director of a literacy program, commented that some of her tutors had found the commercial readers they had been supplied with entirely unacceptable. Some, they had said, actually promoted violence against women through blatant forms of sexism. These were strong charges. I could remember the discomfort I and many of the teachers I used to work with felt toward many of the reading books provided for our adult basic education (ABE) classrooms. And we did then what these tutors were doing now: we left many of the commercial readers on the shelf and instead turned to books from the library, to local newspapers, and to student-authored stories. We searched endlessly for adult-oriented, less judgmental reading materials. Coles (1977) found that the stories in ABE readers of the early 1970s were sexist and racist and displayed distinct prejudices toward certain socioeconomic classes. His article was consistent with my own experience during that period, but what about today?

The graduate student and I decided to update the Coles study to see if anything had changed. What follows is a discussion of what Coles found and what we found, together with a consideration of what the texts represent in classrooms and the influence—both symbolic and literal—that they can have on learners. To jump ahead in this story, after the study was completed, my (now former) student presented our findings at a state literacy conference. She told me afterwards that a program administrator had come up to her, taken her aside, and asked her to stop talking about this sort of thing. She had asked why. "If you keep this up, you'll scare off tutors," was the reply. In a field held together by promotion of the popular perspective and goodwill, the thing most to be feared was "someone causing trouble." But worse trouble may be in store if we fail to ask, What is the perceived reality contained in our texts?

The Unexamined Text

The topic of the texts used in our programs is a curiously unexamined one. It is rare to find an article, a book chapter, or even an evaluation study that discusses the reading materials used in the literacy and ABE curricula. It is even rare to overhear a discussion among teachers of the reading texts given to their students (Fingeret, 1984; Quigley and Holsinger, 1993). The administrator who took my co-researcher aside may have part of the answer to why this is so. In any case, it is an unfortunate blind spot, particularly in view of the growing interest in new ways to facilitate and teach literacy education with genuine humanism (for example, Fingeret and Jurmo, 1989) and similar interest in critical approaches to literacy (for example, Beder, 1991; Fingeret and Jurmo, 1989; Kazemak, 1988a; Kretovics, 1985; Lyman and Collins, 1990; Stuckey, 1991).

It should be added that the public school literature has developed a substantive body of work on issues of the "text" (for example, Gordon, 1988; Martin, 1976). Questions such as what books are "appropriate," who should make the decisions about reading materials, and what students should gain from reading certain texts, as well as the many issues surrounding "neutrality" in texts, are now the basis of a flourishing discourse in the schools literature (for example, Apple, 1990, 1991; Gee, 1989; Giroux and McLaren, 1987). Issues of the text are, in fact, part of an older debate over the stated and unstated values presented to America's children (for example, Bourdieu, 1977; Giroux, 1983a, 1983b). Unfortunately, there is no sign of any such debate in the adult literacy literature (Quigley and Holsinger, 1993).

It is perhaps useful to begin this discussion with Apple's reformulation of Spencer's famous question, "What knowledge is of most worth?" Applying the question to public education, Apple asks, "Whose knowledge is of most worth?" (1991, p. 195). This is a volatile point in the public schools. Schooling has historically been a battlefield on which school boards, parents, and other citizens have fought over the issue of "best" content. Among the debates in the current public school literature is a heated one between cultural literacy—discussed in this book under the heading of liberal philosophy—and critical literacy, which would fall under the rubric of liberatory philosophy.

According to Apple, "students need more than information about what it means to get a job or pass standardized tests that purport to measure cultural literacy. They need to be able to critically assess dominant and subordinant traditions so as to engage their strengths and weaknesses. What they don't need is to treat history as a closed, singular narrative that simply has to be revered and memorized. Educating for difference, democracy, and ethical responsibility is not about creating passive citizens. It is about providing students with the knowledge, capacities, and opportunities to be noisy, irreverent, and vibrant" (1991, p. 374).

Although this discussion could be conducted from the point of view of the vocational, liberal, or humanist philosophy, I think it is worth looking at the adult literacy classroom through the lens of the liberatory approach. Doing so will help us to appreciate how the text plays a part in the messages we apparently expect learners to hear and absorb. Taking a "devil's advocate" stance makes the anomalies particularly clear. It forces us to ask about the powerful influences our texts have on learners. We have to consider what it means when we are advised simply to "live with" what may be inappropriate in our readers and in our myths rather than upset tutors. A closer look at what we do and what tools we use helps clarify the condition of literacy education and also sets the stage for the challenges ahead.

The Political Perspective in Literacy Curricula

What should adult texts and readers contain? Unlike child literacy education, which is largely engaged in the preparation of students for later life and a world not yet arrived, adult literacy education is involved with people who are already engaged with the world.

Adult literacy students are often the teacher's age or older. Most have been out of school for a few years—some for half a century. One might think, therefore, that the texts used in adult literacy would not be preparatory primers but would strive to reflect the type of world learners actually inhabit.

Although the ways adult literacy teachers give, share, exchange, and manage knowledge with their students has never been well researched, the research we do have tends to contradict the foregoing expectation. As one ABE teacher interviewed in the study by Fingeret stated: "ABE's purpose is . . . 'preparing a person for life'" (Fingeret, 1985, p. 88). Although adult learners in mainstream adult education are normally recognized as bringing years of useful experiences to the classroom (Knowles, 1980), many literacy teachers, as we saw in the last chapter, consider the past and even present lives of their adult literacy students to be so painful, so sordid, so irrelevant, or so radically different from their own that they rarely explore or discuss the realities of those lives. Why? Why would the world of the learner play such a small part in so many literacy programs?

The question Apple posed—"Whose knowledge is of most worth?"—is useful here. This chapter argues that characteristics of the political perspective pervade many of the commercial texts and readers used in America's literacy and ABE classrooms. Despite the sincere humanism of teachers and their concern for self-esteem and learner growth, the deficit perspective in maternalistic humanism somehow tolerates a hidden text agenda based largely on fear of and contempt for the illiterate adult. Many of the readers and texts of literacy are social instruments obviously meant to change the values and lifestyles of low-literate adults for the good of society as well as for the good of low literates themselves. If children's texts carry didactic messages aimed at the internalization of the values of upstanding citizens (Coles, 1977), many of the stories studied here carry punitive messages seeking to correct and remediate wayward literacy students.

Giroux defines *hidden curricula* as "unstated norms, values, and beliefs embedded in and transmitted to students through the underlying rules that structure the routines and social relationships in school and classroom life" (1983a, p. 47). Vallance defines them as "those non-academic but educationally significant consequences of schooling that occur systematically but are not made explicit at any level of the public rationales for education . . . [A hidden curriculum] refers to the social control of schooling" (1973, p. 12).

Two Studies of Adult Literacy Readers

The following analysis of what is in our readers is based on the findings of two studies, one conducted by Coles in 1977, the other conducted by Holsinger and this author in 1993. Coles reported the findings of a content analysis of five of the most widely used ABE reading series used in the United States at the time: *Cambridge Adult Basic Education Series* (1969); *Go*, published by Educational Development Laboratories (1966); *Mott Basic Language Skills Program* (1965); *Steps to Learning* (Steck-Vaughn Company, 1974); and *Programmed Reading for Adults* (Sullivan Associates, 1966) (1977, p. 39). Coles said of this early study: "Thirty stories, representing approximately grades one through three, were randomly selected from each set for a total of 150 stories. . . . In each set 30 stories comprised over 60 percent of the stories at these beginning levels" (p. 39). In his conclusion, Coles stated, "What we have in these adult basic education texts . . . are political statements about the social relations in society, statements which, unfortunately, are predominantly against the interests of adults who use the texts, many of whom are minorities and poor" (p. 52).

Coles categorized these "political statements" under three headings: sex roles, racial stereotypes, and class differences. He further subcategorized class differences into "employee and employer characteristics and attitudes toward agencies of authority and hierarchical control"; "blaming the victim"; and "problem solving." Later, yet another subcategory appears and becomes an overarching theme for the entire study: "happy consciousness."

In our own study, we replicated Coles's methodology with contemporary texts to see if there was any difference in the findings. We selected three of the most popular reading series in adult literacy: *Laubach Way to Reading* (Laubach, Kirk, and Laubach, 1984), *Challenger Adult Reading Series* (Murphy, 1985) and *Reading for Today*, published by Steck-Vaughn (1987). The three series contain 146 narrative stories from pre-primer to the fifth-grade level. The fact that there were no inconsistencies in the reports of the two reviewers in our pilot study and none among Coles's reviewers suggested that the situations found in the stories in both time frames were of a very consistent nature and matched the given themes across time (Kerlinger, 1964). In our study, thirty-seven stories (25 percent) were randomly selected across the three series. (Volumes featuring expository passages and stories adapted from literature were excluded.) Steck-Vaughn was a publisher consistently used; two different series from Steck-Vaughn appeared in both studies.

It is hoped that others will pick up this line of research in literacy—and mainstream adult education—and explore it further, as there are new series coming out all the time.

About the 1993 Study and the Definitions Used

To accurately replicate the earlier study, two trained researchers independently read, analyzed, and coded the same stories according to agreed on, standardized criteria. The following definitions were used as points of reference:

Racism: "A doctrine or teaching, without scientific support, that claims to find racial differences in character, intelligence, etc., and that asserts the superiority of one race over another or others" (*Webster's New World Dictionary,* 1982, p. 1170).

Sexism: "The economic exploitation and social domination of members of one sex by the other, especially of women by men" (*Webster's New World Dictionary,* 1982, p. 1305).

Racism and sexism were studied as they appeared in stereotypical familial, social, and/or employment roles. Following Coles, the socioeconomic class factors in employee/employer characteristics and attitudes to authority were also studied for indications of specific ideological patterns:

1.   *"Harmony of interests"* (Coles, 1977). In this pattern, business, government, labor, and the public are portrayed working in perfect harmony toward mutual goals, and employees and everyday citizens act in predictable ways under the benevolent protection of authority institutions.

2. *"Blaming the victim"* (Ryan, 1976; Coles, 1977). Here, social problems are attributed to the alleged failings, shortcomings, or deficiencies of those who are themselves the primary victims of those problems (Coles, 1977, p. 41).

3. *"The individualist ethic"* (Rischin, 1968; Coles, 1977). In this pattern, individualism is preferred over group or cooperative action, and problems are resolved in isolation.

4. *"Happy consciousness"* (Marcuse, 1966). This perspective says, "The established system is rational and, in spite of aberrations, provides people with satisfying lives. To achieve this 'satisfaction,' however, people surrender their moral and critical faculties" (Coles, 1977, p. 41). "Happy consciousness" was found so frequently that it became the major theme for both studies. The pattern of blind acceptance of the order of things, the complete absence of critical thought, and the belief that the system "delivers the goods" (Marcuse, 1966) was perceived as the overarching "hidden curriculum" by both research teams. As Coles concluded in his study:

> When the story characters, including the majority of white males, are examined in terms of how they perceive themselves qua employees, citizens, and social beings, the results are appalling. . . . the characters are overwhelmingly isolated, conformist, uncritical, and frequently filled with self-blame. . . . Through thick and thin, they adhere to implicit or explicit beliefs that agencies of authority and hierarchical control are working in harmony with them, and that when problems arise they have their own individual fortitude to rely on (or in the case of women, that of their men)—overall, they exude . . . [the] "happy consciousness" and absence of contradictory thought of which Marcuse speaks [pp. 49–50].

Content analysis was the methodology used (Holsti, 1968; Berelson, 1954). Coles employed chi-square analysis to test for significance, and comparative analyses were conducted in the more recent study through scissors and sort analysis (Miles and Huberman, 1984). In both studies, the stories were first analyzed to determine the number of male and female characters (as well as characters for whom gender was not identified). Occupations, when stated, were ranked by gender according to three categories: domestic occupational roles, subordinate/labor occupational roles, and managerial/professional/entrepreneurial roles. Story themes were categorized as romantic, domestic, vocational, and "other." Characters' races were determined whenever possible through direct statement in the text, clear implication (for example, family relationships), or through precise illustration.

What Is in the Readers?

A close examination of content in the sample of commercial adult literacy readers that we and Coles studied reveals a sort of mindless "literacy land" with a distinct hierarchy. The tone and purpose of the stories studied suggest a paternalistic, even punitive, view that appears to derive from the political perspective.

Texts are authoritative and are handed out by authority figures—in this case, whether we like it or not, the administration and the teachers or tutors are such figures. As Apple has put it, texts "help set the canons of truthfulness and, as such, also help create a major reference point for what knowledge, culture, belief, and morality really *are* (1991, p. 4). The authority contained in the texts and implied in our roles were far from what most of us would feel proud of when issues of gender, race, and class were examined.

Gender Issues

Coles found that "much more than 'pure reading' is taught in these literacy readers. Sexism and racism abound. . . . Women and nonwhites are presented in predominantly subordinate and stereotypical roles, and white males are largely portrayed as dominant, active, and competent figures" (1977, p. 50). Coles examined the portrayal of race and sex roles by tabulating numbers of male, female, and minority characters, and domestic and nondomestic story themes, and "analyzing how the admirable personal characteristics of competence, bravery, and rationality were portrayed for each group" (p. 39).

Coles found that of the 253 story characters in his study, 192 were male and 61 female. This 3:1 ratio was "remarkably the same as that found for adult male-female characters in a comprehensive study of children's readers" (p. 42). What sorts of occupations are the two genders involved in? "Enumeration of occupations showed that 106 males were engaged in 73 different occupations, from truck driving to medicine. In contrast, 39 females were engaged in 11 occupations; however, 19 (almost one-half of the females) worked as housewives" (p. 42). Coles also found that "women managed little and owned nothing; on the other hand, men, while holding a large number of unskilled jobs, were the predominant occupants of skilled, managerial, and ownership positions" (p. 42). In short, for Coles, men were depicted as being more rational and competent than women, who were often portrayed as "imbecilic" (p. 49).

Among several examples of such female characters is Ann, who appears in Sullivan Associates, book 7: "Ann suddenly awakens Jack, who is napping, to tell him the apartment is burning. He calls the fire department while Ann rushes around to save things. The firemen arrive and discover a burning chicken Ann left on the stove. Ann blushes 'red as a rose'" (Coles, p. 49).

Others such as Dolly, who appears in level BA of the Educational Laboratories series *Go*, are obsessed with notions of romance and exhibit childlike immaturity: "Dolly, a milkmaid, is given a pail of milk to take to the village. While carrying it she muses over the possibility of parlaying the milk, using the money she receives for it to buy eggs and in turn buy a chicken, and so on, so that she finally will be able to buy herself attractive clothes to wear to the fair to attract Ben, the object of her affection. While thinking about all this she drops the milk and thus loses the chance to achieve her goal of catching Ben" (Coles, p. 43).

Coles found women to be "vain and preoccupied with themselves" (p. 49). May, for instance, was always "curling, dyeing, spraying, and redoing her hair." Her husband is "good-natured" about it even when it makes them late for an engagement since "'The way May fusses with her hair makes me glad I'm a man'" (p. 49). In the Coles study, women often lead men astray and cause them to be the "bunglers." In the 1965 Mott series, book 1305, Coles reports how "Ann and Pat [female] beg and coax Ted into taking them out in a boat. When they are some distance from shore Ted realizes there are too many people in the boat and it may capsize. He jumps into the water and pushes the boat to shore, while the girls do nothing. At last they make it safely back and Ted refuses to let them 'coax him back into the boat all afternoon'" (Coles, pp. 42–43).

By comparison, in our 1993 study, 143 characters were analyzed: 56 female and 79 male—a ratio of 7:10 as opposed to the earlier 1:3. (Eight characters could not be identified by gender.) However, in the 37 stories analyzed, only 26 female characters had a stated occupation. Of these, 8 (31 percent) were engaged in domestic occupational roles such as babysitter or homemaker. The remaining were in highly stereotypical roles at the low end of the occupational ladder, such as receptionist, store clerk, or secretary.

The hidden curriculum in both the Coles study and in ours is that women make blissfully mindless wives and mothers. Specifically, *Laubach Way to Reading* depicted 4 of 16 (25 percent) female characters whose occupation was domestic. They were content in the home at all times. They question nothing; they are critical of nothing. *Challenger Adult Reading Series* featured 1 woman in 5 (20 percent) in such a domestic role—always blissful. *Reading for Today* featured 3 of 10 (33 percent) women in blissful domestic roles. The message in one-quarter to one-third of the cases is still that women can always find euphoric fulfillment if they just stay in the home. The tasks are easy, the role is entirely rewarding. As mentioned, of 18 women with a stated occupation outside the home, 15 (83 percent) held subordinate/labor occupational roles such as store clerk or secretary. *Reading for Today* featured 5 of 10 (50 percent) in subordinate occupational roles; *Laubach* featured 5 of 16 (31 percent) in subordinate/labor roles. *Challenger* featured no specific subordinate occupational roles for women per se, but it needs to be noted that working women were invariably depicted as intellectually inferior to males. In the *Challenger* series, for example, Jerome tells Ginger, "I'm studying up on yoga." She replies, "Yoga. Isn't that something you eat?" (Murphy, 1985, bk. 3, p. 18). Only 8 of 26 women (31 percent) whose occupations were stated were given anything approaching a professional role. Though this is an improvement over the 1977 findings, 2 of these characters were teachers, 4 were librarians, and 1 was a nurse—stereotypical roles for women.

It was normally assumed that females would perform the domestic activities in the home. This role was essentially unquestioned by anyone, including the women themselves. Women were depicted cooking, cleaning, and mending; they were always entirely competent in these activities and happy to do them. The only "nontraditional" female character was Fran, who owned a snack shop

(Murphy, 1985, bk. 3, p. 3). By contrast, male characters were depicted doing domestic chores in only two stories, and in both the male characters were disdainful of such chores or comically incompetent at them. Females are the weaker sex who have unquestioningly mastered household chores; males become humorous clowns while playing the stereotypical "women's roles."

As for the males in our study, a total of 29 of 79 (37 percent) male characters had a stated occupation. None were engaged in domestic occupations. Instead, they had the laboring jobs of society. Seventeen (59 percent) were engaged in subordinate/labor roles, including truck driver, factory worker, city sewer worker, and van driver. Only 12 (41 percent) of the male characters were engaged in more professional occupations; these included pet shop owner, employment officer, police officer, pressroom manager, author, and nonspecific "boss" and "manager." Women were never "boss," except Fran in her snack shop. Thus, laboring or blue-collar positions were the main jobs held by the males in "literacy land" depictions, while most of the women held support roles or were seen thriving on household chores. Given the range of abilities and talents of our learner population, and their wide diversity, one has to ask if these messages are conveying as much as a vocational, liberal, liberatory, or humanist philosophy would seek to inspire in adult learners.

Race Issues

In the Coles study, black and Hispanic characters constituted 13 percent of the total, "a percentage corresponding to that of these minorities in the general population" (1977, p. 44). However, according to Coles, racism was expressed in the depiction of minority male-female relationships and can be seen "when comparing personal characteristics of nonwhite males and females" (p. 45). Among white characters, males were competent and assertive (even if utterly uncritical). However, minority male characters were depicted positively only when they dominated minority females, thus reinforcing ethnic or racial male stereotypes. Coles describes Carmen, a "hot-tempered Hispanic," who is jealous because she thinks "Miguel, her boyfriend, went out dancing after work instead of seeing her." Although "Miguel explains, repeatedly and patiently, that he had to work overtime . . . Carmen does not believe him. She is totally unreasonable, angry, and distrustful." Luckily, Roger, a white hero figure, comes along "and Carmen learns that Miguel is in fact telling the truth. She calms down and they make up" (p. 44).

For Coles, "blacks displayed strength and heroism in three stories, but in two of the three they did so as boxers, the stereotypical athletic career for blacks" (p. 44). Blacks as athletes were actually a continuous theme in the Coles study: "Three of the ten blacks in the stories were boxers. . . . When compared with white males, and even racially and ethnically unidentified males, it is readily apparent on which rungs of the occupational ladder we find nonwhites. Perhaps the most graphic example of this is the three black boxers who have two white managers" (p. 45).

Of three of the stories depicting cowardice, two used minorities to play the coward's role. Racism did not end with Hispanics or blacks in the 1977 study. Coles provides the following summary of a story featuring a gypsy in the Mott series, which was used extensively in 1970s classrooms: "A gypsy, with 'dark brown skin and brown arms,' comes to a farm house disguised as a woman. When he removes his disguise he frightens a boy on the farm. Granny, the boy's grandmother, leans a broom handle on the window and pretends it is her son with a gun. She outfoxes the gypsy who runs away" (pp. 44–45).

In 1977, "real competence" was reserved for white males, minority males ranked second in the hierarchy, white females effectively came third, and minority females landed at the bottom of the ladder of competence and self-control. Given the high proportions of minority students and females in literacy programs in the 1970s (and today), these were stereotypical messages that should not have been ignored by our field, but the literacy literature was silent except for the article by Coles.

In our own study, of the 143 characters in 37 stories, 65 were identifiable by race or ethnic group. Of these, 25 (38 percent) were white; 18 (28 percent) were black; 21 (32 percent) were Hispanic; and 1 (1.5 percent) was Asian—a clearly improved ratio if 1990 demographics are the criteria. However, although racism is now more subtle, it still clearly persists. In "A New Start" (Laubach Skill Book 4), for example, a young black youth is being tutored by a white professional man. Searching for a relevant example to make a point, and for no obvious reason, the tutor immediately turns to sports so that the black youth might grasp the point (Laubach, Kirk, and Laubach, 1984, p. 35). In "Who Needs to Read? The Report Card" in *Reading for Today*, (Steck-Vaughn Company, 1987, bk. 4), a black father is forced to admit to his son's white female teacher that he cannot read and humbly requests her help—a consistent theme of "inferiority of minorities" across both studies. The humbling of the illiterate male is reminiscent of the simple American worker and the simple African American illiterate seen in Part One.

Hispanics were represented in the occupational roles of farmer, store clerk, babysitter, and police officer. Only one occupation is specified for a black character: that of police officer. By contrast, white characters were depicted as pressroom manager, successful musician, and laborer. Significantly, the laborer was a happy-go-lucky Irish immigrant named Mike O'Dell. Here and in the Coles study it seems the higher end of the status ladder in this land of literacy is reserved for white Anglo-Saxon males, but even they can suffer from ethnic stereotyping.

Social Class Issues

At the level of socioeconomic class, Coles examined the four sub-themes described earlier: "harmony of interests," "the individualist ethic," "blaming the victim," and "happy consciousness."

Harmony of Interests

Coles found employees to be "overwhelmingly content and uncritical in their jobs" in twenty-six of the thirty stories depicting employment situations. As an example, Jim applies for and gets a stock clerk job. He is "always on time," "follows . . . rules," is "friendly but does not talk too much." In Coles's words, he is "a good, obedient, happy worker." At the end of this story, the instructions direct the teacher to ask the class, "How should one treat his [*sic*] boss?" and "How do you feel about a person who is always telling bad things about his [*sic*] boss?" The teacher is then to ask, "Would you hire that kind of person?" (Coles, 1977, p. 45, citing Steck-Vaughn, 1974).

Employees are content and uncritical of employers, leading Coles to conclude that most of the characters examined (white males included) demonstrated a clear "absence of contradictory thought" (p. 51). He found that "price-fixing, government corruption, military deception, inflation, unemployment, pollution, and a hundred other problems may come and go, but it appears as though the story characters will remain oblivious to it all" (p. 51). Harmony of interest was pervasive throughout both studies. For Coles, characters must always accept their circumstances and put all faith in the established systems. In our study, the employer is always right, and the system is unquestionably working in the employee's best interests. "Bad attitudes" are always to be avoided. In one story, a character loses a good job he has held for ten years. When he finds a job with less pay and poorer working conditions, the message is that he (and the reader) are to be grateful and uncritical: "The job paid less than my last job. And, this factory was noisier and dirtier. But I was glad when the employment officer shook my hand and told me to start work the following Monday" (Laubach, Kirk, and Laubach, 1984, bk. 4, p. 96).

This is the "right attitude." Readers are shown what happens when a "bad attitude" is displayed. For example, one cannot be a "goof-off." In "Tony's Day Off," Tony calls his employer saying he cannot come to work because of sickness. In fact, he is perfectly well and goes shopping instead. He is in a men's clothing store when he becomes the victim of his own bad attitude:

> Tony waited in line to use the fitting booth for what seemed like an hour.
>   "Hey, will you please hurry up in there," commanded Tony. "I haven't got all day, you know." All at once, it became very quiet in the fitting booth. "Oh, yeah? That's what you think. You'll have all the time in the world to shop for fancy clothes now, Tony," declared Mr. Dennis as he poked his head behind the curtain, "because you're fired!" [Murphy, 1985, bk. 3, p. 90–91]

Why Mr. Dennis was shopping on company time does not matter. That an employer is shown firing an employee on sight outside the workplace is also irrelevant. "Right attitude" and the belief in a harmony of interests are what count.

As Coles saw it, the preponderant attitude among characters toward authority and hierarchical control was one of "acceptance and belief that they [agencies and authorities] were working on behalf of people and in harmony with individuals and group interests" (1977, p. 45). Coles found eight out of twelve stories about government and eleven out of fourteen stories about police expressing this attitude. Criticism of authority, from police to banks, "was . . . depicted as an unjustifiable attitude" (p. 47). Harmony of interests prevails in the literacy land of the readers in these two studies.

The Individualist Ethic

Individualism was often manifested in problem-solving style. Given a problem, Coles's characters enter a strange state of alienation. They typically do not turn for help to those who care about them, nor do they seek out or use the local resources at hand. The message conveyed is that one should aspire to stoic endurance.

Fifty-six of Coles's stories contained plots about "the solution of life problems such as romantic problems, drug use, unemployment, and physical accidents" (pp. 47–48). Of these, only twenty-seven (48 percent) of the stories portrayed individuals as capable of solving their own problems rather than just accepting their lot. When they did solve their problems, it was always in a state of isolated individualism, neither seeking nor considering others' help. Where a solution was reached (in twenty-five of the stories) by one individual helping another, "20 of the stories were sexist in that the helpee was a woman who was invariably subordinate to her male 'helper'" (p. 48). Coles cites an example from the *Mott Basic Language Skills Program* (1965): "A woman recalls the skating she did as a youth and decides to try again. When she goes out on the rink she is cautious, tense, and uncertain, but these feelings disappear when a man comes up behind her and takes hold of her. She glides along 'with a big strong partner, not conscious of the dangers of falling.'" (Coles, 1977, p. 48).

Coles also found that only two of the stories in this individualistic ethic category went beyond the persons involved in allowing the characters to look for assistance (p. 48). The characters typically do not involve others; rather, they suffer in isolation.

In our more recent study, we found a story, "The Year I Was Unemployed," in which Roy Johnson loses his job. It was not his fault; the plant closed. His response to the situation was to suffer in silence—an individualist. However, his wife inevitably found out: "That news almost destroyed my wife. She was disappointed in me. She felt that I didn't trust her enough to tell her the truth. It wasn't that. I didn't want to worry her. I thought I might be able to find another job soon. I asked Joyce not to tell our boys. I didn't want to worry them" (Laubach, Kirk, and Laubach, 1984, p. 94).

Thus, the best thing to be is a lone individualist, trusting that the system is always on your side. Coles found that where problems were solved by groups or solved collectively, "two stories were sexist and only one presented a family as a group. In only one story was a true group solution reached, i.e., where an aggregate of people came and worked together unselfishly and caringly" (p. 48).

In our study, individualism and problem solving in isolation were frequent subthemes. Twenty-one of the stories involved such problems as romantic squabbles, unemployment, juvenile delinquency, smoking, stress, and robbery. In these, eleven of the depicted protagonists received (although they did not seek) help, while the ten who resolved their own problems did so in isolation. It was in the portrayal of the ideology of individualism that the protagonists seemed most tragically alone. In only five of the twenty-one stories that featured problems do victims turn to organized authorities, such as the police, schools, or city council. They are cast in roles that assume, against all logic, that the systems will somehow look out for them. They need not challenge or even bother the authorities.

An example is "A Good Ending." This is a police-related story that turns out to be perhaps the most incredible of all those analyzed. Ed is arrested in a case of mistaken identity. His mother, talking to him on a telephone through the glass partition in the prison visiting room, gives him some remarkably passive advice, which Ed unquestioningly accepts: "At times they do arrest people by mistake. The wrong people pay for it. We're with you in this time of trouble. The family will stand by you, Ed."

The son replies: "They'll get the man that looks like me. With luck the man will be arrested and do time for this trouble."

The mother assures Ed: "This will have a good ending, and you will win."

Ed concludes: "I feel bad about being arrested. But I'll feel good about this man being in the hands of the law. I'll feel good about going home!" (Steck-Vaughn Company, 1987, bk. 2, pp. 57–59).

Blaming the Victim

With the social, gender, racial, and economic stage set in literacy land, learners are now given to realize that *they*, not the characters, are the people the stories are about, and it is they who are the cause of their own problems. In case the reader misses the point, he or she is spoken to directly by the narrator. The not so subtle implication of the author's silences and choices is that, in a Kafkaesque way, the reader is "guilty"—or on the slippery slope to becoming guilty. The apparent accusation is, "If you are here reading this book, you are obviously illiterate; if you are illiterate, you are a potential menace to society and to yourself."

For example, in "Hank's Lesson," Hank is back in jail. For no obvious reason, two inmates, Sly and the narrator, make a point of "telling the other kids about life in prison" (Steck-Vaughn Company, 1987, bk. 4, p. 65). But "our lesson wasn't sinking in for [Hank]," according to the narrator. Again for no obvious reason, the narrator tells the reader that he was involved in shoplifting, adding, "but my worst mistake was selling drugs" (p. 65). That the narrator speaks to the reader as much as to Hank indicates that the reader is of at least as much interest to the author as Hank is.

The reader is now told by the narrator that he and Sly "talked to the group" and then stayed to talk further with Hank and his social worker. Hank inexplicably divulges how frustrating it is to "hate school," and that "the teachers always pick on me." He says that when he takes his report card home, "I know I'm going to get a licking." Going further, he admits: "My friends and I are sick of school and home. We get our kicks where we can" (p. 66). Hank is now in jail for drug use. The implication is that this is all one slippery slope—hate school, hate teachers, disrespect your parents, and you naturally turn to shoplifting and inevitably either take drugs (like Hank) or, worse, end up selling them (like the paternalistic narrator).

After "a long talk" (the substance of which is apparently of little interest beyond the points already made), the narrator and Sly give their advice to Hank and the reader: "You are right kid, . . . life isn't like the movies. You can make a lot of costly mistakes, but there are two ways to go, and you are responsible for you. You can learn to cope with life's problems or you can end up in here" (p. 65).

Now, as in an old-fashioned morality play, the narrator turns directly to the reader and asks point-blank: "Will the kid go straight, or will he go for a prison sentence? I hope Hank will learn the lesson before it's too late" (p. 67).

Thus, the decision is Hank's, but it is also for the reader to make decisions: "Only *you* are responsible for *you*." This is the political perspective speaking to adult low literates directly. In any other adult educational setting—vocational, college, university, business training on the job—assuming that the student is a potential criminal would surely be considered an outrage. In literacy, hidden curricula, the narrators' direct statements, and chapter-end instructions to teachers basically to assume the worst in learners seem to say everyone is agreed here.

The Implications of Texts in Our Classrooms

If the texts analyzed in the two studies are taken seriously by those who read them, learners will take the blame for their problems; learn their place in society according to race, gender, and economic status; and graduate into a state of happy consciousness— no questions asked now, none to be asked in the future (Foucault, 1972, 1977). These texts instruct illiterates not to be a threat to society's authority figures, employers, or social agencies; not to raise critical questions; not to seek collaborative problem solving; not to impute blame to others or to society for their problems; and to realize that they should be grateful. Ultimately, the hidden curricula are saying, "The system is good and it will provide."

Not all readers will agree with the conclusions arrived at by Coles or this author. For some, the examples may not seem overtly sexist, racist, or suggestive of the type of individualism or harmony of interest discussed. However, as Coles noted, ABE "readers express particular ideological concepts and they leave almost no room to raise divergent views" (p. 52). It seems a "happy consciousness" is needed to accept the ideologies and not raise critical questions. If we pose questions as educators, we must ask what these texts say about the singular purposes of literacy education. It is obvious that teachers, tutors, administrators, book publishers, and researchers need to give thought to the perceptions of reality and the assumptions carried into this field from the political perspective. I personally know of no other way this can be accomplished than by each practitioner clarifying in his or her mind what literacy education should be for—and what it should not be for.

Toward Change in Practice

Graham warns that the content of textbooks "should alert us to a blind spot in our assumptions and textual practices; namely, that if the authority of the textbook and the knowledge legitimated therein remain unchallenged and taken-for-granted, then what we consider our most enlightened and emancipated teaching strategies may be discovered to have their footing in ideological quicksand" (1989a, p. 416).

Our 1993 study suggests that much of the hidden curricula found in 1977 persists in the current texts. It is different in quantity but not in kind. The two studies indicate that the content has shifted from what we would today consider "blatant" sexism, racism, and socioeconomic stereotypes to less overt manifestations. That the tutors my graduate student mentioned earlier found cases of violence toward women suggests that incidents of greater hostility exist in the contemporary readers than we found through our random selection of stories. Further research is needed to help corroborate this study or to challenge it. In either case, it is imperative that we look carefully at the texts we give our learners and consider the hidden curricula in them. And if we are to argue forcefully and coherently against such curricula, we must be guided by a working philosophy.

Other research questions arise. How many literacy teachers accept the hidden curricula without question? The majority? Only a few? If one looks at these curricula through the liberatory lens, as Giroux does, one will probably conclude that the hidden messages must be made "visible to students and others so that they can become the clear object of debate" (1983b, p. 292). It should again be noted that our study was prompted by the refusal of certain literacy tutors to use their current reading materials, which were found to be "demeaning and insulting to students," as one teacher put it. Research is needed to determine how widespread teacher resistance is to commercial texts such as these, and we need to know more about how teachers cope with such materials. Similarly, it is not known how many, if any, instructors/administrators actively raise objections with publishers. To what extent are we as passive as our own learners in simply living with the texts given to us?

Behind all these questions for further research lies the reality that the authors of these stories, the editors who shape them, and the publishers who sell them apparently have a collective idea of who illiterates are and a collective sense of what our profession is supposed to be doing about such people.

The stories are not written from a neutral stance. The chosen and unmistakable message is that a society dominated by white males is not only normal and appropriate, but that females should—and "naturally" do—occupy a lower intellectual, social, and occupational status. In this fictional literacy land, minorities are inherently inferior and excel mainly when they dominate minority females. White females are imbecilic, and minority females are creatures of impulse. An isolated, alienating, individualism is advocated, whereas group or community action is rarely seen or promoted.

Where do these collective perspectives and attitudes come from? I argue that they come from a historically entrenched political perspective that seeks to regulate "subordinate" groups in society. Why are these stories not challenged? I contend that maternalistic humanism does not choose to challenge paternalistic authority in the field. Most teachers and tutors, in all philosophical streams, close their eyes and use the questionable texts, hoping their learners will just go along. In my experience, it is those who have reflected on their purposes who turn to alternative materials.

Suggestions for Practice and Politics

In my experience once again, I believe that most in this field are exceptionally caring but have not been challenged to think critically about their purposes, nor been given enough alternatives to work with. Following are some suggestions that may be helpful.

Selecting Materials for the Classroom

Texts need to be carefully considered by teachers, with input from students. *Appropriate texts* is a relative term. Appropriateness is determined by the philosophy of the teacher and by the lives, experiences, and aspirations of learners. Toward this, the Ohio Literacy Resource Center works to give a short list of reading texts and a brief annotated bibliography to teachers. They build student feedback into their text reviews as well. Those who lean toward the liberal philosophy may want to use rewritten classic literature published at the reading level of their learners. Several publishers have made such material available in recent years. Publishers' displays at conferences provide an opportunity to look at these materials, and sample sets can be requested.

Those who subscribe to a more vocational philosophy or teach in a vocational setting can search for reading materials that include job terminology. If one knows what sorts of occupation clusters learners are interested in and have an aptitude for, one can approach almost any business or company in that field, requesting free literature. Pamphlets, manuals, magazines, and promotional materials will need to be examined for readability levels. There are standard readability tests that can help determine these.

The liberatory philosophy may draw teachers toward novels that explore issues of oppression and empowerment. Such novels can take learners into problems they can identify with. Meanwhile, both liberatory and humanist teachers can attest that learner-written readers and materials can be very helpful (Soifer et al., 1990). There are entire series written by students that are available from publishing outlets.

In most programs, teachers and tutors have the right to select materials—or they should have. It is recommended that new reading texts be tested with a pilot group of students before a commitment is made to them. Often, the learner can see what the teacher cannot. Evaluations of this kind can be a valuable exercise for the entire class.

Where to Find Materials

It was mentioned earlier that the best materials are often the ones teachers discover. I have found that the smaller, alternative publishing houses sometimes provide a much richer selection than the larger firms who can afford to exhibit at conferences. Seasoned teachers of English as a second language have cupboards full of magazine articles, photos, posters, books, and videos. Reading material is where you find it, and learners should play a large part in the search (Fingeret and Jurmo, 1989). In the first literacy course I taught, I took one or two of the learners on an expedition downtown each week. As we walked, they would read the words in the store windows, the posters in the used car offices, the bulletins in churches, the "Men" and "Women" signs on bathroom doors. The idea was that reading should not be confined to a classroom.

Using Existing Commercial Materials

Although some teachers will not be comfortable with the idea, the commercial materials discussed above have great potential for class debate—across all working philosophies. Even negative materials can provide opportunities for critical discussion of "authoritative sources." Such discussion stimulates the type of thinking central to the liberal and liberatory philosophies. Learners can discuss textual biases and assumptions in ways rarely conducted in literacy. My own experience (and see Fingeret, 1983) is that our learners are much more resilient to the political perspective and much more astute with respect to the popular perspective than we give them credit for. Cross has commented that the job of adult educator is that of "challenger" (1992). In my view, this is the exciting side of education—where learners and teachers can challenge what exists and explore new possibilities together.

Recommendations on the Political Perspective

Opportunities for policy input at the state and federal levels were discussed in Part One, but challenges to the policy status quo should not end there; they should extend to publishers and their representatives.

It is perhaps easy, "by the general necessity of things" (Marcuse, 1966, p. 79), to forever accept our printed materials; ignore the uncomfortable questions; dread that we might be the ones not funded next year if we ask "the wrong questions" (Menzies, 1987); or forever fear that we will somehow discourage tutor/teacher participation by pointing to the problems within our field. However, if we do not press for change, we surrender self-determination and personal responsibility for a version of the "happy consciousness" that reader-based literacy land celebrates.

Choosing appropriate readers for our learners is an ideological act—an act that indicates how we regard our learners. As Daloz puts it: "Teaching is . . . pre-eminently an act of care. We must be concerned not simply with how much knowledge our students have acquired but also with how they are making meaning of that knowledge and how it is affecting their capacity to go on learning, framing the world in ever inclusive and comprehensive ways" (1986, p. 237). Choosing texts is a matter of choosing knowledge and choosing the values embedded in that knowledge. Aronowitz and Giroux succinctly state what is involved in making our choices: "To acknowledge different forms of literacy is not to suggest that they should all be given equal weight. On the contrary, it is to argue that their differences are to be weighed against the capacity they have for enabling people to place themselves in their own histories while simultaneously establishing the conditions for them to function as part of a wider democratic culture" (1991, p. 236).

Part Three

Engaging Nonparticipants and Dropouts

Chapter Six

Understanding Attrition and Improving Retention

One of the most pressing problems in the field of adult literacy in the 1990s is student retention (Horsman, 1991; MacKeracher, 1991; Quigley, 1993b). It was estimated in 1979 that the dropout rate from traditional adult basic education (ABE) was approximately 65 percent in adult literacy programs (Cain and Whalen, 1979), with attrition in various individual literacy and ABE programs soaring to 80 percent (Bean et al., 1989; Belzer, 1990). Figures calculated almost twenty years later are even higher. A federal study of the period July 1, 1993, to June 30, 1994, indicated that the overall attrition rate in basic literacy to GED was approximately 74 percent in federally funded programs (U.S. Department of Education, 1995). It should be added that these attrition figures are normally calculated *after* an estimated 20 percent of the population that enrolled never begin programs (Farra, 1988; Leonard and Jackson, 1986; Bean, Partanen, Wright, and Aaronson, 1989). The uncertain future of sponsored ABE and literacy is certainly not helped by such high dropout levels.

When "access" was the challenge in the 1970s and early 1980s, the pressure was on programs to reach and recruit low-literate adults. Works such as Darkenwald and Larson's *Reaching Hard-to-Reach Adults* (1980) focused exclusively on this issue, as have articles such as Fitzgerald's "Can the Hard-to-Reach Adults Become Literate?" (1984). Often, recruitment literature attempted to apply participation models from mainstream adult education and research to the low-literate population (for example, Darkenwald, 1980). With certain exceptions (for example, Beder, 1980; Irish, 1980), it was not always clear that the mainstream models used were appropriate to the recruitment questions being applied to our population (Fingeret, 1984). Today, the growing accountability for funds in literacy has spurred administrators and programs to improve their retention rates, but despite this need, there is a great lack of research on the topic. A few research studies have appeared in recent years on low-literate student participation—an issue that has tangentially borne on the issue of retention (for example, Baldwin, 1991; Beder, 1989b; Cervero and Fitzpatrick, 1990; General Educational Development Testing Service, 1987; Qi, 1986; Ziegahn, 1992). Others have focused on those adults who do not participate at all—nonparticipants in literacy—and these have been of some relevance to the attrition question (for example, Beder, 1980, 1986, 1989a; 1990a; Fingeret, 1983; Quigley, 1989, 1990b). And a few have focused directly on retention in adult literacy itself (for example, Bean et al., 1989; Belzer, 1990; Knibbe and Dusewicsz, 1990; Nurs and Singh, 1993; Quigley, 1993b; Solarzano, 1989; Vannozzi-Knibbe, 1990; Van Tilburg and DuBois, 1989).

There are no mainstream models and no body of adult education research applicable to our current 1990s retention issue. One reason is that mainstream adult educators such as continuing professional education instructors, distance education researchers, those interested in diversity in mainstream programs, and teachers of older adults simply do not confront retention problems at the same level. Nor do they typically face the policy and political pressures to which adult literacy is subject. Second, the issue of literacy retention draws researchers into the very center of the literacy program. By necessity, retention studies look at the operating assumptions and practices used across a program. Retention is a much more emotional issue than, for example, recruitment. There is an element of vulnerability in the search for better ways to retain learners. As a result, there may have been some hesitancy to conduct research in this area. There is no question, however, that variables abound and controls are difficult in this type of research.

One often sees recruitment and retention bracketed together in books and articles. For literacy, the two program functions need to be separated, and much more research attention is needed on the retention of low-literate adults.

The emotional aspects of the retention issue are unavoidable for those who work in the field. Most practitioners will remember most of the faces, even the names, of the first students they taught in literacy. I could name most of those I taught in my first literacy class over twenty years ago. When students drop out of classes, it can be a terribly discouraging, frustrating, even humbling experience for the teacher. In my opinion, dropout is the worst part of teaching and tutoring low-literate adults and is the source of much guilt. The common feeling is: "I tried to do everything right, but they still dropped out. Did I do something wrong? If so, what should I do differently?"

Here is an observation that may help set the stage for this chapter. Interestingly, most literacy teachers can recall the names of their past schoolteachers from grade one through grade twelve. For the vast majority of us in this field, our schooling has made a huge impact, and for the most part, that impact has been positive; it probably accounts for our working today in the field of education. By contrast, in the research to be discussed here and in the next chapter, past schooling was not positive for most of our learners. We asked ABE and literacy program dropouts to name their past schoolteachers. Although they had spent an average of ten (formative) years in a school, none could recall more than two names. Those we interviewed could sometimes remember one teacher whom they said they still "hated" and felt angry toward even in the present. Most could recall the name of one, occasionally two, teachers whom they remembered with great fondness and love. Here is a virtual reversal of recall. Overall, practitioners carried positive memories of school. Their learners did not. Also interesting, only a few of these ABE and literacy tutoring students could accurately recall the names of the literacy teachers who had recently taught them.

The assumption that learners and teachers come from a common schooling background or share a common emotional base of experience is far from accurate. We have two very different perceptions of the schooling "reality." It is extremely unfortunate that this critical area has been so little investigated. However, some of the work conducted in recent years has helped, as will the action research by practitioners that is discussed in Chapter Eight. Nevertheless, research can only "help." The starting point for improved retention is the belief that change is both desirable and possible.

The Relevant Research Groups

It is worth noting that practitioners actually see only a small proportion of those adults who are low literate in this country. We see the participants. The approximately 8 percent of low literates who do attend programs are not necessarily representative of all. The minority who attend are clearly only those who are willing and able to attend. In other words, we cannot assume that those who participate are the same as those who do not. The field therefore needs two different bodies of research here—one dealing with participants and the other with nonparticipants. The next chapter will take a closer look at the issue of resistance to programs among nonparticipants. As far as participating low literates are concerned, we must again be wary of the assumption that those who persist in programs are the same as those who drop out. We need separate bodies of research on these two groups. Unfortunately, some research literature assumes homogeneity across the entire population of low literates: participants and nonparticipants, persisters and dropouts. Those who stay have been asked why others have left. Those who come to programs have been carefully researched to find out why others do not. We cannot learn much from research based on the wrong people. Assumed homogeneity in research has often only served to confuse an already complex set of issues.

If future research would study dropouts more exclusively—both in the formative stages when they begin to consider quitting and at different points after they leave—we would be much better informed. If we could identify the phases in a program when students begin to think about dropping out, we would know when to attempt intervention. If we could predict which new students were likely to drop out later, and why, we could focus our energy on them in constructive ways. Will some drop out no matter what we do? Will some stay and be so self-directed that they will need minimal attention? If there were some predictability, practitioners could focus more of their scarce time on those most likely to drop out. The following discussion tries to address some of these issues.

In Search of a Practitioner Map of the Territory

In light of all the variables, where can a teacher, tutor, or administrator possibly start on the retention issue? There are no "exit interviews" in literacy—students normally just do not return. There are few published follow-up studies with sufficiently wide generalizability (Fingeret, 1984). This is not to say follow-up studies are not conducted. They are, but few are published. When I was an ABE administrator, I diligently tried to follow up on program dropouts through the ubiquitous telephone interview. In the cases in which I was able to reach the student—and it is not unusual to find that phone numbers and addresses have changed after dropout—it was obvious that I was hearing socially acceptable responses. I was often given what the dropouts were comfortable telling me, or the answers they thought I wanted to hear. Literacy programs do not have probing "feedback sessions." No informed dialogue takes place between teachers and students.

How can practitioners build a better understanding of this complex problem? I believe we need to begin by acknowledging that there is not just one literacy attrition issue. Though homogeneity in this area would be convenient for purposes of research or practice, it is not to be found in our real worlds. Attrition can best be understood, I believe, as a cluster of discrete elements within an organizing framework. Some of the elements can be affected by our systematic efforts; some probably cannot.

Statewide research by Beder in Iowa (1989b) and recent studies on participation (Hayes, 1987, 1988) "suggest two major constellations of reasons for nonparticipation. One is structural; the other is attitudinal" (Beder, 1989b, p. 91). One set of reasons, in other words, has to do with the world that low-literate adults live in. The other has to do with the way they perceive the programming we offer them. The structural pertains to potential learners' "outer world," the attitudinal to the lived experience, or "inner world," of the target group. These basic categories are again suggested in national GED research (Baldwin, 1991). They emerge from ABE work by Fingeret in North Carolina (1985) and again in large-scale longitudinal research by Cervero and Fitzpatrick (1990).

The outer world of structures holds few surprises. Here we find issues of transportation, location, money, child care, and the like. However, there is something striking to be found in the attitudinal reasons for nonparticipation: the consistent influence on low literates of past schooling on the decision to avoid or drop out of programs.

How can the growing body of knowledge about nonparticipants' motivations be further developed? Let us begin with what
teachers and administrators have told me over the past ten years
during more than forty structured and informal presentations I
have conducted on retention for teachers, tutors, counselors, and
administrators in Pennsylvania, Georgia, Texas, Tennessee, Washington, and California. Although I am obviously using a sample of
convenience drawn unsystematically from those who attended
these various sessions, I consistently asked the same sets of questions (in written form) at the beginning of the sessions, each of
which had ten to forty participants. The questionnaire asked

1. At what point in time during your program do most of your
   students drop out?
2. In your opinion, what are the top five reasons why they quit?
3. Do those who quit seem to have anything in common?
4. If the dropouts have something in common, how are they different from those who persist in your program?

The four hundred and more questionnaires I have received,
and the discussions about them that I have had, have further convinced me that the two "major constellations" of reasons, structural
and attitudinal, indeed do aptly categorize the plethora of reasons
given for attrition. As will be seen, the structural area—the world
around the potential participants and the dropouts—is the one
where I believe we have the least influence, even if it is the subject
of so much of the literacy literature (Fingeret, 1984). The attitudinal area, in my view, offers more promise for change in retention
and programs. This is where teachers and tutors are most engaged
and where they can do their best work, irrespective of the working
philosophy chosen. Moreover, it is in this area that program
changes can be affected by the learners. In short, I have reached
the conclusion that practitioners and researchers need to pay more
attention to the world as seen by students. In the majority of
instances, it is not the same one we see or have experienced.

Sadly, our history is an account of exactly the opposite practice—
applying societal and professional "solutions" to problems we imagine or believe we deduce, but that learners either do not have or
do not agree that they have.

A Framework for Understanding Attrition

Some years ago, the two constellations of reasons we have just discussed were integrated by Cross (1992) into a well-accepted description of barriers to adult education participation. I have serious reservations about the term *barrier* because I do not think low-literate adults are typically "blocked by a barrier." The metaphor suggests that low-literate students are trying to enter our Fortresses of Knowledge and that we need only knock down the "barriers" for them to flood in. Far from it. In my view, the descriptor *barrier* diminishes the role of learners' personal choice, or "agency" (Candy, 1991). Low-literate learners make their own decisions; events and circumstances merely encourage them to act, or discourage them (Center for Literacy Studies, 1992; Uhland, 1995). As Candy puts it: "Certainly, people have both a genetic and a cultural inheritance, but as Mair . . . points out, 'We are not bound by our conditioning or our family dynamics, or delineated completely by our heredity, unless we choose to be so . . . We can be different if we go out and do differently, we can become different by acting differently'" (1991, p. 258).

If, however, we recognize that we are talking about the learner's *responses* to barriers, Cross's (1982) well-known framework becomes helpful (see also Cross, 1992). She has categorized three types of barriers facing mainstream adult learners, and I believe the categories apply to literacy learners as well. Our learners also face (1) situational barriers, such as a lack of day care, transportation, or finances; (2) institutional barriers, such as inconvenient scheduling, inaccessible location, or excessive red tape for registration; and (3) dispositional barriers, such as a learned fear of academic failure or dislike of school. These three sets of "barriers" suggest a way to conceptualize the external and internal influences on our learners (Figure 6.1).

Informal surveys I have conducted around the country have supported this framework. Every reason for dropout given by program participants could be located by practitioners in one of the three categories. When teachers said that their learners dropped out because of a lack of family or peer support, we could place that in the situational category, which is part of the structural constellation described earlier. When practitioners mentioned barriers created by their own

Figure 6.1. Influences on the Decision to Stay or Drop Out.

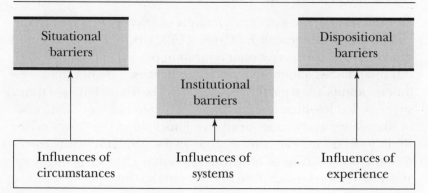

programs—"no wheelchair access," "no appropriate part-time day scheduling available," "center too far from the potential students"—these were located in the institutional category, which is also structural. However, "unrealistic goals," "unwillingness to try something new," and "fear of failing" were examples of dispositional issues within the learners themselves. They cannot necessarily be observed directly, but they are present in the classroom and tutoring situations. We occasionally decided to put a barrier into more than one category, since some appear in more than one way. For instance, is "fear of failing" an institutional or a dispositional barrier? Probably both.

This framework, as will be seen, helps us "get a handle" on the many factors that seem to affect the dropout issue, and it assists us in determining which of those factors are actually within our locus of influence and which are not.

We should be able to acknowledge that there are some things beyond our power to change. At the same time, we do "our best" within our domain of responsibility. I have known many literacy and ABE teachers who would loan or give money to students, take them to live in their homes, give them rides daily to the program and elsewhere, in some cases help with everything from shopping to marital counseling. In fact, I have done many of these things myself. I have also been there when a teacher has had an emotional breakdown on learning from the newspaper that one of her students had been murdered and left in a dumpster. I have seen teachers work passionately with a student, only to witness him or her fall into drug use, disappear from classes, and be glimpsed in alleyways as the teacher walked to work. As will be seen, I do not believe we carry, or should presume to carry, equal responsibility for each of the three categories of barriers.

Further, it was universally agreed by the practitioners I surveyed that the vast majority of low-literate dropouts leave in the first two or three weeks of the program. This is an extremely important observation. Careful study of what discourages learners at the beginning of the program may enable us to boost retention rates significantly.

Because, as practitioners have said, learners typically have made arrangements to overcome most situational barriers just to attend, and because institutional barriers seem not to play a major role early in the program (Quigley, 1993b), it follows that dispositional barriers are important in the first weeks of our programs. The work I have done on the early phase of literacy and ABE programs suggests that there is at least one large group that is profoundly affected by attitudinal barriers and, as will be seen, past schooling plays a major role in this group's decision to stay or drop out.

My interest in trying to identify a predictable dropout group in the first three critical weeks was triggered, in part, by what practitioners told me on their questionnaires. When asked what the early dropouts had in common, some indicated that such students were often "at risk." After inquiring further, the practitioners cited "at risk" behaviors that were demonstrated by a significant number of students who dropped out early in their programs. Such "signs of potential dropout" may be part of the key to addressing the retention issue.

Before moving on to ideas for possible solutions, it is important to look more closely at the nature of the barriers themselves. It was said earlier that learners and practitioners often see different worlds. If we have typically come from different backgrounds, now live in different worlds and, as Fingeret demonstrated in her work in North Carolina (1985), often have radically differing goals in mind in the literacy classroom, it is essential that we understand what might give low literates cause to quit.

Situational Barriers

Situational barriers are those that exist in the objective "lived situations" of our learners outside the program environment. It is these that, in the popular perspective, stir compassion for "victims," and in the political, prompt demands for "bootstraps action." When I ask practitioners around the country to name those factors that seem to affect learners' decision to quit, 38 percent of the responses begin with the phrase "a lack of": learners are said to have a lack of babysitting or day care, transportation, living funds, health, personal time, or spousal or family support. Such lacks are obviously not unique to literacy students. Most undergraduate and graduate students in college face similar problems. How well such problems can be managed is the real issue in the situational category. And for practitioners, there is the more perplexing question of how much one teacher or one program—even with community support agencies working alongside—can do within this category of barriers. It is important for our own mental health, if for no other reason, that we be aware of just how many of these barriers are actually beyond our direct control or influence. Despite the popular press and the sentiments we may share with it, the sad fact is that we typically can do very little in this domain of our learners' lives on an individual basis.

In this area of literacy education, the liberatory approach is more powerful than models built on humanism, liberalism, or vocationalism. Liberatory literacy would want to build curricula and learning around real situational barriers in the lives of learners. A "discourager" becomes a "challenger." People I know who work at the Highlander Research and Education Center in Tennessee have pointed out that illiteracy cannot be overcome unless adults are engaged in their real-life issues. Anything less is institutionally framed and artificial. The decision to engage with such issues needs to arise out of one's working philosophy. Administrators of programs should be prepared to help practitioners—individually and collectively—work through their philosophies and determine the limits of their personal influence.

Still, every practitioner and administrator has a professional if not moral responsibility to try to connect learners with the community agencies that can help them. And we also need to continue to bring pressure on public figures and social policy makers to improve the lives of our learners.

It is important to realize that learner situations are often not as simple as they appear and do not necessarily conform with our assumptions. In one southwest Texas program, the staff came to the conclusion that transportation was the single largest problem, or situational discourager, facing their perpetually absent students. The local military reserve agreed to pick up and deliver the students every morning. However, after just one or two trips, the drivers arrived at the students' homes only to find that the students were not there. If only human behavior were as simple or predictable as we would like it to be!

Institutional Barriers

More promisingly, institutional barriers place the locus of control with the program structure. Red tape, poor geographic access, lack of handicapped access, inconvenient scheduling, and irrelevant courses are all systemic problems that can discourage potential or enrolled students from participating. It is notable that this type of barrier was named the least significant of the three in the informal surveys I conducted among teachers and administrators. Practitioners' own programs—from the content they chose to the teaching style they used—were cited in no more than 10 percent of the responses on why students quit. Moreover, institutional barriers do not figure prominently in the participation literature mentioned earlier. The reason may be that there are actually fewer such barriers than others—at least, fewer constructed by educators. Another factor is that researchers and practitioners often do not see the world through the eyes of their students and may therefore be misinterpreting learner behavior. Finally, it should be borne in mind that no research methodology can absolutely control for the tendency of subjects to give socially acceptable responses.

Given poor administrative mechanisms to collect the views and feelings of those who decide to drop out, and haphazard, often weak, administrator follow-up studies, it is entirely possible that we do have institutional barriers that we are not aware of. For example, learners may not want to continue to attend programs in old school buildings, church basements, or makeshift facilities because they are insulted by them or are somehow reminded of the worst aspects of their "situation." Perhaps "paper paradise programs" based on the printed word—words on handouts, books, chalkboards, tests—do not constitute the best learning environment for a highly aural-oral group of learners (Fingeret, 1984; Anderson and Niemi, 1970). To take another possibility, in one of the first programs I worked in, all teachers assisted during intake by giving students a basic eye chart test. A remarkable three out of seven students desperately needed glasses just to see the blackboard. We referred them to the local optometrist, but not all of them went. How many program participants have learning disabilities, learning style differences, physical challenges? Despite the deep concern for learners, the fact is that we certainly have fewer variations and alternative systems in ABE and GED programs than do the school systems. This category of barriers is a rich field for future research.

Dispositional Barriers

We now turn to dispositional barriers, which I believe are the most promising of the three types in terms of potential improvements in retention rates. The affective domain, to refer to Bloom's taxonomy again, is one where good teachers make a profound difference in learners' lives. This is where more practitioner energy needs to go, whatever the chosen working philosophy. When the teachers and tutors in my surveys were asked why most students quit, dispositional barriers came out on top. In this (less than scientific) sample, they accounted for well over half of the explanations for dropout.

Dispositional influences refer to learners' attitudes in general, to their attitudes toward education in particular, and to their attitudes toward our programs specifically. In this area, the student is typically subject to a good deal of stereotyping. This is where low literates have traditionally been singled out as having "poor motivation," "poor attitudes," "wrong values," or "no interest" (Anderson and Niemi, 1970). Some of the earliest research touching on low literates and their lack of participation in adult education appeared in the mainstream literature and, playing into the stereotypes of the political perspective, undoubtedly did our field more harm than good. Reissman argued there was "pragmatic anti-intellectualism" (1962, p. 12) among the "deprived." Johnstone and Rivera (1965) set the field of adult literacy back by studying mainstream adults in formal adult education programs and concluding there was a "lack of interest" among the poorly educated. In recent years, studies and analyses involving nonparticipating low-literate adults have not suggested that undereducated adults are intellectually lazy or hostile to education. They point instead to cultural and value differences (Fingeret, 1983, 1984, 1985; Quigley, 1990a, 1990b) and to the potential for learning from them in areas such as self-directed problem solving (Center for Literacy Studies, 1992; Uhland, 1995). As mentioned earlier, several national and state studies also point to the influences of prior schooling (for example, Baldwin, 1991; Beder, 1991; Cervero and Fitzpatrick, 1990; Kirsch and Jungeblut, 1986).

Whereas in earlier years, undereducated adults were included in many mainstream studies without receiving close attention to their specific circumstances or dispositions, we are now seeing the emergence of a body of research that is concerned with our own population of participants and nonparticipants. And as discussed earlier, more recent literacy research makes the point that it matters a great deal *what* questions are asked, *who* asks them, *to whom they are posed,* and *how* the asking takes place.

The Dropout Process

My own research and experience, the experiences of other teachers, tutors, and administrators, and the research discussed earlier all indicate that there is a dropout sequence or process that can be identified in most traditional ABE, GED, and basic literacy programs that occurs in the first two to three weeks of programs. As mentioned earlier, according to a Development Associates study (1993) the dropout rate is a full 18 percent before twelve hours of instruction has occurred. Though further research is required on this point, it seems that the barrier that most influences early *at-risk learners* during the first three critical weeks is the dispositional; the others typically appear to come into effect later. After making the decision to attend a program, after "standing in line" on a wait list for several weeks, after making all the arrangements needed to attend the program—child care, transportation, finances, family members' schedules—a student rarely encounters a situational barrier that forces him or her to quit within the very first days or weeks. Both situational and institutional barriers obviously had to be overcome before the student arrived at the program. It seems that, often, dispositional barriers are the ones that motivate learners to drop out early, and it is in this area that we can have a real impact (Cross, 1982; Quigley, 1991b).

I believe that the ability to identify those who may exit in the first weeks because of the influences of dispositional barriers is part of the key to turning our high attrition rates around.

Retaining At-Risk Learners in the First Three Critical Weeks

The significance to the dropout phenomenon of variables such as race, gender, age, cognitive style, and learning style is still far from clear. These factors need to be studied further, and in concert with the dynamics of the teaching-learning situation. However, in the quest to isolate variables, we have too often ignored the reality of learners. Among other things, they have agency—free will, free choice, and the capacity to grow and change. A friend of mine used to say that a good teacher with the right students can make anything happen. Ultimately, the key challenge in overcoming retention problems is that of matching learner needs, objectives, and strengths with teacher needs, objectives, and strengths in a supportive and stimulating learning environment.

It is suggested here that learners' prior schooling—often neglected in literacy research—is of significance in the dynamics of literacy programs, particularly those of the first three critical weeks. This is an area of influence that we often cannot see or easily identify with, but it is a source of many of the decisions made by at-risk learners on their way to dropout. In the hope that it may help some practitioners deal with the difficult issue of retention, and will perhaps encourage a few researchers to go further along the same line, I offer the results of a small-scale pilot study that I conducted on retention. The study can be replicated in almost any ABE or literacy program. As will be explained in Chapter Seven, this pilot emerged from six years of investigation into the concept of resistance to literacy education (Quigley, 1989, 1992b).

Dispositions of At-Risk Learners and Possibilities for Improving Retention

The Development Associates study (1993) cited earlier found that 18 percent dropped out during the first twelve hours of instruction.

This could constitute the first week of many ABE programs. It may be estimated that this rate doubles over the ensuing two weeks, meaning that approximately one-third of those students who will drop out in literacy education programs are "at risk" of dropping out in the first three weeks (Quigley, 1989). What distinguishes early at-risk learners from other students or other dropouts? As seen in two studies conducted during initial intake (Quigley, 1992b, 1993b), certain behaviors can usually be observed by the counselor or intake person that are indicators of early dropout (see Figure 6.2).

In the 1993 study, the intake counselor (call him "Tim"), first showed the new student around the facilities. He then described the ABE program and answered the student's questions. During this initial interview, he watched for signs suggestive of an at-risk learner: negative body language, little eye contact, shifting or pauses in student responses, very low self-esteem, hostility, skepticism or uncertainty about the program. Tim looked and listened for messages from the student that he or she might not make it in the program. In general, such students were obviously wanting to "please" the counselor but were less than comfortable in the interview. On the basis of his observations, Tim made an early assessment that certain incoming students were potentially at risk and might not last longer than a couple of weeks.

This study took place in a major institutional ABE program in Pittsburgh, Pennsylvania. The institution has two program counselors and a variety of student numbers in classrooms. Step one, the first identification level, simply looked for indications of early "at risk" behaviors during the intake interview. At this institution (as at most in the United States today), students completing the intake interview are asked to wait until an opening occurs in the program. When that happens, normally after about two weeks, students return for placement. This was the point at which we marked the next identification level. A second experienced counselor at the institution (call her Tina) interviewed only those whom Tim had initially thought might be potential at-risk students. The involvement of both a male and a female counselor helped to enhance control and validity.

Tina used the Prior Schooling and Self-Perception Inventory (Quigley, 1993b; see also Resource A) in her interview. First ensuring that the counseling environment was experienced as non-threatening, she asked the potential at-risk learners to reflect back

Figure 6.2. Identification of At-Risk Learners.

Level One: Counselor No. 1 Observes for Intake Behaviors

Hostile   Skeptical   Withdrawn   Hesitant   Uncertain

◄──►

Level Two: Counselor No. 1 Sees Particular At-Risk Behaviors

Little eye contact, negative body language, uncertainty about
performance, doubts about making in-class friends, doubts about
teachers, lack of enthusiasm

Level Three: Counselor No. 2 Investigates School Background

Tested on the Prior Schooling and Self-Perception Inventory
Uncertain about:

• Succeeding in subjects failed back in school

• Making new friends, as in school

• Getting along with teachers, as in school

• Receiving outside support, as in school

Level Four: Counselor No. 3 Conducts Embedded Figures Test

High levels of field dependence, indicating a need for acceptance
by peers and teachers

on their experiences in school. They were invited to complete the
inventory and were then asked

1. How they thought they would perform in ABE in the subjects
   they had experienced in school
2. If they had made friends in school and if they thought they
   would make friends in ABE
3. How they related to their past schoolteachers and how they
   thought they would relate to their new ABE teachers
4. How they related to counselors back in school and how they
   thought they would relate to those in ABE

The inventory is structured so that even the lowest-level reader can fill
it in with little difficulty—the size of the font for the numerical
responses gets larger as the level of agreement grows larger. The inven-

tory is visually easy to fill in with only a little guidance and acts as a future basis for discussion. It helped take the potential at-risk student back to his or her past schooling experiences. Tina then asked the student to imagine how he or she would do in the new program. This casual but purposeful interview was a way to systematically explore the learner's past in relation to his or her present expectations.

Most of those whom Tim had thought were at-risk students indicated to Tina that they were in fact at risk. These students went on to the next identification level, never longer than one week later, at which my graduate assistant, Mary, administered the "Witkin" Embedded Figures Test (Witkin, Oitman, Raskin, and Karp, 1971) with those we thought were at risk. The purpose of this test was to determine if this group displayed any appreciable differences from the norm. It was thought that perhaps at-risk learners were being influenced both by past schooling *and* by a somewhat different set of perceptions of the world from those that had emerged as the test's norms. The cognitive differences were tested on the basis of field dependence and field independence (Donnaruma, Cox, and Beder, 1980). Being *field dependent* means that one has a dominant need for acceptance, a desire for belonging, and a strong need for harmony in the environment. *Field independence* denotes a condition in which a person relies less on his or her world for a sense of harmony or well-being. Field-independent learners will typically move ahead on their own with little support from teachers or peers.

The unexpected outcomes that we found on the Witkin test will be discussed in a moment, but the primary result of the research was that the at-risk students were identified. I believe they can be identified in most programs during intake by an astute counselor. The inventory has since proved helpful to others in this identification process. The question now was, What type of teaching or tutoring structure can we use to encourage early at-risk learners to stay in the program longer—preferably, not to drop out at all? On the basis of a prior six-year line of research, we decided to try three types of teaching/tutoring settings: "team-supported," "small group," and "tutored."

The three hypotheses that were to be tested were

1. Early at-risk learners will stay in ABE programs longer than a control group if highly supported by the counselor and teachers.

2. Early at-risk students will stay longer than the control group if placed in small ABE/GED classes of five or six learners.

3. Early at-risk learners will stay in longer than the control group if they are taught by tutors one on one within the institution.

In formulating these hypotheses, we were wondering whether the at-risk student would be most influenced to stay in the program by the teachers and counselor, by peers, or by a one-on-one tutoring relationship.

A limitation of the study was the small number of subjects. Because of a recent influx of gang members to the center, the program's administration was worried about getting too many at-risk students together in one place at one time. And as it turned out, several of the identified at-risk students were indeed gang members. Thus, a total of twenty at-risk learners participated in the study—half of what we had wanted. This study is presented only for the possibilities it suggests. As stated earlier, it is hoped that others will take this line of research further.

Our control group consisted of five randomly selected, early at-risk students who were referred to the ABE mainstream (with classes of fifteen to twenty students) and treated normally (Campbell and Stanley, 1966). There were three study or treatment groups, also containing five randomly selected students. The first, known as the "team-supported group," was given much more than the usual amount of counselor and teacher in-class attention and support (Quigley, 1993b).

To step back a moment, earlier studies this author had conducted (Quigley, 1992b) in this same institution had found that early at-risk students were underchallenged and did not receive enough teacher attention. Because that group of at-risk learners went to the counselor frequently— up to seven times in one case— the question was raised if the counselor and teachers together could provide the challenge and attention needed to retain students longer than a control group. In an attempt to answer this, Tina followed up the team-supported group at least once a week and used the Prior Schooling and Self-Perception Inventory to talk about individual progress to date. All the teachers involved with this group were made aware of who the early at-risk "treatment" students were so that special attention and as much academic challenge as possible could be given them. Tina met with these teachers regularly.

Students in the second treatment group were interspersed among the institution's small-group teaching classes, which had approximately six students each and one instructor. The question we sought to answer was whether a small classroom with more peer interaction would help.

The third treatment group was provided one-on-one volunteer literacy tutoring at the ABE institution.

When I present this study to various groups, I ask them which of the three models they guess will be the most effective. There is never a clear majority of votes for any one of the models. It is interesting that all who are asked this question assume that one of the three will be better than nothing (the control group). Perhaps these observations suggest that we need much more experience with alternative matches between program models and needs of learners. In fact, the small-group approach turned out to be the most promising for retention in this study. The team approach was close behind, and the tutoring proved the least successful—but it was still more successful than the traditional classroom experienced by the control group (Quigley, 1993b).

How can the success of the small group be explained? We normally put great faith in a sensitive counselor and caring teachers to hold learners. Implemented well, the one-on-one tutorial model should be the epitome of care and attention. The reality, of course, is that not all learners are alike, and teachers or counselors are less important to some learners than to others. Especially where dispositional barriers and the past effects of schooling are concerned. What we found on the Witkin test was revealing. The field dependence level of the early at-risk learners in our treatment groups was *much* higher than the test's norm for "college age" adults. A similar result was reported years earlier by Donnaruma, Cox, and Beder (1980), who also used the Witkin test. As seen in Table 6.1, the overall mean for the male at-risk learners in our study was 117.3, compared with the Witkin norm of 45.5 (with a standard deviation of 28.5) for male college-age adults. The overall mean for at-risk females was 142.3; the corresponding Witkin norm was 66.9 (with a standard deviation of 33.6). Such extremely high field dependence can be debilitating.

If, in fact, many early at-risk learners are highly field dependent, and more study is needed, the success of the small group—

Table 6.1. Field Dependence: College-Age Norms and At-Risk Student Means (Embedded Figure Test).

| | *Witkins Embedded Figures Norms*[a] | | | | | *AR Study Results*[b] | | |
Age	Sex	N	Mean	S.D.	Age	Sex	N	Mean
	Witkins College Age Norms				Group #1: Control Group			
College	M	51	45.5	28.5	18–25	M	4	96.3
age	F	51	66.9	33.6	None	F	None	None
	Witkins College Age Norms				Group #2: Team Approach			
College	M	51	45.5	28.5	17–28	M	2	137.5
age	F	51	66.9	33.6	20	F	1	167.0
	Witkins College Age Norms				Group #3: Small Group Approach			
College	M	51	45.5	28.5	18–36	M	2	101.5
age	F	51	66.9	33.6	20	F	1	180.0
	Witkins College Age Norms				Group #4: One-on-One Approach			
College	M	51	45.5	28.5	22–34	M	2	135.5
age	F	51	66.9	33.6	20	F	1	80.0
Means	M		45.5					117.7
	F		66.9					142.3

[a] *Source:* Witkin, Oitman, Raskin, and Karp, 1971, p. 18. Seconds taken by student per item.

[b] *Source:* Quigley, 1993b.

a particularly accepting and supportive "field"—is easy to under-stand. Their chronic need for a high level of acceptance and support was apparently met by their peers, not just the teacher, in the small group. In this setting, early at-risk students were observed as being engaged in parallel and collaborative learning with the other four or five group members.

The variations provided by smaller classes, team support, and one-on-one tutoring are not the answer for every student. The point here is that we need to begin to identify varying learner needs that arise from learners' backgrounds, perceptions, and cognitive differences (Uhland, 1995). A small sample of this at-risk group was tested for learning style preference (Flannery, 1989, 1993). There appeared to be a preference for "global" learning over "analytic" learning. Such suggestions also need more research.

Witkin (1967) has suggested that ethnic and racial diversity often makes psychological differentiation more apparent in the teaching setting. He advocates that the field dependence and field independence of learners of diverse race and ethnicity be considered in such settings. Meanwhile, studies of African American and Hispanic children are suggesting that they exhibit higher levels of field dependence than Caucasian children (Anderson, 1988). How race and ethnicity interact with teaching style in the adult literacy setting, and how significant they are in attrition, are matters still to be researched. Still, as useful as this line of inquiry is, no study of ethnic or racial learning difference based on the Embedded Figures Test has thus far discovered learner scores 200 percent above the test norm, as our own did.

There is a great need to provide program alternatives in literacy that match learners and teachers in more appropriate structures. Is this possible in such an underfunded, understaffed, and typically overworked field? Following are some suggestions for the control of attrition that I think are suitable for many low literacy, ABE, and GED settings.

Program Suggestions

I have heard many literacy teachers say that the way to hold students longer in programs is to talk with them right away, encourage them, tell them how well they can do if they just try, and bolster their self-esteem. This is not the formula for every learner. As Fingeret and Danin put it: "Simply working with a caring individual is not enough" (1991, p. 90). If we are to increase retention rates, we will need much more accurately to see literacy and the world through the eyes of learners. There are clearly some who need greater support, and these, I believe, can be identified. But it does not follow that more care and attention by teachers is the "answer," even for this group. It is suggested that learner peers, program structures matched to individual students needs, and good matches with teachers may turn around an estimated third of the potential dropouts in the early weeks of programs.

However, more than this can be done. Following are some more detailed suggestions that bear on issues discussed in earlier chapters as well as on the matter of retention.

Matching Philosophy, Purpose, and Learner

The first step toward better retention is, I believe, creating a program whose primary mission is well defined and whose teachers and administrators are clear about their working philosophies. This does not mean that everyone must be of the same philosophical orientation—quite the contrary. But we should know if we are working at cross-purposes as a staff, if we are sending mixed messages to learners, if we are trying to be all things to all people in our mixed intentions and goals. I believe we need focused programs with understood missions and purposes that fit our learners' needs. Even if there are only two or three instructors in a program, that program should attempt to have an overall purpose that is consonant with the majority of the people who work in it. Alternatively, if a program is funded and given an overriding, stated purpose (in fact, most are not given such a stated purpose), the teachers should be clear on how their own purposes meld with that of the program.

If mission and philosophy are not dictated by the funding agency, the senior administrator should help identify teachers' philosophies and build on their talents by carefully placing them where they are likely to be most effective. For example, after a process of identifying teacher philosophies, as discussed in Chapter Four, the program may decide to take an overall vocational thrust. In this case, the majority of the teachers will work to prepare learners for the job market, help with placements in employment, and even follow up on students after they have found work. Learners coming in should know that this is the primary purpose of the program. Ideally, another section of the program, perhaps conducted at a different time, or even held at a different location, would provide a more liberal education, a more humanistic education, or a more liberatory education. One stream can support another. The humanist can, for instance, prepare certain students for the vocational stream if everyone involved, including the learner, deems it appropriate.

If a particular alternative philosophical approach cannot be provided within a program and the institution deems it necessary for some of its learners, it may be possible to structure a cooperative venture with another institution in the community or region that has the necessary resources. For example, if the decision is to emphasize a liberal stream and a humanist stream, another agency might be able to cooperate in providing the vocational. A community-based group might take on the liberatory approach. Students can be referred to alternatives if they exist. I do not think a single program can provide "all things to all people"—not only because it is extremely difficult to mount such a program successfully, but because our learners are simply too diverse. If students in K–12 can elect to join, or can be referred to, various streams—vocational to special education—for particular reasons, and if adults in the mainstream can go to a vocational or liberal arts college for courses, cannot we, too, provide some options within the mainstream of funded programs? Cannot we develop better referral networks?

Those learners who come in mainly to advance themselves to further education, or want simply to learn more, or acquire a GED to be "better educated," should not be required to take courses on how to prepare for a job. I once taught such a required class in an ABE program. It was based entirely on the institution's assumption that "it's good for them." Low-literate mothers, grandparents, those already employed did not see it that way, but we basically forced them to take the course anyway. We assumed our curriculum was what they needed—no exceptions.

Similarly, not every student needs to be nurtured for self-esteem building and self-actualization. However, teachers who have training and talent in this area should work with students who do need such nurturance. (Beder, 1991, discusses self-esteem tests and the literacy research on this topic). Such teachers might be the ones to work with at-risk learners in the smaller group settings. If small groups simply are not possible as a separate structure in a program, they can be created in classrooms. One or two at-risk students can be added to a supportive group of two or three who form a community within the classroom. They can work on common questions, and conceivably a volunteer assistant could be added. Because it seems that peers may be more important than teachers for at-risk learners with high field dependence, small collaborative learning groups can be a successful approach for some learners. Teachers who have an aptitude for supporting learners with low self-esteem can also work with the program counselor to provide greater team support. It would be useful to conduct an action research study (as discussed in Chapter Eight) that followed those in the humanist stream to the vocational or more liberal stream to see if they are retained more effectively.

An entire set of classrooms or just one teacher can have a separate curriculum that emphasizes a liberal education—from the classics to critical thinking. As a separate stream, some teachers might engage with learners who are facing major situational problems, encouraging them to take a more liberatory approach to their learning. A knowledgeable, trained teacher who seeks to gain further expertise in community literacy and problem solving can help these learners with real problems in and outside of the program. Unfortunately, the political and popular perspectives tend to distort the idea of placing more focus on learners' expressed or assessed needs. Perhaps we have developed few options in funded programs because we are so often influenced by the societal domain and the traditions of our own profession.

Governments are not typically interested in funding liberatory programs for purposes of personal or collective empowerment (Beder, 1989a). However, certain churches, unions, and advocacy or community groups may be. A communitywide collaborative of various interested agencies can help build such options. It can also help develop a regional referral system, and with employer involvement, at least some job opportunities can be made available to graduates.

Effective Intake and Orientation

The first three weeks are critical in literacy, ABE, and GED programs. Initial placement of learners is often based entirely on reading and math levels. I am not convinced that this is the best starting point. If our aim is to stem attrition, matching the needs and goals of learners with program options and program strengths is more critical than identifying the knowledge that learners do not have. Much depends on the skill and ability of the intake counselor or teacher to determine those needs. Also critical is the range of options we have to offer.

As suggested by the research in this chapter, for many who come to us, the future will be determined by the past. I believe we should generally trust the information given by the learner during intake, but we need more sophisticated ways of selecting the questions we ask. After a tour of the facility and perhaps conversations with teachers or other learners, the first intake discussion might concern itself with the new student's achievement goals and with what the program has to offer. Later in the process, interest and aptitude tests—administered by either the intake counselor or the vocational teacher(s)—may be used with those interested in vocational literacy. For those headed toward a liberal education, cognitive tests may be important. In this first stage of information exchange, there is a need to match interests, goals, and options. The intake counselor needs to be alert to indicators of "risk." Attitudinal barriers will often be the reason for early dropout among those who are at risk; situational and institutional barriers may appear later. Moreover, there is little we can do about situational barriers, although every program should be aware of available community resources, and each teacher should have the phone numbers of local agencies for referral purposes. As far as institutional barriers are concerned, we need to be willing to challenge those we have ourselves created. However, in the early stages of intake with those identified as at risk, the discussion needs to turn to how the new student sees himself or herself progressing in the program.

The second stage of discussion should look more closely at students' past experiences in school. School is the only framework most of them will have as they enter our programs, and it will be against this frame of reference that many will decide if the program is "better" or "worse" than previous sites of failure. The Prior Schooling and Self-Perception Inventory in Resource A may provide help at this stage of evaluation, eliciting how learners imagine their experiences in the new program will compare with those of the past.

Matching Purpose, Teacher, and Learner

Effective matching means determining, first, teacher strengths and interests, and then making informed choices with learners about their strengths and interests. Many learners will be very able to articulate their choices given concrete alternatives. And learners should have the opportunity to make changes from one stream to another if their goals or interests change.

The vocational stream should look for ways to build cognitive knowledge and psychomotor skills related to work; the liberal should emphasize material that will be a stimulus to cognitive enhancement; the humanist should concentrate on helping those who need high levels of support in building the affective domain; and the liberatory should focus on problem solving and on methods of interpreting and influencing the world around the student.

The Challenges of Time and Resources

Program administrators and teachers will ask, "Where can we find the time and resources to create new alternatives? How can we spend more time on intake when we have so little time now?" The key lies in incremental change, systematic exploration of the best ways to structure programs, effective use of community and funding resources, and above all, program time management. One principle that should be kept clearly in mind is that, for retention purposes at least, some learners need more attention, challenge, and support than others. Some will persist with almost no support.

A small ABE program in rural Pennsylvania—a program with which I once worked—provides an illustrative example. It had three excellent, hard-working teachers: Rita (who coordinates the program), Mary, and Stephanie. There were no "streams" and no counselors. Each teacher had her own classroom. Classes were held at night on the top floor of a red-brick former high school near the center of town. Through action research (described in Chapter Eight), the three teachers determined who was most skilled at job preparation, who had the greatest interest in liberal literacy, and who was most talented in giving high support to learners. They decided to take turns for intake. Rita met new students on Mondays, Mary on Tuesdays and Thursdays, Stephanie on Wednesdays and Fridays. They each looked for learner interests compatible with their own strengths and philosophies and made referrals to the others as appropriate. They especially looked for at-risk students during intake and used the Prior Schooling and Self-Perception Inventory when needed. Apparent at-risk learners were referred to Stephanie, who had a talent and interest in building self-esteem.

She kept her class sizes small, and eventually created two classes—one in the early evening and another in the late evening. New students who were looking for more immediate work advancement went to Rita, who was prepared to work with employers in the town to get students into the workforce. Meanwhile, Mary worked with those who wanted mainly to "advance their education" and were simply unsure of their future plans.

None of the three teachers was the "GED teacher" or the "basic literacy teacher." Each worked at a range of academic levels in her classroom, and each transferred students within the program, depending on how learners changed in their interests, self-esteem, and goals. The three kept careful track of the learners and met weekly to exchange progress and program data—particularly on retention. In one academic year, their retention rate showed a 36 percent increase over the prior three years. The last I heard, Rita was attempting to develop a community referral and employment network among the town's employers, schools, colleges, and social assistance agencies.

Making a More Significant Impact on Retention

What do at-risk students want from a program? The outcomes of an earlier study (Quigley, 1989) of at-risk learner dropouts gave us the basis for the experiment discussed here. As seen in this chapter, a place to begin on the complex issue of retention is with the high numbers of at-risk learners who drop out in the first one-to-three weeks. The experiment described here was with a small sample, but it shows promise if early at-risk learners can be effectively matched with the appropriate teacher(s). There are many other approaches to be tried and much more research is needed. To this end, the following list of characteristics and behaviors of the early at-risk group that this author has found through research over the past several years is provided (Quigley, 1990a, 1990b, 1992a, 1993b). Of those literacy and ABE dropouts who apparently quit because of dispositional barriers, it was revealed that

1. They had had little interaction with their teachers back in school and had also not interacted with their teachers in ABE before dropping out.

2. They had had considerable interaction with counselors back in school, and the same was true in ABE.
3. They had felt underchallenged in school and again felt underchallenged and "bored" in ABE.
4. They had felt "ignored" by their teachers back in school and felt the same way in ABE.
5. They had had very few friends in school (but the few they had were very close). They did not make, nor did they expect to make, many friends in ABE.
6. They had had little support from family or friends while in school, and this was often, though not always, the case in the ABE program.

These were some of the findings that led us to construct the Prior Schooling and Self-Perception Inventory, which includes questions designed to contrast and compare past schooling with expectations for the future. These findings also led us to experiment with the three treatment models discussed earlier. Overall, it seems clear that the past is of great significance to the future success of our learners and should not be neglected (Fingeret and Danin, 1991). History tends to repeat itself until the cycle is broken. While we invariably focus on learners' needs, the reality is that we often need to break with the history of our own assumptions and some of our own practices if learners are to have the chance to break their own negative cycles.

This chapter has looked at retention; the next discusses those low literates who refuse to attend our programs and the question of recruiting some of the truly hardest to reach. If we can go beyond the issue of retention to reach and involve more of those who previously have rejected what we have to offer, our field will surely have begun a new, exciting chapter in its history and its mission.

Chapter Seven

Why Many Resist, and Ways to Recruit Them

This chapter takes us a step away from the everyday operations of programs and discusses low-literate adults who are eligible to attend but who never do enroll. We now look at programs from the outside—through the eyes of the "unconverted."

The research I and others have conducted over the past decade and the experience of hundreds of practitioners I have talked with across the country clearly confirms that the vast majority of low-literate adults in the United States, even the "hardest to reach," do want an education. In fact, many dream of completing at least high school. Despite the fact that they all quit school, despite the fact that many who do not come to our programs carry emotional scars and traumatic memories from the schooling experience, the vast majority indicate that they greatly value "education" and say they wish they could somehow complete their own (Quigley, 1992a, 1992b; Beder, 1991, Beder and Valentine, 1987). Considering this fact, the existence of a large body of caring and committed literacy practitioners, and the (ostensible) desire of the wider society and of political leaders for a fully literate population, why is the program participation rate in our basic literacy, ABE, and GED programs so low? How is it possible that after almost twenty years of marketing and "consciousness raising," the U.S. Department of Education found in 1990 that traditional literacy, ABE, and GED programs attract only 8 percent of those eligible (Pugsley, 1990)? The National Center for Education Statistics found in 1979 that fewer than 5 percent of those "targeted" for literacy and ABE go to the programs offered (Cain and Whalen, 1979).

How can it be that we have seen only a 3 percent gain during the eleven years of some of our nation's most aggressive campaigning? If the "no-show" rates of 20 percent (Bean et al., 1989) and attrition numbers of 74 percent (U.S. Department of Education, 1995) are put together, it becomes obvious that we are barely denting the tip of the illiteracy iceberg. Surely some fundamental questions need to be asked.

The Hardest to Reach

What can be concluded after almost two decades of continuous literacy campaigning and recruiting? First, we must conclude that the vast majority of low-literate adults are no longer unaware of program opportunities. The time-honored explanation that low literates are not able to read or understand recruiting campaign information has worn hopelessly thin. We should also reject the old argument that low literates are so unmotivated, or so obsessively caught in the "here and now," that they cannot be bothered to attend (Anderson and Niemi, 1970). And finally, it is surely too simplistic to believe that most low literates are so dyslexic or so otherwise learning disabled, or so terribly fearful of further failure, that they instinctively see no reason to attend our programs. To borrow Kozol's phrase (1985), we cannot keep accepting that nonparticipants are either crazy or lazy. In fact, the familiar explanations for low participation have a strong element of rationalization. "Blame" for low participation often falls on the nonparticipating low literates who, coincidentally, have no voice in the discussion (Ryan, 1976).

The conclusion that should be reached, I believe, is that we need to evolve a more critical—indeed, a more self-critical—set of explanations for the low attendance in our programs. We need to ask about the programs we are offering and what they mean to those who are not attending. To gain a fresh perspective, we need a vision founded on something other than the old metanarratives. And this is the postmodern condition. For all of their internal disagreements, postmodern scholars "all respectively concede that we are living in a transitional era in which emerging social conditions call into question the ability of old orthodoxies to name and understand the changes that are ushering in the twenty-first century" (Aronowitz and Giroux, 1991, p. 66). As discussed in Part One of this book, we may intellectually recognize what we can no longer believe in, but we are unsure of what should be in its place. However, if there is a loss of faith in the old "orthodoxies," there is also an opportunity for our field to use its present circumstances as the springboard for a process of constructive change. In my view, it is the responsibility of those of us in this field to identify the right questions and make those questions more "discussable."

This chapter will argue that the voice consistently absent in so many policy and practice decisions is the voice of the learner. Keddie put the challenge well: "The issue is not whether individuals have needs nor whether they should be met but how those needs are socially and politically constituted and understood, how they are articulated and whose voice is heard" (Keddie, 1980, p. 63).

The position taken here is that the nonparticipation of low literates in literacy education can provide valuable information for future program and policy guidance. However, I have no illusions about how difficult it will be for some to accept this assertion. When I was working in a senior government office some years ago, we had a meeting on the idea of starting a literacy campaign. I made the suggestion that the programs we had at the time needed additional alternatives. The civil servants around the table began thinking of what alternatives would cost. When one began moving the discussion to "What is wrong with our schools, anyway?" I tried to bring us back by suggesting that alternatives should be based on what our target population was "willing to accept." To involve more adults, I said, "we need more acceptable programs." A pregnant pause followed. I was then informed that "illiterates should accept what they are given and be grateful!" A senior governmental official added, "If they want a better life—have what we have—they can damn well go to the programs provided now by the taxpayers!"

I later realized that this was a predictable response from the political perspective, given the context I was working in. For decades, low participation in literacy education has been seen in the political perspective as a problem inherent in the low literate himself or herself. Some, as in this example, focus on the school system. But the essence of the political perspective is: "Schools are there, they should not have quit; literacy programs are there, they should go back." The issue is not whether programs exist. Of course literacy programs exist—they have done so for over a century. Mere access is where we need to begin, not end, this issue. As Greene put it: "The notion that men are equally free to act if only the same legal arrangements apply equally to all—irrespective of differences in education, in command of capital, and the control of the social environment which is furnished by the institution of property—is a pure absurdity" (1988, p. 18).

A university colleague of mine once said he was "fed up" with the discussion about why there are so many illiterates and "sick to death" of so many of his college students writing papers on the issue. "Here's my suggestion," he offered. "Instead of wasting money on new programs, give a cash voucher to all those who are illiterate and tell them to go to a literacy or ABE program. They can have the voucher redeemed there. Let's say $500 each. There's your incentive. There's your answer to getting people into programs."

If it were simply a matter of making programs available and if indeed people were "equally free to act," adult illiteracy would probably never have occurred in the first place. As for my colleague's proposed incentive, $500 multiplied by the ninety million low literates identified in the NALS study (Kirsch, Jungeblut, Jenkins, and Kolstad, 1993) produces a figure that would sink any budget, even if 8 percent is subtracted for those who are already participating (Pugsley, 1990). And, as any literacy practitioner knows, all would not participate. It is not a simple question of providing external incentives. There still exist a myriad number of dispositional, situational, and institutional barriers.

Let us begin with what we actually know. There is a small but growing body of literature on nonparticipants (Beder, 1991; Fingeret, 1983; Quigley, 1992b; Ziegahn, 1992). This literature argues, among other things, that we need to allow for the possibility that there is a level of ideological resistance to the programs being offered. But why? And how can we understand this phenomenon? Fingeret has said we need to turn to the adults themselves: "If we do not learn to work with them, many illiterate adults will continue to refuse to work with us" (1983, p. 145).

But what have we learned thus far? As will be seen, one point that has become clear from the research is that many nonparticipants may still dream of an education, but they also still have nightmare memories of past schooling. Here are the dispositional barriers discussed in Chapter Six. We have learned that what is now offered is very often seen as a repetition of school, thereby raising questions of trust, relevance, and sheer acceptability in the minds of many nonparticipating adults (Beder, 1991; Fingeret, 1989; Gowen, 1992; Stuckey, 1991).

This issue is far more complex than incentives or punishments, carrots or sticks. For example, a mandatory program for low-literate welfare recipients was instituted in Cook County, Illinois, in the mid-1960s. If they did not attend classes, they would be removed from welfare. Literacy or starvation. The program collapsed (Cook, 1977). Evidently, starvation was the preferred option.

The Nature of Resistance to Schooling

To put the discussion in context, one of the first presentations I ever made on the topic of resistance to literacy education was to military educators from the navy and army. I was filled with self-doubt. "Surely the army and navy is made up of those who conform to authority," I thought. I was convinced the idea of resistance would be "too far out, too radical" for this audience. The exact opposite was true. Members of the audience soon identified with the issue. They raised questions about the hundreds of military personnel who flatly refuse to come to training and educational programs until forced to do so. Later, several came up to say that they themselves had been "resisters" of education, not just as adolescents, but throughout their lives. In private, and lowered voices, many "confessed" that they, too, had continuing feelings of resistance to the formal schooling process.

There is no doubt that everyone is, in some manner, a "resister." America was created out of resistance, and active populist democracy depends on it. There is an existential human impulse toward justice—an inexplicable resistance to the denial of freedom that is visceral and the stuff of rebellion (Greene, 1988). Camus (1956) has said that the rebel experiences a sense of physical and spiritual revulsion at the infringement of personal rights, while at the same time feeling an unquestioned loyalty to other, more rebellious, aspects of himself and other forms of support from his world. Thus, "he implicitly brings into play a standard of values so far from being gratuitous that he is prepared to support it no matter what the risks" (p. 13).

Resistance occurs regularly on every school playground and in every school building on a daily basis. As Aronowitz and Giroux (1985) state: "Schools are miniature societies more than centers of technical and scientific education. In schools students learn how to operate within the historically evolved culture with particular modes of organization at different levels of the occupational and social hierarchies" (p. 166). History and resistance theory tell us that not all who are called to conform to a set of normative values or are expected to buy into the views and beliefs of a dominant culture or religion actually do what they are expected to do. Resistance to beliefs, values, views, and the authoritative power of another begins at an early age.

An established school of discourse has grown up around resistance theory in sociology and the "new sociology of education." Aronowitz and Giroux have applied such theory to schooling this way: "To the extent that an oppositional group or class culture generates symbolic relations that constitute a counterlogic to the dominant 'cultural arbitrary,' students may 'choose' to oppose the system of school-induced rewards by fighting authority. In effect, they respond to another authority system, one that places high social and economic value upon factory labor, street life, or participation in the underground economy which is another labor market. Of course, students may not always be aware of the specific options they are choosing" (1991, pp. 168–169).

The nonparticipation of adult low literates is not simply a policy issue in search of a better program. A recent linear study of eighteen thousand children who attended twelve hundred schools with a special focus on those who dropped out of school revealed that the school dropouts had low participation levels in adult education for the rest of their lives (Cervero and Fitzpatrick, 1990). The authors concluded, "Schooling provides a powerful set of social circumstances [which] . . . shapes the individual" (p. 92). Their recommendations for literacy education included the following: "Governmental policy makers who offer programs such as adult basic education and job retraining need to recognize that participation in these programs is not simply a matter of individual choice . . . These officials, educators and other researchers must better understand the long-standing and enduring nature of the factors in which a decision to participate is embedded before they decry the low participation rates in these programs. But these factors must be recognized before they can be acted upon" (p. 92).

Here is the connection to the lifelong dispositional barriers discussed in Chapter Six. Kirsch and Jungeblut (1986) found in a national survey of 3,600 teenagers who quit school that almost two-thirds did so because of boredom (36.5 percent) and personal reasons (27.1 percent). Following those who quit school early, Baldwin (1991) surveyed 7,800 adults who had taken the GED exam and asked, among other questions, why they had abandoned school in the first place. Twenty-four percent of those surveyed said it was because of dislike, boredom, or being unhappy—"disengagement"—with school.

Hayes's investigation of teachers, teachers' aides, and student participants in ABE programs (1987, 1988) revealed that negative attitudes toward classes was one of five main factors leading ABE students to leave school early. In a study by Beder of 1,321 adults in Iowa who had quit school and were not participating in ABE or literacy, two-thirds said their reason for not attending was the nature of school itself. As Beder put it, when we are discussing the nonparticipation of low-literate adults, negative attitudes "seem to pertain to school itself—and to all the things associated with it" (1989b, p. 95).

Fingeret (1985) gives us a closer look at what so many adults recall as being unacceptable: "Data . . . suggest that schooling was alienating for a number of reasons, foremost among them the inability of the culture and structure of schools to respond to the concerns, pressures and life circumstances of individual students. From this perspective, individual student 'failure' becomes simply one result of the broad conflict between individuals whose characteristics and cultural backgrounds differ from those valued by a system which is organized around middle class norms" (p. 54).

It seems very clear from every angle of study—quantitative, qualitative, and theoretical—that schooling has a lifelong impact (McDonald, 1974). For countless nonparticipating adults, that impact has been so extremely negative that resistance to schooling is a persisting element in their lives (Cook-Gumperez, 1986; Courtney, Jha, and Babchuk, 1994).

I have been asked, "If resisters are indeed so determined to resist ABE and literacy programs, why not just leave them alone?" In fact, Beder asked a similar question in his Iowa study when he found consistently low interest in ABE/literacy among the older population of adults in his sample (Beder, 1989b). However, as will now be seen, resistant adults have also said that they have never stopped valuing an education—for their children, for their friends, and for themselves. Despite what school and schooling have come to stand for among resisters, there is a dream called "education." Why can we not fulfill this dream for more adults?

Resistance to Literacy Education

The first study I conducted on resistance was in 1985 (Quigley, 1987a, 1987b). After many years in practice, I asked in my doctoral dissertation, "Why do so few participate?" I followed this seemingly simple question "by addressing those who refuse to continue participating in school systems" (1987b, p. 15). For reasons discussed earlier, it seemed that the research literature was part of the problem in answering this question. Quantitative studies were of little help. As Hunter and Harman (1979) have noted, researchers who work in the area of illiteracy and who typically present their findings in the form of statistics "run the risk of perpetuating stereotypes [because] we tend to simplify complex lives into cases to be analyzed, or problems that need solutions, or statistics to be studied." As they stated, "This tendency, and our inability to interpret with understanding the first-hand information that people give us about their aspirations and their lives, are serious blind spots." They concluded that a "truer picture or at least a fuller understanding" (p. 55) might be obtained from fictional and nonfictional literature.

Glaser and Strauss (1967) promoted literary works as a rich basis for grounded theorizing. Berger (1977) wrote on the value of such works for research, saying, "They ring true; that is, they conform to the readers' general sense of things, to their common sense about themselves as social beings" (p. 161). Literary fiction has long been recognized in the school literature for purposes of research and student values guidance (for example, Amato, 1957; DeHart and Bleeker, 1988; Lenknowsky, 1987; Russell and Shrodes,

1950; Shrank and Engels, 1981; Whipple, 1968; Zucaro, 1972). In adult education, Merriam conducted research on male life stages using novels as a source of data (Merriam, 1980), and McKenzie argued forcefully for using literature for research across the field. As McKenzie put it, through literature, "Whole new fields of research will open up for the adult educator, and knowledge about adult development and learning will be expanded in a way that is uniquely humanistic" (1975, p. 215). More recently, Kazemak has argued that "fiction can be truer and offer us better ways of being and acting in the world than scores of statistically driven or thickly described studies" (1995, p. 100).

In their discussion on "the politics of literacy" in *Postmodern Education* (1991), Aronowitz and Giroux argue that traditional knowledge is being challenged and that there is great value in literary works: "Their narratives were inevitably drawn from the everyday lives of their readers, as well as from the lives of those who had not yet gained their voices" (p. 37). It is the voice not yet heard— the nonparticipant's voice—that can be found in examples of enduring fiction. I believe it is a rich source for theory building in otherwise unexplored areas of resistance to literacy education (McKenzie, 1985; Merriam, 1980, 1988b).

In the first major study I conducted on resistance (Quigley, 1987b), I asked *how* resistance to schooling takes place, *why* it occurs, and *what* the consequences of resistance appear to be from the resisters' perspectives. This early study gave a theoretical basis for trying to understand the dispositional questions seen in the previous chapter. In it, each novel and short story that was used contained a resister, operationally defined as an "adult maturationally capable of making considered life choices based on value systems, and of sufficient chronological age to be societally permitted to act upon those choices, who overtly or tacitly challenges the traditional school system" (1987b, pp. 19–20). *School*, for this study, referred to traditional sets of normative practices in educational institutions from the dominant culture. Public schools, parochial schools, a military school, a preparatory college and a university were settings found in the novels and short stories. Resistance to schooling was investigated by applying Spiegelberg's steps of the phenomenological method (1960) to various works of literary fiction. The works were selected by American and

Canadian professors of literature, using McKenzie's literary canons (1975).

The works chosen were modern American and Canadian novels and short stories that contained young adult resisters in traditional school settings, from high schools to parochial schools to colleges:

The Adventures of Huckleberry Finn, by Mark Twain ([1884] 1958)

"The Conversion of the Jews," by Phillip Roth (1959)

The Apprenticeship of Duddy Kravitz, by Mordecai Richler (1974)

Studs Lonigan, by James Farrell (1935)

Grain, by Robert Stead (1926)

Who Has Seen the Wind, by W. O. Mitchell (1969)

In Search of April Raintree, by Beatrice Culleton (1983)

Half-Breed, by Maria Campbell (1979)

The Catcher in the Rye, by J. D. Salinger (1951)

Too Far to Walk, by John Hersey (1966)

Each of these ten selections contained a resister in settings ranging from urban ghettos to remote rural settings. Two of the protagonists were female. Ethnic identities included Metis (for example, of mixed Caucasian and Indian ancestry), second-generation Irish, and second-generation Jewish. The school settings of the novels and short stories that were the battlegrounds of cultural and racial clashes included parochial and public schools, a college, and a private university. The works were published over a period of 101 years. Despite the range of time, geography, ethnicity, and gender, a remarkable consistency was discovered in how and why young adults resisted schooling.

The limitations of the study included the fact that only works containing resisters were selected, so comparison with persisters was not undertaken. The study focused specifically on resisters' response to schooling, not on their other many concerns. And the ages of the protagonists ranged no higher than the early twenties. Actually, this age range is representative of a considerable component of the ABE population. In 1988, 38.1 percent of all adults who participated in funded literacy and ABE programs were between the ages of sixteen and twenty-four; the largest group (44.4 percent) was in the twenty-five to forty-four range (Pugsley, 1990).

It became obvious that in each of the novels and short stories, the protagonist's resistance to school was more than just a rejection of school. Mirroring the descriptions of Camus and researchers such as Fingeret (1985), it was a positive quest for freedom that each protagonist undertook with absolute conviction and, in some cases, with risk to reputation and even life. In their eyes, resistance to school meant a determination to stay true to the beliefs and values of their own culture, their own race, or their religious heritage. Instead of conforming to what they saw as the spurious values promoted by schooling, they resisted authority as they saw it. The protagonists were seeking to gain the liberty (Stanage, 1986) to follow a culture, value system, or lifestyle that they held to be superior to that of the school.

The Steps of Resistance

A pattern of sequential steps was found in the development of resistance. It is essentially this pattern that was described in Chapter Six in relation to our ABE programs. Dispositional barriers make themselves felt during the first three weeks of a literacy or ABE program, and it appears that there are steps in the resistance process leading to the decision to quit. The process, both in the fictional works and in our own programs, grows out of a awareness that what is being presented is not acceptable when compared to the known world (see Figure 7.1).

The phenomenon of resistance and its sequential steps was clear throughout the study of resisters in novels and short stories. "Learning," "objective knowledge," and "education" were never resisted. What was resisted was the infringement of rights "to be otherwise": to think otherwise, to live otherwise, and to determine one's destiny otherwise. These resisters were capable learners who wanted to learn. Not all caused agitation or made "noise" in the system. Those who were the most determined to quit school at the earliest opportunity were also the least "visible"—that is, they were quiet and pensive, and like so many who drop out of literacy education in the first weeks, were just biding their time until they could escape. There were also those who took the path of least

Figure 7.1. The Process of Resistance to Schooling.

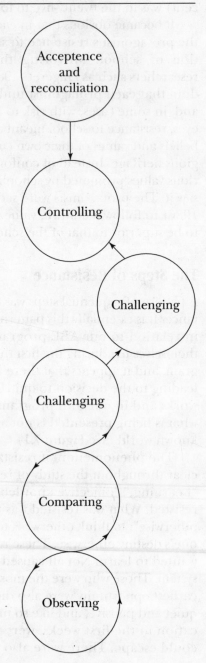

5. Accepting myself as holding a specific liberty and accepting others not holding it

Acceptence and reconciliation

4. Actually having and "holding" a specific liberty

Controlling

Challenging

3. Knowing that I possess a specific liberty

Challenging

2. Knowing that I do not have a specific liberty

Comparing

1. Not aware that I do not have a specific liberty

Observing

resistance by staying in school and suffering through to the end, though always staying mentally disengaged.

Resisters carefully observed the world of the school. In comparison with their own "outside" world, they found it oppressive and hypocritical. Observing, comparing, and challenging were cyclical steps building toward breakaway. The characters in these works also underwent transformation as they realized the nature of liberty and discovered that their freedom to choose liberty was being devalued, even denied (Stanage, 1987). The breakaway step became inevitable and was invariably followed by a euphoric sense of control over oneself. This "holding" of the liberty was as far as some resisters went. Others took a further step into reconciliation with those peers they left behind. Most looked back either in anger or indifference (Quigley, 1990a).

The final step in Spiegelberg's method of phenomenology, interpreting the meaning of the phenomena, indicated that the meaning of resistance extended beyond its "how," its "why," and its consequences. Resistance was finally seen to mean "a struggle to become free in the eyes, mind and heart of the resister on the basis of a specific liberty which must be attained and held at any cost" (Quigley, 1987b, p. 241; 1990a).

Implications for Literacy Practice

Giroux (1983b) has stated, "The concept of resistance must have a revealing function that contains a critique of domination and provides theoretical opportunities for self-reflection and struggle in the interest of social and self-emancipation" (p. 290). In the theory building and in my interview-based studies that followed there has been found a consistent critique of domination—domination of people and of systems. In interviews since with actual resisters (Quigley, 1992a, 1992b), self-reflection was seen when low literates compared themselves with others in and outside of the schooling world. However, when these adult resisters to literacy were interviewed, subjects invariably feared that their stories and experiences were meaningless, their opinions worthless. Far from being hostile to interviewers, they were delighted that someone was interested in what they had to say (Ziegahn, 1992). Neither the schools nor the adult literacy world seems to hear this voice. When it is assumed that no one will listen, nothing is said. When nothing is said, nothing changes.

The early theory-building study and several subsequent ones with resisters have several implications. First, it is apparent that nonparticipants in ABE are not "the same" as participants. As discussed in the previous chapter, programs for resistant learners that are based on what willing participants see may fail. Second, none of the resisters resisted objective knowledge or learning. Each was a capable learner who wanted to learn. My work with resisters led to the conclusion that because each nonparticipant was resisting normative values and cultural systems, there was a need for "learner-grounded" basic education models—models that match learners and teachers, for instance, as seen in Chapter Four. Although some may resist any model, it is suggested that program models designed *with* learners and with their unique perspectives and needs in mind will be the most acceptable. Learner-grounded models should involve relevant, stimulating knowledge keyed to the identified needs of the learners (Fingeret and Jurmo, 1989). Here is where the studies on disposition and matching, seen in the previous chapter, began (Quigley, 1993b).

"Why Did You Quit?"

The early theory-building study was tested later in Pittsburgh with twenty low-literate resisters: eight males and seventeen females, ranging in age from 57 to 18 (mean 34.35). The question of why so many evidently resist literacy education was explored with in-depth interviews. Three of the resisters were more than 50 years old, one was in his 40s, ten were in their 30s, five in their 20s, and one was 18. The group was predominantly African American (eighteen black, two white). Eleven had lived in Pittsburgh their entire lives, the rest for no less than one-third of their lives. Thirteen were on public assistance or were unemployed. The remaining seven were self-employed (two); employed part-time (one); working in the home (two); or employed full-time (two). Fourteen had children. Four were married; the rest were single (nine); divorced (two); separated (one); living with a partner (two); or of unknown status (two). Total years in school ranged from 8 to 17, with an average of 10.72 years. The highest grade level achieved ranged from 7 to 11 (mean 10.05). They had been out of school from 1 to 42 years (mean 16.88). All had previously attended schools in Pittsburgh and left those schools early (Quigley, 1992b).

The subjects were asked about one of the largest literacy and ABE institutes in Pittsburgh. It was first determined that each knew of it and where it was. All were aware that they were probably eligible to attend literacy or ABE programs. They said they probably could make the necessary arrangements to attend the institute (meaning there were no overriding situational barriers) and had no particular objection to it as a school (no overriding institutional barriers).

It would be a mistake to say that most subjects were free of significant situational barriers. These ranged from deep poverty to time constraints. Half of those interviewed lived in housing projects where drug-related shootings were common. However, in-depth interviewing conducted by two trained African American research assistants who were comfortable with the environment and culture and able to gain the subjects' trust revealed that the primary reasons for not attending literacy classes were neither situational nor institutional. These resisters held an unswerving belief that ABE or literacy would be no different from school. The resulting data were coded, weighted, categorized, and examined for consistent response patterns.

When subjects were asked, "Why did you quit school?" the over-arching reasons were teachers, the injustices of the school system, and sheer boredom—reasons not unlike those given by dropouts in the attrition study discussed in Chapter Six. Following are some responses to a series of semistructured questions (Quigley, 1992b). Unfortunately, the rage and tears accompanying the answers are lost in transcription.

Teachers

Insensitive teachers were identified by eleven of the twenty subjects as the most important reason for quitting school. Typically, responses included dissatisfaction with the amount of time and interest devoted to the student—a finding repeated with adult literacy dropouts, as discussed in Chapter Six.

DESIREE: "They didn't spend enough time with the people that needed it. The people that were easy, they picked up things easy, they spent more time with them it seemed because it wasn't, I don't know, it was like their star students and people like me that needed extra things they would just fluff over you, you know, so you just didn't care. If they didn't care, why should you?" (p. 7).

WALTER: "The attitudes and the values were very shallow. The attitudes and the values of the teachers were very shallow, as I said before. They only taught what they knew, they did not go beyond that. They did not try to actually reach out to the students, it was like rote learning. . . . there were only like a few teachers that actually extended themselves just a little bit further. Then that was really teaching" (p. 6).

CHARLES: "Some were ignorant. Some of them had this personal thing about the way they didn't like certain people, because you didn't bow down. There were some who were the teacher's pet. They did, like, they were told. I have never been taught like that. You know, I've always been a free thinker. It's how my mom raised me. Think for yourself because if somebody else is thinking for you, they're gonna lead you somewhere where you don't want to be and that is how society is right now today" (p. 6).

YVONNE: "Well, see that was how I was back there when I was younger. It seem everything somebody told me to do, I did the opposite. It was because, it seem like everybody was always trying to run my life. You know, do this, do this, do this. Nobody ever asked me, you know, what did I want. You know, I may have wanted to stay in school. I might, I can't understand it, you know, explain it, you know. I was just, like, so confused. Everybody stayed in school and I always wanted to do opposite, the opposite of everything" (p. 6).

No resister could recall more than two teachers' names, although the average time they spent in school was ten years. When they remembered a teacher's name, it was often someone they held in high esteem—or still hated. Lyle expressed it this way: "She didn't want me to quit. She said, 'You're too intelligent to be so dumb.' She told me I wasn't supposed to quit school because I had too much intelligence just to walk away" (pp. 6–7). Anna praised her math and science teachers and added, "Those kind of teachers are hard to find"

(p. 7). Four African Americans, with rage in their voices, described the role that prejudice and racism played in their school experience:

KAREN: "At the time, [my school] was very prejudiced. I had a teacher, Business English teacher, that was really giving me problems. He made a lack of confidence in myself. Just, just destroying me personally. He made me hate school and lashing out at him. I either had an option to either drop out or be kicked out. . . . What made me drop out of school was the problems I was having with the one teacher. I had got, let him gotten me so angry with things he was saying to me that I wasn't, I wasn't important, I was just another Black person and Black people wouldn't go far and especially Black women and I felt so much anger and hate for that man until I lashed out at him and I know now that I was wrong for letting him make me that angry, but it happened. I was young and couldn't control my temper and was mainly because of listening to him belittle me so much I lost my self confidence" (p. 7).

DONNA: "The teacher was, I didn't like the teacher. She talked down to Black people. Especially if you didn't understand or you weren't at the level which she was. Teachers can turn you off. Teachers can turn you on or off" (p. 7).

YVONNE: "[My school] was a very prejudiced school. I did not like the teachers" (p. 7).

SHIRLEY: "It wasn't the learning. It was fun. But there was a lot of racism in school" (p. 7).

The School System

Not all of those interviewed pointed to specific teachers. Some immediately recalled the injustices of what can only be called "the school system." Or they recalled how they simply did not "fit." The reluctant learners seen in Chapter Six also did not engage with the ABE program and did not expect to do so. The anger that some interviewees felt toward the school system's authority, values, and culture is expressed in the following examples:

KAY: "The school district forced me to change schools when my parents moved. Why did they do that? I hated the new school and quit after three months. Who gave them that authority to ruin my education?" (p. 6).

CHARLES: "It didn't give me nothing about my culture. It didn't teach nothing about my ancestors. It taught me a good philosophy of another man's society. See? And I could never conceive that. How could I understand that? A White man was teaching me to do this, do that, do this. But when I did what he did in this society, he incarcerates me. See, I'm wrong, but look how his society came out" (p. 7).

WALTER: "I didn't like school. I knew too much from the streets, you know. It was mainly real, like, it was mainly like one of the movie things, you know. This gang on this corner, this gang on that corner, come and go as you please. And this is my turf and this is your turf. . . . I didn't do too bad in school but it was mainly up to [grade] five. I mostly ran the classes in the school, whatever. I was so, what you would call 'bad' that the teachers would ask me did I want to learn or whatever, you know. And if I didn't feel like it, I would tell them no, I didn't wanna do it. I mean to me that was more like being a macho man, being with the gang or whatever. And if I felt like that I didn't wanna do it, I wouldn't do it. If I applied myself to it, I could pass. But to me that was what you called 'square.' I felt that I had more important things. Gettin' smart with the teachers or whatever, you know, or playin' hookey. Like I said before, I regret now but I have had quite a few of my teachers tell me if I applied myself, you could go ahead and do it. Somebody would say somethin' then, you know, and 'Look at that dummy' and or look at somethin' that would throw me off and I'd be angry and, you know, this is for chumps. But I have been told if I'd apply myself, I had the ability to continue . . . if you sat up there and tried to learn something, you'd be square . . . if you was a square, you wasn't in the clique" (p. 8).

JOANNE: "I think that it was the system [that failed] because it had to do with their planning stage, with their perception, OK, with their perception in governing, so called governing the people, making up rules and laws, for the people. But then yet they were not able to see and to understand all of the different aspects of people and their needs and how people could help the system. The system did not really gear themselves to be able to, you know, to look at everybody, like you're on the same level or maybe on different levels of values" (p. 15).

Boredom

The third major theme to appear was boredom. The courses, the teachers, the school environment were simply not challenging, and what was done often seemed repetitive. This is a theme that emerged also with the reluctant learner dropouts discussed in Chapter Six. Boredom was a reason identified by Fingeret and Danin (1991) for learners leaving traditional literacy programs and going to the Literacy Volunteers of New York City program. This is how the adult resisters recalled boredom in school (Quigley, 1992b):

> YVONNE: "It seems once I got past a certain grade in high school, like the seventh grade, I felt once I got into eighth and ninth, they was just repeating over the year before and adding a little bit more to it and, you know, I felt I had better things to do with my time than sit in class and learn something I already learned" (p. 7).

> SHIRLEY: "I was bored. I didn't like school." [INTERVIEWER: "You like to be challenged?"] "Yeah. Definitely" (p. 7).

The Compartmentalization of Education, School, and Learning

When asked about "education" in the abstract, all those interviewed were adamant that they saw an absolute value in education for their children; each stated that they wanted their children to get an education. Most also added that they saw real value in education for their friends and certain peers. Later, subjects were asked if they had continued "learning" since leaving school. Each could name areas where they had made progress—child raising, work-related areas, "economic survival." But when asked if they would attend the ABE/literacy programs at the major institute, or at any other location, the subjects heard and understood "school" and consistently stated that they either "did not want to return to school" or "would not return to school." When the topic was raised again later, some said they "should" go back to school. However, it was like having to take bitter medicine. They feared the cure more than the disease.

There is significance for the field and for nonparticipation research that these interviewees did not see the terms *school, education,* and *learning* as interchangeable, as is so often the case in the literature. Each of the three terms had a distinct meaning. "School" was at the negative end of a continuum of connotations, "education" at the positive.

This study suggested three types of resistance: (1) personal/ emotive resistance grounded in trauma and a specific critique of individuals and their actions; (2) ideological/cultural resistance grounded in a critique of macro systems and dominant ideologies; and (3) resistance of older adults who perceived schooling to be irrelevant. These three categories may help to expand and inform the discussion of resistance. As Giroux has said, theories of resistance "have not given enough attention to the issue of how domination reaches into the structure of personality itself" (Giroux, 1983b, p. 288).

Three Types of Resistance, Three Types of Recruitment

Following are some of the findings of this resistance study and the strategies that are suggested by them.

Personal/Emotive Resisters

The personal/emotive resisters who remembered school as personally traumatic said that teachers and peers were the most significant influences in their decision to quit. They felt betrayed not by systems themselves but by individuals within those systems. Overall, members of this group firmly believed they had been "ignored" in the classroom, and they were often "different" in the school hallways and playground. Their perception of insensitivity from teachers was, in many cases, compounded by their perception of insensitivity from peers.

At the close of the interviews, they were asked what sort of literacy programs could ever prompt them, or others like them, to resume their education. It was clear that only a major breakthrough in trust could bring about their return. After some soul-searching, many suggested that small classrooms, a lot of individual attention, friendly and accepting peers, teachers who would treat a learner like "a human being, a grown man" would help. They were describing a learning environment with a knowledge of their cultures, their values, their needs, and their aspirations.

It is my suspicion (an entirely untested one) that after programs have attracted those who are not particularly hampered by situational, institutional, and most dispositional barriers—the "cream," as Mezirow, Darkenwald, and Knox (1975) once termed them—we will be able to draw in only a small percentage of these personal/emotive resisters. There was some positive response to the question about returning, and sincerity in the expressed belief that other personal/emotive resisters would go to improved programs, but the fragility of this group's personal feelings can hardly be overemphasized.

That many low literates demonstrate low self-esteem in our programs has been discussed by Beder (1991), and the research on self-esteem and literacy is still inconclusive. Some personal/emotive resisters may be highly field dependent, and without the attention they continually told us they need, they may well fall again into silence and quit in the first three weeks of a program. Probably, no specific "incident" or "teacher problem" would be needed to induce this group to quit. If they were bored once more, why would they not quit early? Adults have other lives and responsibilities beyond "school."

What other suggestions did subjects have for programs and recruitment? The need for geographic proximity and child care assistance were commonly mentioned. The marketing suggestions they gave included making courses known in rental offices and places "where people congregate." Significantly, several people recommended making announcements in churches. Churches may have been named more than any other type of gathering place because they are closely associated with trust. Word-of-mouth publicity was stressed. This has long been a widely accepted marketing approach. Martin (1989) states that "for many adult literacy programs, personal contact with the people and organizations in their target area is the most effective recruitment technique employed" (p. 86). Radio and television advertising, with personal testimony from peers, was suggested. Flyers and printed material were also mentioned occasionally.

When I give presentations on this research project, I often notice that the "shopping list" of suggestions causes pens and faces to fall. Many in the audience say they are already doing all these things, and they leave rather disappointed. There is no magic wand hidden in our findings. However, is it the job of twenty interviewed resisters to give our field "the final answers"? As one of our subjects, Frederick, put it, "I really don't know, to tell you the truth." What is significant here is that this group related only to past schooling when they were interviewed on specifics. Past schooling formed the entire basis for their responses. Terms like "adult education" are our terms, not theirs; we are talking across a chasm of differences. And they were able to give directions that, for personal/emotive resisters, involved trust. Trust is the bridge that needs to be rebuilt if there is to be a dialogue between programs and nonparticipants. Perhaps the most valuable suggestion to have emerged is that an appropriately drawn sample of nonparticipants and participants form an advisory group. The possibilities for informing ourselves and improving our programs are there if we ask the right people the right questions.

Ideological/Cultural Resisters

Like the previous group, the ideological/cultural resisters were indelibly marked by past schooling. Both males and females in this group resisted primarily out of an ideological culture clash. More than one African American recalled school as a "white world." Timothy assumed that the major literacy institute we asked about was "for white men." The view of past schooling as culturally biased, even racist, was bolstered by omissions in the curricula. Consistent with research by Fine (1982), both white and black members of this resister group were exceptionally sensitive to perceived injustice. Teachers and peers were frequently named, but for reasons that differed from those found among personal resisters. Teachers, as Donna put it, "had a certain life-style. They don't understand that other people have grown up differently" (Quigley, 1992b, p. 23, and see Donnaruma, Cox, and Beder, 1980). Peers, unlike teachers, were the measure for appropriate lifestyle and self-image. Consistent with Willis's research (1977), to do well in school was to give over to the dominant culture.

In this group, memories of schooling led to suspicion of systems and motives in the white adult world. Charles, for instance, assumed that what was wrong with school would still be wrong with the literacy and ABE institute he was asked about: "Well that school's based on grants. Don't they give grants, government-funded? Well that's the only reason that they have these things, they they're gonna make all Black people mechanics, all Black people body and fender men. I mean, but here's Black people that should be in research, these people should be in the space program, electrical programs, they should be in NASA, but here they want all of us to be just fender and bodymen, tire changers, gas pumpers, cleanin' up this house, cleanin' up that house. It's garbage" (Quigley, 1992b, p. 15).

The clear message from ideological/cultural resisters was that programs must invite a degree of learner input into content and structure. There was little trust of "the system." Among obvious mechanisms for building input are preliminary assessments of learner needs, student advisory groups, formative evaluations for feedback to the program as well as the teacher, and summative evaluations that are skillfully conducted and acted on by the program. Being recognized and included as adults with valuable opinions was critical to the ideological resisters in this study.

The marketing suggestions offered by this group stressed the need for connections to the culture that potential learners belong to—in particular, the black culture. One resister suggested marketing through a radio station that plays primarily African American music.

Some literacy and ABE programs have achieved success by adding computers to the classroom. Because technology has a certain "acceptable status," particularly among males, computers may help to overcome some of the skepticism toward traditional classroom and institutional systems. A similar point came up at a meeting I chaired of GED administrators in Northern Saskatchewan, Canada, in the late 1980s. In that area, GED tests were offered mainly to Indians who lived in remote communities accessible from "the outside" only by bush plane. But the administrators faced a serious logistical problem: in that culture, adult male Indians almost never went onto school grounds, even to pick up their children, because doing so was seen to incur a serious loss of dignity. To hold GED tests or GED preparation courses in the area's school, the only building available for such purposes, was just not acceptable. I asked what kinds of courses these men wanted in their remote communities. The answer was, "How to use their PCs better." As it turned out, most had a personal computer, even in this remote area and even in the late 1980s. The administrators came to the conclusion that if the men's own computers were part of a program in the school building, they would probably be persuaded to participate.

Several colleagues of mine who work with Hispanic communities in the southwestern states have raised the possibility of using computers to better advantage in literacy programs for men in various settings—school and otherwise. This needs to be researched further along cultural and gender lines.

Older Resisters

The final and smallest group in this resister study was that of subjects over the age of fifty. To these individuals, just as those in Beder's Iowa study (1989b), literacy was a matter of little significance. This may well be the group we will not reach in large numbers, regardless of what we do. Those over fifty were neither sad nor mad toward past schooling. If anything, they were somewhat nostalgic about it. The best route to learning for this group was evidently trial and error. "Listening and doing a lot of things" was described as "the best teacher" by fifty-eight-year-old Melanee (Quigley, 1992b, p. 11). Many of these subjects had been unable to attend school as children, and all had considered it irrelevant even back then. "School" was yet more irrelevant now. For sixty-year-old Raymond, who quit school to earn money, "I saw no future at all by staying in school. All my friends were joining the service as soon as they became of age. I saw money as a cure-all for *all* of my problems" (p. 12).

For literacy programs to become relevant to these over-fifty low literates, they would need to have immediate impact on the learners' businesses, work situations, or grandparenting duties. Overall, these subjects felt they had continued learning successfully throughout their lives. However, they were acutely conscious of their limitations. As Anne said, "I'm never going to go any place else or do anything else because I didn't make it, I didn't get that paper" (p. 20). Hope was transferred to the next generation. Anne said she would "push my daughter . . . and my youngest son" (p. 20). In these cases, education remains important at an abstract level; learning is necessary for continued survival, and school is for the children.

Recruitment Issues for Future Change

Improved marketing efforts for literacy programs might begin by asking which of the three groups discussed here the program is trying to reach. The next question would be, How is the program being portrayed? What language and images are being used? In general, the research I am drawing on suggests that our advertising needs to be stripped of its school imagery and that much more emphasis needs to be placed on education and adult learning. The question we must ask ourselves is, How can we project exciting, relevant adult education possibilities, not through the lens of the popular perspective, but with the help and guidance of those we are trying to serve? As noted above, we might ask a sample of nonparticipants to be an advisory group and a test group for recruiting. However, recruitment does not mark the end of the marketing process. Serious internal discussion must precede the arrival of new learners, asking if the program is likely to confirm the personal/ emotive resisters' worst fears. Will it again be boring and irrelevant to some, and how will we know if it is? Will we be experienced by some as "insensitive," and how will this be observed and evaluated? Will we replicate the "injustices of individuals" from past school programs in some learners' eyes? How will this be discovered?

The earlier discussion on working philosophy will, I hope, be of assistance here. By building in program options, internal evaluation, and external input, we can guard against many of the hazards of personal/emotive resistance. Ideological/cultural resisters will, in my view, be more difficult to include in our programs. In fact, it may not be possible to attract this group in any significant numbers without even more radical change than is being presented here.

Can We Fulfill the Dream of an Education?

Anna Louise, a woman we interviewed in a housing project, looked over at her children playing on the concrete floor and put it this way: "Financially, I can't do anything . . . but as far as emotionally, they're watching me and I, I try to help them with their work and I'm always expressing education as so important to do, you can do anything if you have an education" (Quigley, 1992b, p. 19). Walter, an ideological/cultural resister who ended up a gang member, said his attitude now was regret:

> I say I regret that now, I really do. Because to me, the biggest thing in my life, if I had a choice, would be to learn to read good. It hurts a lot you know, when you have a child come up to you and ask, "Daddy, what's this?" "Go ask your mother, I don't, I don't got time now." You could of learned to do this a long time ago. There's been a lot of times me and my wife have been together and she says "What does that say? I don't have my glasses." Then I have to look at her and say, "You know I can't read" [p. 8].

These and other statements on education and its value told us that adults want what education promises. They want what it has provided for others. Most said they felt ashamed to admit that they did not have an education and could not demonstrate a basic skill like reading or elementary math. Their children played a significant role in this valuing of education. It was important in parental modeling. Charles said, "I want them to be better than I am" (Quigley, 1992b, p. 18). Donna explained it this way: "I have two little ones, yeah, it's important. What kind of mother would I be if it wasn't important?" (p. 18). As mothers and fathers, they all wanted their children to have a better education and a better future than they had. In every respect, the resisters were not resistant to objective knowledge or the concept of learning. They believed education could add to their children's lives. They said they valued it for their friends.

Despite all the policies of the past four decades that have been based on the political perspective and have insisted that literacy should be for job preparation, our subjects saw education as something important for its own sake. As Joanne put it, education "helps to enhance or polish the mental level or intelligence that one already has" (p. 19). Career advancement was a bonus—a by-product.

Given the complexity and emotionally charged nature of recruitment in the resistant population, it is hoped that more qualitative research will be undertaken, using ethnographic methods such as in-depth interviews, participant observation, and heuristic studies of fiction and nonfiction, both oral and written. The field of investigation should be expanded to include comparative studies on resistant adults of various age cohorts, races, ethnicities, and religions. Refinements of these studies should be taken into our programs to further our knowledge of attrition and dispositional barriers, as suggested in the previous chapters. The many missing links between schools and literacy programs have rarely been discussed or even identified (Quigley, 1992a). Despite the fact that virtually every North American master's and doctoral degree program in adult education is housed in a university college of education, joint adult and child education research in the area of literacy is a rarity (Fingeret, 1984; Quigley, 1992a). It can only be hoped that the concept of "lifelong learning" may one day be a mutual source of research for child and adult researchers to understand better the complex decision process that takes place among adolescents and young adults regarding their future in formal education. Why are some adults leading literacy and ABE classrooms while other adults are sitting there learning basic skills? Why are so many other adults unwilling to be part of this process at all? Why can we not bridge the school-adult education gap with joint research?

Part Four

Taking Action to Transform Literacy Education

Chapter Eight

Grounding Programs and Policies in Practical Knowledge

Part One of this book looked at the need for change at the macro level. Part Two examined the need for change in our own classrooms and tutoring settings. Part Three considered the need for change in the areas of retention and recruitment.

Some will say change depends on external conditions. Others argue that the world we see is, in large part, constructed by ourselves as we try to interpret external forces (Apps, 1973; Candy, 1991). What is important in this "constructivist" view is the firm belief that individuals can act out of free will, or "agency." Individuals are not victims of circumstance. People can bring about change in the world as they see and define it. They do not have to wait for the externals to change—they can change the externals. Change, according to Greene, takes place when we are willing to envisage something better: "It is partly a matter of being able to envisage things as they could be otherwise, or of positing alternatives to mere passivity. And it should remind us of the relation between freedom and the consciousness of possibility, between freedom and the imagination—the ability to make present what is absent, to summon up a condition that is not yet" (Greene, 1988, p. 16).

Ethics and Change

Literacy practitioners are constantly caught in ethical dilemmas, in large part because of the all-consuming influences of the political and popular perspectives. As discussed in Chapter Four, the working philosophies we bring to our students and programs should be a guide to the ways we teach and administer, and by extension, should be a guide to the types of knowledge we seek. They can give us ways to at least formulate options in the midst of ethical dilemmas, even if sometimes we feel we cannot act on them. Cervero and Wilson (1994) have shown how personal and professional ethics are at the very heart of responsible practice. Cervero states: "Our understanding of adult and continuing education practice is impoverished by not discussing its ethical dimensions. Ethical understanding is central to the practice of all professionals and is an important criterion by which they make decisions in many situations. If adult and continuing education educators are to fully understand and improve their practice, ethical dimensions must be made explicit in the context of their own practice knowledge as well as in the ongoing discussions of good practice in the literature" (1989, p. 110).

The ethical dimension of what we do in adult literacy education, and why, can be illuminated by working philosophies. As Apps put it: "A working philosophy can help the adult educator deal with 'what should be' questions" (1973, p. 3). What we want for our field has deep ethical roots. And these, it has been suggested, are the product of well-considered working philosophies.

Without considered philosophical purposes and the ethics inherent in them, and without practice-based data to make our cases for change, we are left helpless in the face of the status quo. Decisions are made for us. But it is my firm belief that this need not be so—that we have the capacity to choose our directions as practitioners.

How? Practitioners can decide which questions are of greatest value. They can test old assumptions. They can test others' findings. They can observe the changes brought about by new ideas. They can collect the data needed to argue for change. Rather than wait for experts to define and answer questions, teachers, tutors, counselors, and administrators can pose questions based on their own sense of what is appropriate. They can seek to have questions answered through opportunities provided by their own programs. For example, they can create individual courses, program streams, combinations of options, dedicated programs, or program thrusts across neighborhoods or whole regions that emphasize the vocational, liberal, humanist, or liberatory philosophy (Beder, 1990b). Such programs could strive for appropriate matches between learners and teachers. Even in times of cynicism concerning literacy education, we can introduce alternatives, and we can break from the singular perceptions and beliefs of the past. As the postmodernists argue, we can bring adult literacy into the era of the "pluralism of the post-modern, that heterogeneous range of lifestyles and language games which has renounced the nostalgic urge to totalize and legitimate itself" (Harvey, 1989, p. 9).

As a former professor of mine used to say, "Don't get mad, get data." To do this in a program setting, I know of no better method than action research. Action research is sometimes called "practitioner inquiry," "participatory research," even "case study" within the qualitative research domain of ethnographic and phenomenological methodologies (Isaac, 1971; Merriam and Simpson, 1984; Runcie, 1980; Schumacher and McMillan, 1993). There are small and large differences between these that are beyond the scope of this book. The method and approach I want to discuss here is action research (Kemmis and McTaggart, 1984; Lees and Smith, 1980). I and a number of others have been involved since 1992 in training literacy teachers, tutors, and administrators across Pennsylvania through a statewide grant initiative. We have come to believe that this type of activity could be the key to change in our field.

Action Research in Adult Literacy: Background

In 1991, the Adult Literacy Act obligated states to "set aside" for professional development and innovative projects in literacy not the usual 10 percent of the federal funds they received for literacy programs, but a full 15 percent. A U.S. Division of Adult Education and Literacy follow-up review of what was happening with the additional 5 percent found that, of the forty-eight states and five protected territories reporting, all had sharply increased their practitioners' professional development activities (Division of Adult Education and Literacy, 1993). However, the follow-up review also found that two states, Virginia and Massachusetts, had challenged the usual model of professional development. They had decided that the allocation of the additional funds would not be based simply on needs assessment questionnaires—statewide or local—or on the advice of an expert advisory group. Virginia reported that it had used an "'inquiry-based decision' [process] as opposed to [an] 'expert-driven system.'" The state added that it would go further to "conduct [a] study of [its] staff development system" (p. 14). Massachusetts reported that it had used "collaborative planning" (p. 5) among practitioners. Virginia has since implemented practitioner action research and so has Massachusetts (Cockley, 1993). This was a challenge to the traditional "school model," where experts first decide who will get what training, then go out to deliver workshops or courses, or insist that practitioners journey to them.

The school model, or what I will call the "received knowledge" model, was challenged in Michigan at the statewide level in 1994–95 and in Pennsylvania in 1995–96 on a statewide basis. Two major initiatives were put in place to train and mentor practitioners, who then went on to identify and work on their own individual questions. Meanwhile, action research institutional projects have grown out of Literacy South in Georgia (Drennon, 1995) and North Carolina (Pates, 1992); the Institute for Literacy at the University of Tennessee (Gaventa and Horton, 1981); Columbia University (Columbia University, 1993); and action research work based in various adult education centers in California (MacDonald, 1994). Consortia and Internet web sites have been established around action research. This is a "grassroots movement" striving to support practitioners in defining questions, answering them, and owning the results of their research. Here, I believe, lies some of the promise for building data and knowledge to support change.

Practitioner action research is modeled on successful K–12 research using similar methods (Allen et al., 1988; Hubbard and Power, 1993; Lytle and Cochran-Smith, 1990). It has international recognition in both industrialized countries (for example, Kemmis and McTaggart, 1984) and developing countries (Fernandes and Tandon, 1981). The action research process of problem posing and problem solving will either adapt and test established theory or research in the practitioner's own setting or will allow the practitioner to systematically test his or her own hypotheses (Cochran and Lytle, 1993). This research empowerment of practitioners and their learners is beginning to have a wide impact on practice. Findings are shared and then retested by others, thus strengthening test validity over time (Merriam, 1988a).

What Is Action Research and How Does It Work?

Developed by Kurt Lewin in the 1940s and 1950s (Weisbord, 1987), action research is most straightforwardly defined by Isaac (1971): "to develop new skills or new approaches and to solve problems with direct application to the classroom or working world setting" (p. 27). Kemmis and McTaggart (1984) have provided an especially useful definition: "Trying new ideas in practice as a means of improvement and as a means of increasing knowledge about the curriculum, teaching, and learning. The result is improvement in what happens in the classroom and school, and the better articulation and justification of the educational rationale for what goes on. Action research provides a way of working which links theory and practice into the one whole: ideas-in-action" (p. 5).

Action research is thus a form of inductive experimentation. In a sense, it is systematic trial and error (Whitehead, 1989).

Looked at more closely, action research is seen to follow a spiral. One "cycle" of investigation is conducted with the aim of bringing about a desired change; then, on the basis of what is learned from this first cycle, a second will be initiated, and so on.

Action research does not exactly have an "end point," because it is conducted in the action-based world of daily practice, not in "static" or controlled conditions. This research seeks to bring about change in the everyday world. A further distinctive element is that participants, rather than being kept unaware that they are engaged in a study or experiment, are fully informed (Hall, 1979).

Where do we begin? The motivation to try a project usually resides in what I call an "itch." There is a sense of frustration about something we are doing or seem unable to do. We cannot get something to "work" properly. We then begin to visualize a way of solving the problem.

Planning

The planning phase of action research is perhaps the most difficult because it begins with an attempt to identify the *actual* problem. This task is rarely easy and does not always conform to one's expectations. The process of discovering and defining the "itch" often requires the involvement of others familiar with the situation being explored. There is usually a series of questions and refinements to get at what the nature of the perceived problem is, what factors help to cause it, and what aspects can, perhaps, be changed through an action research "intervention." When one is clear on the question, it is advisable to conduct a literature search before taking any other steps, to determine what research has already been done on the topic. A specialist library may be of help here, but equally important is the state resource center (maintained by most states), which can advise on various literacy databases. An "ERIC search" is also considered to be essential in research of this kind. ERIC is an information clearinghouse and on-line database of adult education and related research that can be searched at almost any major library, with professional assistance if needed (Mekosh-Rosenbaum, n.d.).

If the literature search indicates that the problem has not already been addressed, the next step is to decide if the problem is "researchable"—that is, if the necessary research can be managed, and if it will in fact lead to an answer. One has to consider where as well as how to intervene in the problem situation. At this point in the planning phase, discussions with colleagues can be extremely helpful.

Some of the key questions to be addressed are

- What actually is "the problem"?
- Do I understand why the problem exists?
- Is this a problem I want to spend time on?
- How can I intervene to see if a different approach would make a difference?
- Can I conduct this project in a way that allows me to manage the research activities?

Organization

Once a problem and an intervention are decided on, the next step is organizational. Normally, those who are to be studied in a research project must be made aware of the fact, and their permission obtained. Research universities and some other institutions require that a full plan be submitted that includes a procedure for written consent from every subject. The exact requirements of the institutions one is working with need to be determined early on.

Among the questions to be answered in this phase of action research are

- When will I begin the project?
- How will I inform those in the project?
- What approvals will I need?
- What resources, if any, will I need?
- To whom can I turn to talk about my problems and progress as the project moves through its various phases?

Methodology and Structure

Before beginning the research, one must decide how change is going to be measured and how outcomes will be evaluated. Typical questions to be addressed are

- How will the results of the new approach be compared to the usual outcomes of the old approach?
- What will be the criteria for a successful project?
- How long should the project run?

There are many ways to collect data in action research. Among the most common and useful tools are

The reflective journal. An ongoing record of thoughts on the project, updated at least three times a week. I always recommend that such a journal be kept from the very outset because observations that might be considered minor at the time may later reveal important patterns.

Objective tests. For example, pre- and post-intervention exams.

Records analysis. For example, analysis of attendance records in the administrative office.

Logs. Systematic contemporaneous records of events.

Field notes. Immediate, usually nonreflective, observations.

Anecdote cards. Index cards on which the actions of an individual or group in the same or similar concrete situations are detailed over time. Special attention is often paid to the "before and after" of the concrete situation to see what apparently causes outcomes and with what effect.

Interviews. These may be nonstructured (like a conversation), semistructured (with the same opening question given each interviewee, following which certain information is "probed for"), or structured (with a set list of questions). Arranging for a neutral party to conduct the interview may reduce the chance of getting "acceptable answers."

Tape recorders or video cameras. Audiotapes and videotapes permit careful study of what is said by research subjects—and how it is said. They can reveal much more than contemporaneous observation.

Cross-checking of data is facilitated and the validity of results is enhanced if at least three forms of observation are employed (Merriam, 1988a).

Monitoring

As the research proceeds, it is important to continually ask a set of questions that turns a spotlight on one's own performance:

- Am I keeping close track of what is going on in the data collection systems I have put in place?
- Am I keeping in touch with my colleagues for support and insight?
- Am I staying true to the initial plan?
- Am I collecting the data the way I said I would?

The key is to think and act with objectivity. Keep track of events like an anthropologist. The very act of objectifying a situation that may be very close to one's daily experience can be illuminating—and even therapeutic.

It is important to stay with data collection until the scheduled completion date of the project. Sometimes a teacher is tempted to abandon the task of making entries because of the burden of other work. Or an administrator may come to feel that conditions have changed so drastically that the situation being studied is no longer "typical." But this is why we use action research; we observe "in action." Frequently, the "atypical" is just the typical showing itself. Keep at it. To quit is to waste all the thinking and work that have previously been invested in the project.

Even if the intervention does not produce the changes one had hoped for or does not meet the set criteria, completed research cannot be considered a waste of time because at least some negative information has been generated, and future research will avoid the discredited approach. In any event, there is such a commonality of problems across literacy education that one can be reasonably sure findings will be of interest to others. They can be shared by means of a conference presentation, a newsletter article, a monograph, a workshop for peers, a computer bulletin board, E-mail, or even a web site.

Reflection

At the conclusion of the project, I suggest pulling the data together and asking colleagues to help analyze them. Going over the results systematically with others can produce significant insights. Often, colleagues will notice patterns that the researcher has overlooked. At other times, they may offer valuable advice on whether a second cycle of research is called for.

Questions one needs to ask oneself include

- Did the results I received actually reflect what happened?
- Did the intervention make a difference?
- Was the difference sufficient to meet the criteria I set?
- How can I have this study repeated to strengthen validity?
- What could I do differently if I tried this again?

It is very common to initiate a second cycle based on what was learned in the first. This is systematic discovery. The purpose of the second cycle may be to adjust the original intervention or to experiment with an entirely new one. This cycle is normally easier to conduct than the first because questions such as how and where to conduct the study and what pitfalls are likely have already been answered.

Action Research: Some Examples

A case study of action research is provided by the rural Pennsylvania ABE program discussed briefly in Chapter Six.

There were three teachers involved, each with approximately fifteen adult students. When the program was originally organized, one teacher was responsible for all of the lower literacy level, another for the "middle" ABE level, and the third for the senior GED level. The coordinator, Rita, was typically in charge of the intake of new students. This occurred every evening, Monday through Friday at 6:00 P.M., as new students either dropped in to enroll or came in on an agency referral. General information was normally given over the telephone in the late afternoon by all three teachers, while they prepared for the evening classes.

Despite their best teaching efforts, they experienced a dropout rate higher than they wanted. Though it was no more than about 30 percent, far lower than the U.S. norm of 74 percent (U.S. Department of Education, 1995), the teachers were far from satisfied. They wanted to improve the situation. But how? They attempted something we called "Operation Match."

A number of at-risk adults participated in the program, and the teachers decided to focus on these individuals to see if they could be kept in the program longer. The strategy was to try to match the teachers' personal working philosophies, and their interests and strengths, with compatible learners. The idea arose when it was noted that Stephanie seemed able to keep her learners longer than anyone. As we talked about this, it was evident that she had a talent for working with those whom the others were agreed were the early at-risk learners. She jokingly said, "Maybe I should only work with the at-risk students." No one laughed. "She knows how to encourage and how to help that group," one of the other teachers said. Stephanie said she was committed to and comfortable with a humanist approach to teaching, but she was quick to point out the strengths she had noted in the other two teachers. Rita was skilled at working with those who wanted to enter the world of work. She knew a number of employers, and by virtue of her work as coordinator, had a good idea of what jobs were available in the community. "We can't all be like Stephanie," said Mary. She was interested in "teaching"—nothing more. But when we talked further, it emerged that Mary's real interest was in teaching critical thinking skills. Her degrees were in English, and she often used a reader series featuring classic novels rewritten in a low-vocabulary, high-interest format to raise challenging questions. The three decided that they would try to match new learners with the working philosophy each was most comfortable with.

The action research "intervention" was to be a new assessment system and a new process of referral to a program structured around working philosophies. New students were to be identified by their interests and needs during intake through observation; those suspected of being at risk then took the Prior Schooling and Self-Perception Inventory (Resource A). The at-risk group, considered likely to be highly field dependent although the teachers did not use Witkin's Embedded Figures Test, was referred to Stephanie.

To give the small-group model a chance, it was decided that Stephanie should not try to work with more than six students at any given time. She placed the at-risk learners among others who happened to be assigned to her small groups. To accommodate more at-risk students, she later began to teach a "double shift," with one group in the late afternoon and one in the evening.

Those who said they were interested in a general education—mothers wanting to help their children with homework, those desiring to go on to college or further education, those who sought a GED—were referred to Mary. And as mentioned, those wanting to go directly from the program to work went to Rita's classroom.

The teachers decided to dispense with the internal schooling levels of low literacy, ABE, and GED. As in the old rural schoolhouse, each teacher took on all academic levels. Although the spread across cognitive abilities was not so very wide that it became a problem, it did occasionally happen that Stephanie, Rita, or Mary would have a basic literacy student in with a GED student. In these cases, the teachers would go over to each other's classroom to help on a particular question or topic. Mary was the "English and grammar" expert. Rita was the program's "math expert." They helped each other out when someone got stuck or was in an area they were not entirely comfortable with. Interestingly, Mary's liberal classroom and Rita's vocational one saw a good deal of "participatory" processing, with more and more input from the learners (Fingeret and Jurmo, 1989). Stephanie's remained more pedagogical in terms of internal decision making, but her groups became extremely supportive for their members.

As described in Chapter Six, the three teachers took turns with the intake. By doing so, each became familiar with the types of student needs that presented themselves. As they put it, they were no longer subject specialists but "student specialists." This was a project they could all manage without outside assistance or new expense. They had identified their problem—attrition—and were eagerly waiting to see if matching would improve retention. Their criterion of success was a 20 percent improvement in retention as compared with the prior three years. If they could retain 20 percent more learners than the average of the past three years, they would feel they were on the right track. They calculated the average dropout rate for January through June of previous years and tried the new approach over the next six-month winter-spring period. In fact, they achieved an improvement of more than 20 percent. But this was not the only outcome of the project. The teachers' reflective journals revealed that their enjoyment of teaching had risen to a new level.

Others I have worked with whose "itch" was retention have paired at-risk learners in a "buddy system." One teacher created an after-class support group where students could talk about problems they were facing—usually situational and institutional barriers, but not always—with a teacher and counselor sitting in. Several others tried variations on the intake process for at-risk learners. For example, one program decided to stream at-risk students to create small classes within classes; such students and two or three other non-at-risk learners would have a special area of the classroom during the afternoon to work on common subjects. Another teacher decided to create a closer tie between the intake counselor and the teacher responsible for an at-risk student. The counselor talked with the student at least once a week, and the teacher made a point of working closely with the student in every class. Yet another teacher, working in English as a second language, thought retention might improve if she put Hispanics together in their own classroom rather than across the program with a mix of international students.

In all of these instances, there were good reasons to try the selected intervention. However, it was not always easy to settle on the selection. Some I have worked with have taken months to decide on the problem and the intervention. In one case, the coordinator of a literacy tutoring project that spanned a rural area at least four hundred miles in diameter was having great difficulty getting tutors to send in their time sheets. This was important because she had reporting obligations to the state. Facilitating a short course on action research with this coordinator in it, the group of adult literacy practitioners in the class came up with more than thirty different suggestions for intervention. One person suggested giving some sort of recognition, like certificates or newsletter kudos, to those reporting consistently. Another said that if a phone tree of volunteers were established, they could remind each other to send in their time sheet each month. It was very difficult to know how best to begin with this one. Finally, a decision was made that the coordinator would compile a list of all our suggestions and, at the upcoming volunteer recognition dinner, would ask an advisory committee to help her make a choice—or come up with an even better intervention. Ultimately, the advisory committee decided to try a postcard mailing followed by a phone call. There was now a new ownership of what had previously been "the coordinator's problem." The advisory committee became a standing group on this and other problems.

When Should Action Research Not Be Used?

If a teacher, program planner, or administrator can identify a clear problem—an "itch"—and come up with a clear and reasonable intervention for effective change, he or she is on the right road. But if the problem and intervention are not manageable or "researchable," he or she will surely drive off that road. The problems for action research are normally practice problems that the researcher can manage without undue involvement from external parties. However, not all topics are "researchable" with this method. There is a difference between trying a new math technique, a new counseling method to improve retention, or a different recruitment approach and trying to resolve difficulties with an obstructive employer or board member. Similarly, trying to investigate retention in a neighborhood that is hostile to the program's very presence may be taking on more than one can manage. Employer resistance and community hostility are emotionally and politically charged realities that will not change simply as a result of a single teacher's research efforts, at least of the type described here. There are other qualitative research methodologies for effecting community change—for example, advocacy efforts involving participatory research (Dilts, 1986; Hall, 1979; Hall, Gillette, and Tandon, 1982).

Improving practice through action research means testing new ideas. Sometimes, these are ideas one picks up from reports in the literature or from conference presentations. Often, they are just our best "hunches" for change. Discussions with peers can be vital when making a decision on which idea to pursue.

Questions for Action Research

The following are questions concerning literacy practice that action research may help answer for the benefit of the wider field. Several are actually challenging the myths of the popular and political perspectives. They are grouped according to working philosophy.

Vocational Working Philosophy

- How do learners become better prepared for the workforce?
- What are the effects of holding a course at a job site as opposed to a traditional literacy center? Does follow-up show that, in the former case, more graduates get employment at that site or a similar one?
- What happens when we teach vocabulary directly relevant to a specific workplace? Does this actually help learners on such a job? Does it help to retain learners in a literacy course? How important is relevant vocabulary?
- Does teaching a class with job simulation enhance retention or subsequent employment?
- Does the use of computers and other technology help recruit or retain males?

Liberal Working Philosophy

- What do different types of learner ownership of courses do to retention? For example, do participatory courses where there is a much higher degree of input to course decisions improve retention or cognitive gain (Fingeret and Jurmo, 1989)?
- Do participatory courses in which learners are matched with teachers by interest provide measurably higher levels of student satisfaction?

- Does the encouragement of critical thinking improve reten-tion or cognitive gain?
- How does critical thinking as a classroom objective change the dynamics in the classroom or student satisfaction?
- Does a teacher aide—volunteer or paid—contribute to reten-tion or cognitive gain?
- Can we identify a list of reading texts that will be of interest to most within the liberal stream?
- Are there high-interest novels or nonfiction works for differ-ent genders, races, and other groups?

Liberatory Working Philosophy

- What happens to retention rates and cognitive gain when stu-dent advocacy projects are undertaken—for example, working as a group to change a learner's life situation?
- What happens over time as a result of liberatory classes? Does momentum die as the class ends? Or does it build? What are the dynamics apart from and following liberatory classes?
- Are graduates more empowered in observable ways well after the course ends?
- What techniques, methods, ideas, or attitudes carry beyond the class, and how are they used in the learner's world?

Humanist Working Philosophy

- What are the actual self-esteem levels of learners in and out of classrooms?
- What are at-risk learners' self-esteem levels before and after they are placed in the humanist stream?
- Do at-risk students with low self-esteem improve their self-esteem most in contexts with fewer peers, more teacher or counselor support, or additional tutoring support?
- Do humanist programs with at-risk students improve retention in both rural and urban settings?
- Does a humanist approach have different effects with different races and genders? How does this manifest itself with, for instance, retention and cognitive gain?
- How does learners' self-esteem change when classes have field trips, open discussions, debates?

- What are the learning differences between males and females? (Kazemak, 1988b).
- Does cognitive gain follow matching?
- How can we identify those who are at risk, and how can we determine which of the barriers—situational, institutional, or dispositional—are at work?

A Research and Policy Plan for the Future

Consider for a moment how many teachers and tutors have basically the same questions, the same frustrations, every day. The problems of illiteracy are not isolated incidents but patterns present in every classroom in every state. Given this fact, why not establish action research strategies across and among states and regions? The validity of findings would be enhanced by multiclassroom repetition of outcomes (Isaac, 1971).

Imagine a planning group that would facilitate and support a statewide initiative. It could be composed of one or more state policy makers, a range of literacy teachers and administrators familiar with action research, and at least one seasoned action researcher. On the basis of its own field experiences in literacy education, the group would draw up a prioritized list of statewide issues, taking into account the needs of the state itself. The group would then ask various literacy programs across the state to engage with the three or four issues at the top of the list. Each of these programs would then use action research to investigate its assigned problem while maintaining communication with other programs also working on that problem. Four or five programs might, for example, be working on a new way to teach math. Another three or four might be experimenting with a method to retain learners. One group might be working on the issue of learning style. Another might be challenging self-esteem assumptions by using different settings or activities or by drawing on student input.

What if each placed its findings in its state literacy resource center, creating a critical mass of pooled judgment on these various issues? What if the seasoned researcher made suggestions on what was still needed in each area for fuller validity and if, with the planning group's support, designated programs initiated new cycles of research to fill these gaps? Monthly monographs might be distributed, and the outcomes of the research projects might be discussed at annual state conferences and regional meetings. Attending teachers could then absorb the new knowledge, apply it in the classroom, and report back to the planning group. We might see real alternatives, informed by measured outcomes, emerging across states and regions.

The state would thus provide input to and help pursue a field-based agenda of value to all involved in literacy education. Findings would inform policy (Nelson, Haggerson, and Bowman, 1992), policy would be based on what the field itself experienced, and internal validity would be constantly enhanced.

For the sake of our learners and the advancement of our field, I am advocating here that we "work locally and argue globally." We can own our own knowledge at the classroom level. We can contribute this knowledge to regional or statewide programs of action research. We can use this research to argue for program change and program funding on a small or large scale. And finally, we can bring increased, valid knowledge to the issues that our ethical frameworks tell us are of greatest importance. Will this ever happen? As Greene put it, "change comes only when we are willing to envisage change" (1988, p. 16).

Chapter Nine

Literacy Educators as Leaders of Effective Change

Adult illiteracy has been called the "most fixable" of all social problems, a "disease to be cured," a "war to be won," "a blight," "a curse," a "doorway" through which everything from sin to social uprising has been said to pass. For practitioners, the field is also, in my opinion, the area within adult education where it is easiest to grow cynical. As mentioned at the beginning of this book, we have lost excellent teachers, tutors, and administrators over the years not because they were uncommitted but because they saw no professional future in literacy or because they had grown tired of uncertainty (Beder, 1994).

As literacy policy moves into the twenty-first century, those many tutors, teachers, and administrators who continue to work in the field and to believe in the value of literacy education need reassurance. They need hope. Hardly a week goes by without practitioners telling me how fearful they are for the future of their programs. No one I know in the field plans beyond the end of the current fiscal year. No state is immune, no governmentally funded program remains untouched. Now, even further federal cuts are likely, and state-level "block grants" will throw literacy funding decisions into the fray of state legislatures. Deprived of the legislative support of the National Literacy Act, practitioners need to be assured that this field will not be pushed further and further into the margins of social policy.

From the governmental perspective, adult illiteracy is surely one of the most exasperating of all social problems. No amount of literacy campaigns, "consciousness raising," declarations that illiteracy will be "eradicated," or accountability measures seems to make a substantive difference to the statistics. Almost two decades of campaigning under Presidents Reagan and Bush left the nation's low literacy rate virtually untouched (Califano and Berry, 1978; Kirsch, Jungeblut, Jenkins, and Kolstad, 1993). At no point in the history of literacy has there been agreement on definitions; therefore, from a governmental point of view, it continues to be unclear as to what literacy actually is. This all adds to the exasperation.

Hope for the Twenty-First Century

This book has attempted to examine assumptions, raise new questions, and make certain topics "discussable" for the future. Let us conclude by asking if all of the grim speculations about low literacy and our uncertain future deserve credence.

First, an anecdote. A close friend of mine who was vice president for training at a huge electrical corporation used to tell me about the hard-bitten district foremen and managers he worked with, each supervising several thousand employees and negotiating with up to four unions. The issue for him in the late 1980s, as now, was how to do more with less. He was always arranging courses and training for managers and their staff, and they invariably touched on downsizing. One day, he was conducting a workshop dealing with employee morale when he was challenged by one of the senior foremen, who had grown tired of cutbacks and "pep talks." This man looked up, glowering, and asked, "And who exactly is supposed to motivate the motivator?" My friend gave him a straightforward answer that I never forgot: "You are. As the leader, people expect you to motivate yourself."

In the final analysis, the motivation to sustain and change adult literacy education cannot be expected to come from any source but ourselves. The field must be led by those working in it, not by political pundits or media-induced public sentiment. Ultimately, what will count is a commitment to stay in the field and to work at changing it. Is this possible? The times we live in offer new possibilities—new opportunities for fresh thinking. As we approach the twenty-first century, our postmodern society has placed most of our traditional beliefs and values under attack. For literacy, this creates hope. The caring and commitment of the practitioners who have sustained this field will carry us into the future. The opportunity afforded by postmodernism—the opportunity for real leadership—opens the door for practitioners to find their voice.

Four themes that have run through this book are directly relevant to the renewal of commitment: new perceptions, belief in our purpose, awareness of historical context, and the power of knowledge to change what is into what should be.

The Power of Perception

The perceptions of illiteracy and low literates held by the public and those in political life were the focus of Part One of this book. It was seen there that the media and popular literature have typically viewed low literates through the lens of what I have called the "popular perspective," with its emphasis on a romanticized "heroic victim." Like minor characters in a Faulkner novel, heroic victims in the American perception of illiteracy are depicted as steadfast but simple immigrants, simple American workers, simple African Americans, and simple white southerners. It was also noted how the heroic victim was occasionally turned into "natural man" to make a social statement.

There were varying responses to these public images, and different degrees of caring about heroic victims. In my experience, most of us who came into this field did so because we have a high degree of caring for low-literate adults, and we should be prepared to challenge the worst aspects of the media stereotypes. Responsible practice should demand no less (Cervero and Wilson, 1994). The same holds true for the political perspective. Low literates remain one of the few acceptable scapegoats of late twentieth-century American politics. To this day, political literature and rhetoric depict illiteracy as an economic burden, a drain, and an insidious disease of ignorance inexorably leading low literates to acts of despair, such as crime and violence, and to susceptibility to dangerous ideologies. As was seen in Chapter Three, the political perspective has argued that illiteracy could lead to communism, Nazism, the unwanted acts of undesirable immigrants, or immoral behavior. For practitioners and researchers, such hostile and simplistic analyses and the assumptions behind them are an insult both to our learners and to our profession. In any other present-day context, these assertions would be deemed racist or sexist or worthy of litigation (Beder, 1991). Distorted stereotypes should not go unquestioned, either at policy-making levels or in the media. Our learners and potential learners are our sources of strength. Their intrinsic worth to our society as a whole needs to be affirmed. It is time for our field to clearly and forcefully articulate a new set of realities. Figure 9.1 indicates how both the participant and nonparticipant who still dream of an education should be practitioners', researchers', and practitioner–action researchers' sources of strength and knowledge, if we are to challenge the enduring political and popular perspectives of our society.

Building Our Own Reality

As we gain insight into the limitations of the popular and political perspectives and recognize the restrictiveness of the myths they generate, we will develop a much clearer sense of our own purpose and reality. It should not be acceptable that macro-level

Figure 9.1. A Field Model for Influencing Political and Popular Perspectives.

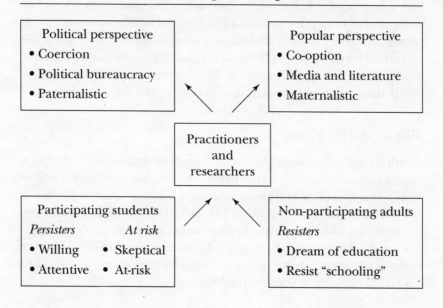

myths oversimplify our practice as well as our learners. Those who work in this field need to be like the magician's assistant who, standing in the wings, sees how illusions are created. Unlike the assistant, we need to speak up when the illusions are taken to be bona fide truths (Garvey, 1995). As long as we are subject to inherited perceptual distortions, our field will continue to be marginalized at the public and political levels.

Understanding our context more deeply should give us new confidence that practitioners hold the truest perspective on the field and those we serve. From this base of knowledge and power, we can work for widespread changes in perception and for increased stability in the field. We should be able to argue that our field is like other professional development disciplines and not simply a stepchild of "adult remedial schooling." Those who have a vocational working philosophy bring the same orientation to adult education as any vocational or continuing education program. Where our programs embody liberal education values, they should be seen as comparable to other forms of liberal arts postsecondary education. Where a humanist philosophy guides our efforts, we should be bracketed with other helping agencies. The long liberatory tradition in our field should be recognized and supported for its achievements and potential in advocacy and social change. Adult literacy is not schooling for failed adults. Nor is it a "second chance to get an education." Our work for adult learners should be seen as a point along the continuum of lifelong learning. It is like any other phase of formal learning in an adult's life. Having a clearer view of literacy reality in our own practice and in the lives of our learners and potential learners should help strengthen our resolve for change.

History and the Future

Adult literacy has been the cornerstone of organized and volunteer adult education for centuries. In fact, some histories tell us that adult literacy was where organized adult education began in the Western world (Grattan, 1955). With this longevity behind us, why succumb to the paranoia that says that funding and support for our field is about to be erased? Literacy education began before today's adult education programs and long before the emphasis on youth education (Grattan, 1955).

What is sadly missing in the training of practitioners is a sense of where literacy education has come from, how other practitioners have flourished in the face of greater odds than those confronting us in this decade, and how innovation in funding and practice has been the touchstone of so many of our predecessors. If we had better knowledge of our past, and were not caught in the myths of the popular and political perspectives, we would undoubtedly take greater pride in our field. The history of our field is still to be written. It is hoped, however, that the discussion in this book of some of the key events and shifts in attitudes that have shaped adult literacy education will encourage researchers and practitioners to write more and speak more about our rich heritage. If we take the longer view, we will see a field that has endured despite the capriciousness of political favor and public sympathy.

Matters of the Heart

In every one of the chapters in Parts One, Two, and Three, there was encouragement to change. But why work for change? As Lindeman put it in the 1920s: "In what areas do most people appear to find life's meaning? We have only one pragmatic guide: meaning must reside in the things for which people strive, the goals which they set for themselves, their wants, needs, desires and wishes" (Lindeman, 1961, p. 8). Our working philosophy and sense of purpose take us to the emotional foundation of why we do what we do—to life's meaning and matters of the heart.

Obviously everyone has asked at one time or another: "Why continue? Why work for change?" The electrical company supervisor asked: "Who motivates the motivator?" Reasons to stay in this field and work for change have been suggested throughout this book, but I believe the core reason is simple: It is worth doing.

Why are even the most cynical of our veteran practitioners touched by the success stories of learners? In my view, it is because many of us who work in this field are "seriously afflicted" with idealism—a condition only made worse by sudden flashes of romanticism induced by student testimonies at state literacy conferences. We hear political bombast, we work surrounded by literacy rhetoric. Yet, most of us are incurable optimists and would like our work to contribute to a better future for the nation.

These deep feelings for individuals and our society are part of our strength.

However, I have come to think that emotional strengths such as these also make our field highly vulnerable. They encourage us to believe that others will ultimately come to realize the value of our good works and will somehow reward us—or at least, not abandon us in our efforts. There is an innocence of faith at work in literacy education, including a degree of naiveté. In the cynical 1990s, naiveté does not help us or our learners very much.

Knowledge and Change

Lindeman has said, "Melancholy is temporary. Human nature is predisposed to optimism" (1961, p. 23). Our ability to see our own world of practice more clearly should predispose us to a greater optimism. Today's melancholy of postmodernism is also accompanied by the ushering in of new perspectives, new voices, and new possibilities. As Fingeret has said, "If programs are going to change, people who create them must change" (1984, p. 44). I take this to mean "The way people *see* programs must first change." I hope this book may have helped toward such a goal. The sustained argument of this book has been that we lack no degree of caring, no amount of commitment. As Beder has pointed out (1994), we also have no lack of learners who could lobby for change, and we would have ample funds if even half of our practitioners joined a single professional organization (see Resource B). Furthermore, we have the means to accumulate new knowledge on better ways to conduct practice and provide new realism in order to challenge old myths.

Guided by our own considered working philosophies, we have the potential to build a better future. If we put the passion of our commitment together with the power of knowledge, we can bring about the changes that we and our learners need. To try is always worth it.

Prior Schooling and Self-Perception Inventory

Learner Name _____   Intake Person _____

Date _____

1 = very negative ←→ 7 = very positive

1. How valuable do you believe
   this program will be for you?   1 2 3 4 5 6 7

2. How different do you think this
   program will be from school?   1 2 3 4 5 6 7

3. How well will you do in:
   Math?   1 2 3 4 5 6 7
   Reading?   1 2 3 4 5 6 7
   Social Studies?   1 2 3 4 5 6 7
   Science?   1 2 3 4 5 6 7

4. In school, how well did you do in:
   Math?   1 2 3 4 5 6 7
   Reading?   1 2 3 4 5 6 7
   Social Studies?   1 2 3 4 5 6 7
   Science?   1 2 3 4 5 6 7

5. How helpful will:

The teachers be here?   1 2 3 4 5 6 7

The counselors be?   1 2 3 4 5 6 7

Your friends at home be?   1 2 3 4 5 6 7

6. Back in school, how helpful were:

The teachers?   1 2 3 4 5 6 7

The counselors?   1 2 3 4 5 6 7

Your friends at home?   1 2 3 4 5 6 7

7. How easy do you think it will be
to make friends here?   1 2 3 4 5 6 7

8. How helpful do you think these
new friends will be?   1 2 3 4 5 6 7

9. How easy was it to make friends
in school?   1 2 3 4 5 6 7

10. Right now, how well do you think
you will do in this program?   1 2 3 4 5 6 7

Adult Education Organizations and Associations

Following is a partial list of adult education organizations and associations with an interest in adult literacy.

AFL-CIO, Department of Education
Assistant Director
815 16th Street, NW
Washington, DC 20006
(202) 637-5143
Fax: (202) 637-5058

American Association for Adult and Continuing Education
Executive Director
1200 19th Street, NW
Suite 300
Washington, DC 20036
(202) 429-5131
Fax: (202) 223-4579

American Association of Community Colleges
Director
Education Services
One Du Pont Circle
Suite 410
Washington, DC 20036-1176
(202) 728-7851
Fax: (202) 833-2467

American Association of Retired Persons
Institute of Lifelong Learning
Director
Special Programs
601 E Street, NW
Washington, DC 20049
(202) 434-2470
Fax: (202) 434-6499

American Council on Education
The Center for Adult Learning and Educational Credentials
Director of Outreach
One Du Pont Circle
Suite 250
Washington, DC 20036-1193
(202) 939-9475
Fax: (202) 775-8578

American Library Association
Reference and Adult Services Division
50 East Huron Street
Chicago, IL 60611
(312) 280-4395
Fax: (312) 944-8085

American Reading Forum
Executive Office
Education Department
North Georgia College
Dahlonega, GA 30549

American Society for Training and Development
Vice President for National Affairs
1640 King Street, Box 1443
Alexandria, VA 22313-2043
(703) 683-8160
Fax: (703) 548-2383

American Vocational Association
Executive Director
1410 King Street
Alexandria, VA 22314
(703) 683-3111
Fax: (703) 683-7424

Commission of Adult Basic Education
President
Portland Community College
P.O. Box 19000
Portland, OR 97219
(503) 244-6111, ext. 4667

Council for Adult and Experiential Learning
Director of Institutional Relations
243 South Wabash
Chicago, IL 60604
(312) 922-5909
Fax: (312) 922-1769

Distance Education and Training Council
Executive Director
1601 18th Street, NW
Washington, DC 20009-2529
(202) 234-5100
Fax: (202) 332-1386

International Association for Continuing Education and Training
Associate Director
The Georgia Center for Continuing Education
University of Georgia
Athens, GA 30602
(706) 542-1275
Fax: (706) 542-5990

International Reading Association
Executive Office
800 Barksdale Road
P.O. Box 8139
Newark, DE 19714-8139
(302) 731-1600

Laubach Student Congress
1320 Jamesville Avenue
Syracuse, NY 13210
(315) 422-9121

Learning Resources Network
President
1550 Hayes Drive
Manhattan, KS 66502
(913) 539-5376
Fax: (913) 539-7766

National Adult Education Professional Development Consortium
(NAEPDC)
Executive Director
444 North Capitol Street, NW
Suite 422
Washington, DC 20001
(202) 624-5250
Fax: (202) 624-8826

National Association for Adults with Special Learning Needs
Director of Adult Education
142 Hope Hill Road
Wallingford, CT 06492
(203) 294-5932, 269-3670
Fax: (203) 284-2063

National Coalition for Literacy
Office of Adult Education
Virginia Department of Education
P.O. Box 2120
Richmond, VA 23216-2120
(804) 225-2075

National Community Education Association
Education Director
3929 Old Lee Highway
Suite 91-A
Fairfax, VA 22030-2401
(703) 359-8973
Fax: (703) 359-0972

National Council on Community Services and Continuing Education (NCCSCE)
President
Blackhawk College
6600 34th Avenue
Moline, IL 61265
(309) 796-1388

Teachers of English to Students of Other Languages
Executive Director
1600 Cameron Street
Suite 300
Alexandria, VA 22314-7864
(703) 836-0774
Fax: (703) 836-7864

References

Agee, J., & Evans, W. (1966). *Let us now praise famous men.* (Original work published 1939). New York: Ballantine Books.

Alamprese, J. (1990). Strengthening the knowledge base in adult literacy: The research imperative. In F. Chisman & Associates (Eds.), *Leadership for literacy.* San Francisco: Jossey-Bass.

Alderman. L. (1927). Buncombe County's excellent work for adult illiterates. *School Life, 8*(9), 176–179.

Allen, J., Combs, J., Hendricks, M., Nash, P., & Wilson, S. (1988). Studying change: Teachers who become researchers. *Language Arts, 65*(4), 379–387.

Amato, A. (1957). Some effects of bibliotherapy on young adults. *Dissertation Abstracts International, 17,* 2870.

America needs a literacy corps. (1987, July 2). *New York Times,* p. 27.

Anderson, J. A. (1988). Cognitive styles and multicultural populations. *Journal of Teacher Education, 39*(2), 2–9.

Anderson, D., & Niemi, J. (1970). *Adult education and the disadvantaged adult.* Syracuse, NY: ERIC Clearinghouse.

Anderson, S. H., & Dunlap, D. W. (1984, November 27). $45 million for the fight against adult illiteracy. *New York Times,* p. II-3.

Anderson, V. (1995, July 16). Throwing the book at them: Reading program helps convicts define morality. *Dallas Morning News,* p. 26.

Apple, M. (1990). The text and cultural politics. *Journal of Educational Thought, 24*(3A), 17–33.

Apple, M. (1991). *The politics of the textbook.* New York: Routledge.

Apps, J. W. (1973). *Towards a working philosophy of adult education.* Publications in continuing education: Occasional paper no. 6. Syracuse, NY: Syracuse University.

Arnove, R., & Graff, H. (1987). *National literacy campaigns: Historical and comparative perspectives.* New York: Plenum Press.

Aronowitz, S., & Giroux, H. (1985). *Education under siege.* South Hadley, MA: Bergin & Garvey.

Aronowitz, S., & Giroux, H. (1991). *Postmodern education: Politics, culture and social criticism.* Minneapolis: University of Minnesota Press.

Asante, M., & Mattson, M. (1992). *Historical and cultural atlas of African Americans.* New York: Macmillan.

Ausband, S. (1983). *Myth and meaning, myth and order.* Macon, GA: Mercer University Press.

Bagdikian, B. (1990). *The media monopoly.* Boston: Beacon Press.

Baldwin, J. (1991). Why did they drop out? Reasons GED candidates give for leaving school. *GED Profiles: Adults in Transition,* dedicated issue no. 4, pp. 1–8.

Bean, R., Partanen, J., Wright, F., & Aaronson, J. (1989). Attrition in urban basic literacy programs and strategies to increase retention. *Adult Literacy and Basic Education, 13*(3), 146–154.

Beder, H. (1980). Reaching the hard-to-reach through effective marketing. In G. G. Darkenwald & G. A. Larson (Eds.). *Reaching hard-to-reach adults.* New Directions for Continuing Education, no. 8. San Francisco: Jossey-Bass.

Beder, H. (1986). The basic principles and concepts of marketing. In H. Beder (Ed.), *Marketing continuing education programs* (pp. 3–18). San Francisco: Jossey-Bass.

Beder, H. (1989a). Purposes and philosophies. In S. B. Merriam & P. M. Cunningham (Eds.), *Handbook of adult and continuing education* (pp. 37–50). San Francisco: Jossey-Bass.

Beder, H. (1989b). *Reasons for nonparticipation among Iowa adults who are eligible for ABE.* Des Moines: Iowa Department of Education.

Beder, H. (1990a). Reasons for nonparticipation in adult basic education. *Adult Education Quarterly, 40*(4), 207–218.

Beder, H. (1990b). Adult literacy and the political economy. Symposium paper. In T. Valentine (Ed.), *Beyond rhetoric: Fundamental issues in adult literacy of education.* Athens, GA: Department of Adult Education, University of Georgia.

Beder, H. (1991). *Adult literacy education: Issues for policy and practice.* Malabar, FL: Krieger.

Beder, H. (1994). The current status of adult literacy education in the United States. *PAACE Journal of Lifelong Learning, 3,* 14–25.

Beder, H., & Valentine, T. (1987). *Iowa's adult basic education students: Descriptive profiles based on motivations, cognitive ability, and socio-demographic variables.* New Brunswick, NJ: Rutgers Graduate School of Education.

Bell, B., Gaventa, J., & Peters, J. (Eds.). (1990). *We make the road by walking: Conversations on education and social change.* Philadelphia: Temple University Press.

Belzer, A. (1990). *A research study in retention: A qualitative approach.* Harrisburg: Pennsylvania Department of Education, Division of Adult Basic and Literacy Education.

Berelson, B. (1954). Content analysis. In G. Lindzey (Ed.), *Handbook of social psychology*. (Vol. 2). Reading, MA: Addison-Wesley.

Berger, M. (1977). *Real and imagined worlds.* London: Harvard University Press.

Blakely, R. (1957). The path and the goal. *Adult education, 7,* 93–98.

Bloom, B. S., et al. (Eds.). (1956). *Handbook of educational objectives. Handbook I: Cognitive domain.* New York: McKay.

Blunt, A. (1991a). The effect of literacy on income and duration of employment. *Proceedings of the Canadian Association for the Study of Adult Education.* Kingston: University of Western Ontario.

Blunt, A. (1991b). The effect of literacy on personal income: Evidence from the *Survey of literacy skills used in daily activities.* In M. Langenbach (Ed.), *Proceedings of the Adult Education Research Conference.* Norman: University of Oklahoma.

The bottom line: Basic skills in the workplace. (1988). Washington, DC: U.S. Department of Education and Labor.

Bourdieu, P. (1971). Systems of education and systems of thought: New directions for the sociology of education. In M.F.D. Young (Ed.), *Knowledge and control* (pp. 189–207). London: Collier-Macmillan.

Bourdieu, P. (1974). The school as conservative force: Scholastic and cultural inequalities. In J. Eggleston (Ed.), *Contemporary research in the sociology of education* (pp. 30–42). London: Methuen.

Bourdieu, P. (1977). Cultural reproduction and social reproduction. In J. Karabel & A. Halsey (Eds.), *Power and ideology in education.* New York: Oxford University Press.

Bourdieu, P., & Passeron, J. C. (1977). *Reproduction in education, society and culture.* Thousand Oaks, CA: Sage.

Bowles, S., & Gintis, H. (1977). *Schooling in capitalist America.* New York: Basic Books.

Brandl, J. (1980). Policy evaluation and the work of the legislature. In L. Braskamp & R. Brown (Eds.), *Utilization of evaluative information. New directions for program evaluators,* No. 5. San Francisco: Jossey-Bass.

Brookfield, S. D. The broken dream of illiteracy. (1993, October). *America, 4.* (1987). *Developing critical thinkers: Challenging adults to explore alternative ways of thinking and acting.* San Francisco: Jossey-Bass.

Brookfield, S. D. (1990). *The skillful teacher: On technique, trust, and responsiveness in the classroom.* San Francisco: Jossey-Bass.

Brubacher, J. S. (1969). *Modern philosophies of education.* New York: McGraw-Hill.

Button, H., & Provenzo, E. (1983). *History of education and culture in America.* Englewood Cliffs, NJ: Prentice Hall.

Cain, S., & Whalen, B. (1979). *Adult basic and secondary educational program statistics: Fiscal year 1976.* Washington, DC: National Center for Education Statistics (Department of Health, Education and Welfare), Adult Vocational Education Surveys and Studies Branch. (ED 178 765).

Califano, J. A., & Berry, M. F. (1978). *Report of the USOE Invitational Workshop on Adult Competency Education.* Washington, DC: United States Department of Health, Education and Welfare.

Caliver, A. (1934, September). Outlook for Negro education. *School Life,* 40–41.

Caliver, A. (1946). Adult education of Negroes. *School Life, 29*(1), 26–28.

Caliver, A. (1948). Progress report on the adult education of Negroes. *School Life, 30*(4), 17–19.

Caliver, A. (1951). Illiteracy and manpower mobilization. *School Life, 33*(9), 131–133.

Cambridge adult basic education series (1969). Reading 2, Reading 3, Reading 4. New York: Cambridge Book Co.

Campbell, M. (1979). *Half-breed.* Halifax, Nova Scotia: McClelland and Steward.

Campbell, M. (1991, June). Continuum. *Omni,* p. 33.

Campbell, M., & Stanley, J. (1966). *Experimental and quasi-experimental designs in research.* New York: Rand McNally.

Camus, A. (1956). *The rebel.* New York: Random House.

Candy, P. C. (1991). *Self-direction for lifelong learning: A comprehensive guide to theory and practice.* San Francisco: Jossey-Bass.

Cantor, J. (1992). *Delivering instruction to adult learners.* Middletown, OH: Wall & Emerson.

Carlson, R. (1970). Americanization as an early twentieth century movement. *History of Education Quarterly, 10,* 441–465.

Carnevale, A., Gainer, L., & Meltzer, A. (1990). *Workplace basics: The essential skills employers want.* San Francisco: Jossey Bass.

Center for Literacy Studies (1992). *Life at the margins: Profiles of adults with low literacy skills.* (Final report). Knoxville: University of Tennessee.

Cervero, R. M. (1980). Does the Adult Performance Level Test measure functional competence? *Adult Education, 30,* 152–165.

Cervero, R. M. (1984). Is a common definition of adult literacy possible? *Adult Education Quarterly, 36,* 50–54.

Cervero, R. M. (1988). *Effective continuing education for professionals.* San Francisco: Jossey-Bass.

Cervero, R. M. (1989). Becoming more effective in everyday practice. In B. A. Quigley (Ed.), *Fulfilling the promise of adult and continuing education.* New Directions for Adult and Continuing Education, no. 44. San Francisco: Jossey-Bass.

Cervero, R. M., & Fitzpatrick, T. (1990). The enduring effects of family role and schooling on participation in adult education. *American Journal of Education, 99*(1), 77–94.

Cervero, R. M., & Wilson, A. L. (1994). The politics of responsibility: A theory of program planning practice for adult education. *Adult Education Quarterly, 45*(1), 249–268.

Chamberlain, M. (1988). *Women in academe: Progress and prospects.* New York: Russell Sage Foundation.

Chambers, I. (1990). *Border dialogues.* New York: Routledge.

Chang, K. (1989). Literacy and illiteracy in the workplace. In M. Taylor & J. Draper (Eds.), *Adult literacy perspectives* (pp. 413–422). Toronto: Culture Concepts.

Chazin, S. (1992, October). Up from illiteracy. *Reader's Digest,* pp. 130–135.

Chisman, F. P. (1989). *Jump start: The federal role in adult literacy.* Washington, DC: Project on Adult Literacy.

Chisman, F. P. (1990). Solving the literacy problem in the 1990s: The leadership agenda. In F. P. Chisman & Associates (Eds.), *Leadership for literacy* (pp. 246–264). San Francisco: Jossey-Bass.

Chisman, F. P., & Associates. (1990). *Leadership for literacy: The agenda for the 1990s.* San Francisco: Jossey-Bass.

Clark, R. (1984). Definitions of literacy: Implications for policy and practice. *Adult Literacy and Basic Education, 8,* 133–146.

Clark, R. (1990). Successful illiterate adults. Unpublished doctoral dissertation. Department of Administrative, Adult and Higher Education, University of British Columbia.

Cochran, M., & Lytle, S. (1993). *Inside/outside: Teacher research and knowledge.* New York: Teachers College Press.

Cockley, S. (1993). *The adult educator's guide to practitoner research.* Dayton, VA: The Virgina Adult Educators Research Network.

Coles, G. (1977). Dick and Jane grow up: Ideology in adult basic education readers. *Urban Education, 12*(1), 37–53.

Columbia University, Action Research Professional Development Program (1993). *Exemplary practice file: Critical thinking.* New York: Columbia University, Center for Adult Eduction.

Cook, W. (1977). *Adult literacy education in the United States.* Newark, DE: International Reading Association.

Cook-Gumperez, J. (1986). Schooling and literacy: An unchanging equation? In J. Cook-Gumperez (Ed.), *The social construction of literacy* (pp. 16–44). New York: Cambridge University Press.

Coolidge, C. (1924). New importance is attaching to the cause of education. *School Life, 10*(1), 1–2.

Cooper, G. (1980, December), Different ways of thinking. *Minority Education*, pp. 1–4.

Cooper, G. (1981). Black language and holistic cognitive style. *Western Journal of Black Studies, 5*, 201–207.

Coors ad. (1993, June). *Better Homes and Gardens*, p. 33.

Costa, M. (1988). *Adult literacy/illiteracy in the United States*. Santa Barbara, CA: ABC-Clio.

Courtney, S. (1989). Defining adult and continuing education. In S. B. Merriam & P. M. Cunningham (Eds.), *Handbook of adult and continuing education* (pp. 15–25). San Francisco: Jossey-Bass.

Courtney, S., Jha, L. R., & Babchuk, W. (1994). Like school? A grounded theory of life in an ABE/GED classroom. *Adult Basic Education, 4*(3), 172–195.

Cremin, L. (1964). *The transformation of the school: Progressivism in American education*. New York: Vintage Books.

Cross, K. P. (1982). *Adults as learners*. San Francisco: Jossey-Bass.

Cross, K. P. (1992). *Adults as learners: Increasing participation and facilitating learning*. San Francisco: Jossey-Bass.

Culleton, B. (1983). *In search of April Raintree*. Winnipeg, Manitoba: Pemmican.

Cunningham, P. (1989). Literacy definitions: Who wins and who loses? *Thresholds in Education, 15*(4), 2–5.

Daloz, L. (1986). *Effective teaching and mentoring*. San Francisco: Jossey-Bass.

Darkenwald, G. G. (1980). Continuing education and the hard-to-reach adult. In G. G. Darkenwald & G. A. Larson (Eds.), *Reaching hard-to-reach adults* (pp. 1–10). New Directions for Continuing Education, no. 8. San Francisco: Jossey-Bass.

Darkenwald, G. G., & Larson G. A. (1980). What we know about reaching hard-to-reach adults. In G. G. Darkenwald & G. A. Larson (Eds.). *Reaching hard-to-reach adults* (pp. 87–92). New Directions for Continuing Education, no. 8. San Francisco: Jossey-Bass.

Darkenwald, G. G., & Merriam, S. B. (1982). *Adult education: Foundations of practice*. New York: HarperCollins.

Darkenwald, G. G. & Valentine, T. (1984). *Outcomes and impact of adult basic education*. Research monograph no. 6. New Brunswick, NJ: Center for Adult Development, Rutgers University.

David, L. (1992). Workplace literacy programs: Important part of rescue of U.S. economy. *Adult Learning, 3*(8), 7.

DeHart, F. E., & Bleeker, G. W. (1988). Young adult realistic novels: Model for information transfer? *Journal of Youth Services in Libraries, 2*, 64–70.

Development Associates. (1992). *National evaluation of adult education programs: Profiles of service providers.* (First interim report). Washington, DC: U.S. Department of Education.

Development Associates. (1993). *National evaluation of adult education programs: Profiles of client characteristics.* (Second interim report). Arlington, VA: Development Associates.

Dickens, C. (1911). *Great expectations.* New York: Scribner. (Original work published 1861).

Dickens, C. (1953). *Bleak house.* New York: Doubleday. (Original work published 1853).

Dilts, R. (1986). *Researchers from the village.* Paper presented at the annual conference of the National Rural and Small Schools Consortium, Bellingham, WA.

Division of Adult Education and Literacy. (1993). *New section 353 training activities for state-administered adult education programs.* Washington, DC: U.S. Department of Education, Office of Vocational and Adult Education.

Djao, A. (1983). *Inequality and social policy: The sociology of welfare.* New York: Wiley.

Donnaruma, T., Cox, D., & Beder, H. (1980). Success in a high school completion program and its relation to field dependence-independence. *Adult Education, 30*(4), 222–232.

Dorland, J. R. (1978). A national focus on competency-based education. In *Proceedings of a National Workshop on Competency-Based Adult Education.* Austin: University of Texas, pp. 2–14.

Dougherty, P. (1984, December 13). Drive against illiteracy. *New York Times,* p. IV-29.

Drennon, C. (1995, Winter). There are so many questions: Inquiry-based staff development in Georgia. *Vision, 7*(2), 1.

Du Bois, W.E.B. (1962). *Black reconstruction in America.* New York: World Publishing. (Originally published 1935.)

Eberle, A., & Robinson, S. (1980). *The adult illiterate speaks out: Personal perspectives on learning to read and write.* Washington, DC: National Institute for Community Development. (ED 195 771)

Edelman, M. (1977). *Political language: Words that succeed and policies that fail.* Orlando, FL: Academic Press.

Editors. (1985, May 24). The illiteracy blight. *Publishers Weekly, 227,* 27–48.

Educational Development Laboratories. (1966). *Go: Levels BA, CA.* New York: Author.

Elias, J., & Merriam, S. B. (1980). *Philosophical foundations of adult education.* Malabar, FL: Krieger.

Eringhaus, M. (1990). Media rhetoric and adult literacy education. Symposium paper. In T. Valentine (Ed.), *Beyond rhetoric: Fundamental issues in adult literacy education.* Athens, GA: Department of Adult Education, University of Georgia.

Farra, H. E. (1988). *Demographic, economic and educational characteristics of adults who responded to the adult literacy media campaign: An urban profile.* Unpublished doctoral dissertation. University of Pittsburgh, PA.

Farrell, J. T. (1935). *Studs Lonigan.* New York: Vanguard Press.

Fernandes, W., & Tandon, R. (1981). *Participatory research and evaluation: Experiments in research as a process of liberation.* New Delhi, India: Indian Social Institute.

Finch, J. (1984). *Education as social policy.* London: Longman.

Fine, M. (1982). *Examining inequity: View from urban schools.* Unpublished manuscript, University of Pennsylvania, Philadelphia.

Fingeret, A. (1982). *The illiterate underclass: Demythologizing an American stigma.* Unpublished doctoral dissertation. Syracuse University, NY.

Fingeret, A. (1983). Social network: A new perspective on independence and illiterate adults. *Adult Education Quarterly, 3*(3), 133–145.

Fingeret, A. (1984). *Adult literacy education: Current and future directions.* Columbus: Ohio State University National Center for Research in Vocational Education.

Fingeret, A. (1989). The social and historical context of participatory literacy education. In A. Fingeret & P. Jurmo (Eds.), *Participatory literacy education.* New Directions for Adult and Continuing Education, no. 42. San Francisco: Jossey-Bass.

Fingeret, A., & Jurmo, P. (Eds.) (1989). *Participatory literacy education.* New Directions for Adult and Continuing Education, no. 42. San Francisco: Jossey-Bass.

Fingeret, H. (1985). *North Carolina ABE instructional program evaluation.* Raleigh, NC: Department of Adult and Community College Education.

Fingeret, H., & Danin, S. (1991). *"They really put a hurtin' on my brain": Learning in literacy volunteers of New York City.* Durham, NC: Literacy South.

Fitzgerald, G. (1984, February). Can the hard-to-reach adults become literate? *Lifelong Learning,* pp. 4–27.

Flannery, D. (1989). *Learning style assessment scale.* Unpublished test. Harrisburg, PA.

Flannery, D. (1993). Global and analytical ways of processing information. In D. Flannery (Ed.). *Applying cognitive learning theory to adult learning.* New Directions for Adult and Continuing Education, no. 59. San Francisco: Jossey-Bass.

For the eradication of illiteracy. (1923). *School Life, 8*(7), 151.

Forster, E. M. (1927). *Aspects of the novel.* New York: Harcourt Brace.

Foucault, M. (1972). *The archeology of knowledge and the discourse of language.* New York: HarperCollins.

Foucault, M. (1977). *Discipline and punish: The birth of the prisons.* New York: Pantheon Books.

Foucault, M. (1986). What is enlightenment? In P. Rabonow (Ed.), *The Foucault reader.* Harmondsworth, England: Penguin Books.

Fowler, R. (1992). How to build a successful program in the workplace: A business perspective. *Adult Learning, 3*(8), 17–18.

Franklin, J. H. (1967). *From slavery to freedom: A history of American Negroes* (3rd ed.). New York: Knopf.

Freire, P. (1973). *Pedagogy of the oppressed.* New York: Seabury Press.

Gaiter, D. (1982, September 16). Barbara Bush says illiteracy is an epidemic. *New York Times,* p. II-6.

Garvey, J. (Ed.). (1995). *Through the eyes of teachers: Portraits of adult learners.* New York: City University of New York.

Gaventa, J., & Horton, M. (1981). A citizens' research project in Appalachia, USA. *Convergence, 14,* 30–42.

Gee, P. (1989). Orality and literacy: From "the savage mind" to "ways with words." *Journal of Education, 1,* 39–60.

General Educational Development Testing Service. (1987). *Adult education in Texas: A survey of GED candidates and Hispanic adult education students (major findings).* Washington, DC: Author.

Genovese, E. (1972). *Roll, Jordan, roll: The world the slaves made.* New York: Pantheon Books.

Gersh, D. (1988, June 18). Illiteracy as a poverty issue. *Editor & Publisher,* pp. 20–21, 34.

Giles, D. (1985, December). Why we can't read. *Essence,* p. 34.

Gillette, A. (1987). The experimental world literacy program: A unique international effort revisited. In R. Arnove and H. Graff (Eds.), *National literacy campaigns: Historical and comparative perspectives.* New York: Plenum Press.

Giroux, H. (1983a). *Theory and resistance in education.* New York: Bergin & Garvey.

Giroux, H. (1983b). Theories of reproduction and resistance in the new sociology of education: A critical analysis. *Harvard Educational Review, 53,* 257–293.

Giroux, H., & McLaren, P. (1987). Teacher education as a counter public sphere. In T. S. Popkewitz (Ed.), *Critical studies in teacher education* (pp. 266–297). Bristol, PA: Falmer Press.

Glaser, B. & Strauss, A. (1967). *The discovery of grounded theory.* Hawthorne, NY: de Gruyter.

Goodell, W. H. (1968). *Slavery and anti-slavery: A history of the great struggle in both hemispheres with a view of the slavery question in the United States.* New York: Negro University Press.

Gordon, D. (1988). Education as text: The varieties of educational hiddenness. *Curriculum Inquiry, 4,* 425–448.

Gowen, S. (1992). *The politics of workplace literacy: A case study.* New York: Teachers College Press.

Graff, H. J. (1979). *The literacy myth: Literacy and social structure in the nineteenth-century city.* New York: Academic Press.

Graff, H. J. (1987). *The legacies of literacy: Continuities and contradictions in Western culture and society.* Bloomington, IN: Indiana University Press.

Graham, R. J. (1989a). The Irish Readers revisited: The power of the text(book). *Canadian Journal of Education, 4,* 414–425.

Graham, R. J. (1989b). Media literacy and cultural politics. *Adult Education Quarterly, 39*(3), 152–160.

Grattan, C. (1955). *In quest of knowledge.* New York: Association Press.

Greene, C. (1984, August). The ABC's of courage. *Esquire,* pp. 10, 12.

Greene, M. (1988). *The dialectic of freedom.* New York: Teachers College Press.

Griffin, C. (1987). *Adult education as social policy.* London: Croom Helm.

Griffith, W. (1990). Beyond the old rhetoric. Symposium paper. In T. Valentine (Ed.), *Beyond rhetoric: Fundamental issues in adult literacy education.* Athens, GA: Department of Adult Education, University of Georgia.

Griffith, W., & Cervero, R. M. (1977). The Adult Performance Level program: A serious and deliberate examination. *Adult Education, 27,* 209–224.

Hall, B. (1979). Participatory research: Breaking the academic monopoly. In J. Niemi (Ed.), *Viewpoints on adult education research.* Information Series No. 171. Columbus, OH: ERIC Clearinghouse on Adult, Career, and Vocational Education, pp. 43–70.

Hall, B., Gillette, A., & Tandon, R. (1982). *Creating knowledge: A monopoly? Participatory research in development.* Participatory Research Network Series, no. 1. Toronto: International Council for Adult Education.

Harman, D. (1977). The Experimental World Literacy Program: A critical assessment. [Review]. *Harvard Educational Review, 47*(3), 444–447.

Harman, D. (1987). *Illiteracy: A national dilemma.* New York: Cambridge Book Co.

Harr, J. E. (1988, December). The crusade against illiteracy. *Saturday Evening Post,* pp. 42–48.

Harris, T. L., & Hodges, R. (Eds.). (1981). *A dictionary of reading and related terms.* Newark, DE: International Reading Association.

Harvey, D. (1989). *The condition of postmodernity.* Cambridge, MA: Blackwell.

Hayes, E. (1987). *Low-literate adult basic education students' perception of deterrents to participation.* Unpublished doctoral dissertation, Rutgers University, New Brunswick, NJ.

Hayes, E. (1988). A typology of low-literate adults based on perceptions of deterrents to participation in adult basic education. *Adult Education Quarterly, 39*(1) 1–10.

Heaney, T. (1984). Action, freedom, and liberatory education. In S. B. Merriam (Ed.), *Selected writings on philosophy and adult education* (pp. 113–122). Malabar, FL: Krieger.

Hearings draw excellent response. (1991, April). *A.L.L. Points Bulletin,* pp. 5–6.

Hechinger, F. (1987, June 2). What illiteracy isn't. *New York Times,* p. III-7.

Herman, E., & Chomsky, N. (1988). *Manufacturing consent: The political economy of the mass media.* New York: Pantheon Books.

Hersey, J. (1966). *Too far to walk.* New York: Knopf.

Highlights of the National Literacy Act of 1991, Public Law 102–73. (1991). Washington, DC: Southport Institute for Policy Analysis.

Hirsch, E. (1988). *Cultural literacy: What every American needs to know.* New York: Random House.

Holsinger, E. (1993). Personal correspondence, Jan. 5.

Holsti, O. (1968). Content analysis. In G. Lindzey & E. Aronson (Eds.), *Handbook of social psychology.* Reading, MA: Addison-Wesley.

Horsman, J. (1991). From the learner's voice: Women's experience of il/literacy. In M. Taylor & J. Draper (Eds.), *Adult literacy perspectives.* Ontario, Canada: Culture Concepts Inc.

Horton, M. (1990). *The long haul: An autobiography.* New York: Doubleday.

Hubbard, R., & Power, B. (1993). Finding and framing a research question. In Patterson, Leslie et al. (Eds.), *Teachers are researchers: Reflection and action.* Newark: DE: International Reading Association.

Hunter, C., & Harman, D. (1979). *Adult illiteracy in the United States.* New York: McGraw-Hill.

The illiteracy blight. (1985, May 24). *Publisher's Weekly,* pp. 27–48.

Ilsley, P. J. (1989). The language of literacy. *Thresholds in Education, 15*(4), 6–10.

Ilsley, P. J., & Stahl, N. A. (1994). Reconceptualizing the language of adult literacy. *Literacy Harvest, 3*(1), 29–34.

Improving literacy level is crucial: NAEP. (1987, May). *Phi Delta Kappan, 68,* 711, 714.

Irish, G. (1980). Reaching the least educated adult. In G. G. Darkenwald & G. A. Larson (Eds.), *Reaching hard-to-reach adults.* New Directions for Continuing Education, no. 8. San Francisco: Jossey-Bass.

Isaac, S. (1971). *Handbook in research and evaluation.* San Diego: EDITS.

Jacobs, H. (1980, July). No arts, no letters—no society. *Vital Speeches of the Day, 46,* 562–565.

Jenkins, P. A. (1983). *Southern Blacks: Accounts of learning to read before 1861.* ERIC Reproduction Service No. ED 246 394.

Jenkins, W. S. (1960). *Pro-slavery thought in the old south.* Gloucester, MA: P. Smith.

Johnston, L., & Anderson, S. H. (1983, May 19). A boost for literacy. *New York Times,* p. II-3.

Johnston, W., & Packer, A. (1987). *Workforce 2000: Work and workers for the 21st century.* Indianapolis: Hudson Institute.

Johnstone, J., & Rivera, R. (1965). *Volunteers for learning.* Chicago: Aldine.

Jordan, P. (1987, August). Bertha's triumph. *Reader's Digest,* pp. 55–59.

Judge announces strategy to curb black illiteracy. (1986, June 30). *Jet, 70,* 22.

Jump, J. (1967). Lord Byron. In B. Ford (Ed.), *The pelican guide to English literature from Blake to Byron.* Baltimore, MD: Penguin Books, Ltd.

Karabel, J., & Halsey, A. (1977). Educational research: A review and an interpretation. In J. Karabel & A. Halsey (Eds.), *Power and ideology in education* (pp. 1–85). New York: Oxford University Press.

Kazemak, F. E. (1988a). Necessary changes: Professional involvement in adult literacy programs. *Harvard Educational Review, 58*(4), 464–487.

Kazemak, F. E. (1988b). Women and adult literacy: Considering the other half of the house. *Lifelong learning: An omnibus of practice and research, 11*(4), 15, 23, 24.

Kazemak, F. E. (1995). Dead letters and blank girls: Workplace literacy through the lens of literature. *Adult Basic Education, 5*(2), 98–109.

Keddie, N. (1980). Adult education: An ideology of individualism. In J. Thompson (Ed.), *Adult education for a change* (pp. 45–64). London: Hutchinson.

Kemmis, S., & McTaggart, R. (1984). *The action research planner.* Victoria, Australia: Deaken University.

Kerlinger, F. (1964). *Foundations of behavioral research.* Austin, TX: Holt, Rinehart and Winston.

Kilgore, H. (1952). Literacy and the national welfare. *School Life, 34*(6), 90–91.

Kirsch, I., & Guthrie, J. (1984). Adult reading practice for work and leisure. *Adult Education Quarterly, 34*(4), 213–232.

Kirsch, I., & Jungeblut, A. (1986). *Literacy: Profiles of America's young adults.* Princeton, NJ: Educational Testing Service.

Kirsch, I., Jungeblut, A., Jenkins, L., & Kolstad, A. (1993). *Adult literacy in America: A first look at the results of the National Adult Literacy Survey.* Washington, DC: U.S. Department of Education.

Klein, H. (1967). *Slavery in the Americas: A comparative study of Virginia and Cuba.* Chicago: Ivan R. Dee.

Knibbe, M., & Dusewicsz, R. (1990). *A research study in retention.* (AdvancE Report No. 98–0027). Harrisburg, PA: Pennsylvania Department of Education.

Knowles, M. (1980). *The modern practice of adult education.* New York: Cambridge Book Co.

Koloski, J. (1989). Enhancing the field's image through professionalism and practice. In B. A. Quigley (Ed.), *Fulfilling the promise of adult and continuing education.* New Directions for Adult and Continuing Education, no. 44. San Francisco: Jossey-Bass.

Kozol, J. (1985). *Illiterate America.* New York: Doubleday.

Kretovics, J. (1985). Critical literacy: Challenging the assumptions of the mainstream educational theory. *Journal of Education, 167*(2), 50–62.

Lankshear, C., & McLaren, P. (Eds.). (1993). *Critical literacy: Politics, praxis, and the postmodern.* Albany: State University of New York Press.

Lash, S. (1990). *Sociology of postmodernism.* London: Routledge.

Laubach, F. C., Kirk, E. M., & Laubach, R. C. (1984). *Laubach way to reading,* Skill books 1–4. Syracuse: New Readers Press.

Lees, R., & Smith, G. (Eds.). (1980). Action research in community development. New York: Routledge.

Leigh, E. (1871). Illiteracy in the United States. In H. Barnard, *Special report of the commissioner of education on the condition and improvement of schools in the District of Columbia.* Washington, DC: U.S. Government Printing Office.

Lenknowsky, R. S. (1987). Bibliotherapy: A review and analysis of the literature. *Journal of Special Education, 21,* 123–132.

Levine, K. (1982). Functional literacy: Fond illusions and false economics. *Harvard Educational Review, 52,* 249–266.

Lindeman, E. C. (1961). *The meaning of adult education.* Montreal: Harvest House. (Originally published 1926.)

Lowe, J. (1995). New year's resolution: Tell the facts as well as the stories. *GED Items, 12*(6), p. 2.

Luttrell, W. (1996). Taking care of literacy: One feminists's critique. *Educational Policy, 10*(3), 342–365.

Lyman, B. G., & Collins, M. D. (1990). Critical reading: A redefinition. *Reading Research and Instruction, 3,* 56–63.

Lyotard, J. (1984). *The postmodern condition.* Minneapolis: University of Minnesota Press.

Lytle, S., & Cochran-Smith, M. (1990). Learning from teacher research: A working typology. *Teachers College Record, 92*(1), pp. 83–103.

MacDonald, B. (1994, Winter). Director's column. *The Community Exchange, 3*(2), p. 2.

MacKeracher, D. (1991). Women and literacy. In M. Taylor & J. Draper (Eds.), *Adult literacy perspectives*. Ontario, Canada: Culture Concepts.

Manley, D. (1989, September 25). Until he tackled his illiteracy, the Redskins' gridiron terror lived in fear of his ABC's. *People,* pp. 49–52.

Manning, A. (1983). *Prosperous illiterates*. Unpublished doctoral dissertation. Department of Adult Education, Syracuse University, Syracuse, New York.

Marcuse, H. (1966). *One-dimensional man*. Boston: Beacon Press.

Martin, J. R. (1976). What should we do with a hidden curriculum when we find one? *Curriculum Inquiry, 2,* 135–152.

Martin, L. G. (1989). Recruiting and retaining adult students in literacy and ABE. In P. S. Cookson (Ed.), *Recruiting and retaining adult students*. New Directions for Adult and Continuing Education, no. 41. San Francisco: Jossey-Bass.

Maskin, M. (1973). *Black education and the New Deal: The urban experience*. Unpublished doctoral dissertation, Department of History, New York University.

Maugham, W. S. (1957). *The verger*. New York: Random House.

Mayo, A. (1898, September). The significance of illiteracy in the United States. *Education,* pp. 30–36.

McDonald, R. (1974). Achieving school failure: An anthropological approach to illiteracy and social stratification. In G. Spindler (Ed.), *Education and cultural proces: Toward an anthropology of education*. Austin, TX: Holt, Rinehart and Winston.

McDonald, K., & Wood, G. (1993). Surveying adult education practitioners about ethical issues. *Adult Education Quarterly, 43,* 243–257.

McGovern, C. (1977). The relative efficacy of bibliotherapy and assertion training on the assertiveness levels of a general population and a library personnel population. *Dissertation Abstracts International, 37,* 6954A.

McGovern, G. (May 1980) Illiteracy in America: A time for examination. *USA Today, 108,* pp. 24–26.

McKenzie, L. (1975). Analysis of bildungsroman literature as a research modality in adult education: An inquiry. *Adult Education, 25,* 209–216.

McKenzie, L. (1976, April). *Literary life-cycle research as an atypical research modality for adult education*. Paper presented at the Adult Education Research Conference, Toronto, Ontario.

McKenzie, L. (1985). Philosophical orientations of adult educators. *Lifelong Learning, 9,* 18–20.

McLaren, P. (1988). Culture or canon? Critical pedagogy and the politics of literacy [Review of *Reading the word and the world*]. *Harvard Educational Review, 58*(2), 213–234.

McLaren, P., & Lankshear, C. (1993). Critical literacy and the postmodern turn. In P. McLaren & C. Lankshear (Eds.), *Critical literacy: Politics, praxis, and the postmodern* (pp. 379–419). Albany, NY: State University of New York Press.

The Media Institute (1980). *The public's right to know, communicator's response to the Kemeny commission report: a survey.* Washington, DC: The Media Institute.

Meier, A., & Rudwick, E. (1976). *From plantation to ghetto* (3rd Ed.). New York: Hill and Wang.

Mekosh-Rosenbaum, V. (n.d.). *Action research guide for adult literacy practitioners.* Bethlehem, PA: Lehigh University.

Mendel, R. (1988). *Meeting the economic challenge of the 1990's: Workforce literacy in the South.* Chapel Hill, NC: MDC, Inc.

Menzies, H. (1987). Private and public policymaking: A case study in policymaking alternatives. In F. Cassidy & R. Faris (Eds.), *Choosing our future: Adult education and public policy in Canada.* Toronto: Ontario Institute for Studies in Education Press Press.

Merriam, S. B. (1980). *Coping with male mid-life: A systematic analysis using literature as a data source.* Washington, D.C.: University Press of America, Inc.

Merriam, S. B. (1988a). *Case study research in education: A qualitative approach.* San Francisco: Jossey-Bass.

Merriam, S. B. (Ed.). (1988b). *Themes of adulthood through literature.* New York: Teachers College Press.

Merriam, S. B., & Cunningham, P. M. (Eds.). (1989). *The handbook of adult and continuing education.* San Francisco: Jossey-Bass.

Merriam, S. B., & Simpson, E. (1984). *A guide to research for educators and trainers of adults.* Malabar, FL: Kreiger.

Merrifield, J. (1990). Illiteracy, the workplace, and the global economy. Symposium paper. In T. Valentine (Ed.), *Beyond rhetoric: Fundamental issues in adult literacy education.* Athens, GA: Department of Adult Education, University of Georgia.

Mezirow, J. (1978). Professional misgivings about adult basic education. *Reports Magazine, 17,* 7–9.

Mezirow, J., Darkenwald, G. G., & Knox, A. (1975). *Last gamble on education.* Washington, DC: Adult Education Association.

Miles, M., & Huberman, A. (1984). *Qualitative data analysis: A sourcebook of new methods.* Thousand Oaks, CA: Sage.

Minnick, E., O'Barr, J., & Rosenfeld, R. (Eds.). (1988). *Reconstructing the academy: Women's education and women's studies.* Chicago: University of Chicago Press.

Mitchell, W. O. (1969). *Who has seen the wind.* Toronto: Macmillan.

Morrison, J. (1989). *Camps & classrooms: A pictorial history of Frontier College.* Toronto: Frontier College Press.

Mott basic language skills program (1965). Books 1304, 1305, 1306. Galien, MI: Allied Education Council.

Murphy, C. (1985). *Challenger adult reading series.* Books 1 & 3. Syracuse, NY: New Readers Press.

National Adult Education Professional Development Consortium. (1991). *Annual report: The adult education program.* Washington, DC: Author.

National Advisory Council on Adult Education. (1987). *Annual Report.* Washington, DC: Author.

National Center for Education Statistics. (1995). *The digest of education statistics.* Washington, DC: U.S. Department of Education.

National Literacy Act of 1991. (1991). Washington, D.C.: U.S. Government Printing Office.

National organizations will combat illiteracy. (1924). *School Life, 9*(6), 128.

Neff, M. (1965). Toward literacy in the United States. *Wilson Library Bulletin, 39,* 885–886.

Nelson, L., Haggerson, N., & Bowman, A. (1992). *Informing educational policy through interpretive inquiry.* Lancaster, PA: Technomic Publishing.

Niemi, J., & Nagle, J. (1979). In P. Langerman & D. Smith (Eds.), *Managing adult and continuing education programs and staff.* Washington, DC: National Association for Public Continuing and Adult Education.

Nurs, J. R., & Singh, R. (1993). *Atlanta family literacy collaborative. Interviews of participants: Year 1 and 2.* (ED 365 797).

O'Toole, P. (1985, September). The illiteracy epidemic. *Glamour,* pp. 369, 414–415.

Oxley, H. (1937, January). Meeting problems of Negro enrollees. *School Life, ,* 145–155.

Pates, A. (1992). Collaborative research in ABE. *Vision, 4*(2), 1, 3–4.

Pendered, D.(1991, September 2). The debate rages: What's the best way to teach reading? *Atlanta Journal and Constitution,* p. A-7.

Philipi, J. (1991). *Literacy at work: The workbook for program developers.* New York: Simon & Schuster.

Pugsley, R. S. (1990). *Vital statistics: Who is served by the adult education program?* Washington, DC: U.S. Department of Education, Division of Adult Education and Literacy.

Pugsley, R. S. (1993). *New section 353 training activities for state-administered adult education programs.* Washington, DC: U.S. Department of Education.

Qi, S. (1986, May). *Why did they drop out? And who came back? Comparing high school graduates, dropouts, and returnees using NELS:88.* Paper presented at the Commission on Adult Basic Education Conference, Pittsburgh, PA.

Quigley, B. A. (1987a). Learning to work with them: Analyzing non-participation in adult basic education through resistance theory. *Adult Literacy and Basic Education, 11*(2), 63–70.

Quigley, B. A. (1987b). *The resisters: An analysis of nonparticipation in adult basic education.* Unpublished doctoral dissertation. Northern Illinois University.

Quigley, B. A. (1989). Literacy as social policy: Issues for America in the 21st century. *Thresholds in Education, 15*(4), 11–15.

Quigley, B. A. (1990a). Hidden logic: Resistance and reproduction in adult literacy and basic education. *Adult Education Quarterly, 40*(2), 103–115.

Quigley, B. A. (1990b). *Reasons for resistance to ABE and recommendations for new delivery models and instructional strategies for the future.* Harrisburg, PA: AdvancE Publishing, Pennsylvania Department of Education.

Quigley, B. A. (1990c). "This immense evil": The history of literacy education as social policy. Symposium paper. In T. Valentine (Ed.), *Beyond rhetoric: Fundamental issues in adult literacy education.* Athens: Department of Adult Education, University of Georgia.

Quigley, B. A. (1991a). Exception and reward: The history and social policy development of the GED in the U.S. and Canada. *Adult Basic Education, 1*(1), 27–43.

Quigley, B. A. (1991b). Shaping literacy: An historical analysis of literacy education as social policy. In *Proceedings: 32nd Annual Adult Research Conference* (pp. 218–225). Norman: University of Oklahoma.

Quigley, B. A. (1991c). We the governed: The National Literacy Act of 1991. *Adult Basic Education, 1*(3), 168–172.

Quigley, B. A. (1992a). Looking back in anger: The influences of schooling on illiterate adults. *Journal of Education, 174*(10), 104–121.

Quigley, B. A. (1992b). *Understanding and overcoming resistance to adult literacy education.* State College, PA: Institute for the Study of Adult Literacy.

Quigley, B. A. (1993a). To shape the future: Towards a framework for adult education social policy research and action. *International Journal of Lifelong Education, 12*(2), 117–127.

Quigley, B. A. (1993b). *Retaining reluctant learners in adult literacy programs.* State College, PA: Institute for the Study of Adult Literacy.

Quigley, B. A., & Holsinger, E. (1993). "Happy consciousness": Ideology and hidden curricula in literacy education. *Adult Education Quarterly, 44*(1), 17–33.

Reading for today. (1987). Books 2–5. Austin, TX: Steck-Vaughn.

Recent educational conferences held in Washington, D.C. (1930). *School Life, 15*(5), p. 91.

Reissman, F. (1962). *The culturally deprived child.* New York: HarperCollins.

Richardson, E. (1926). California is making determined efforts to overcome illiteracy. *School Life, 11*(7), 136.

Richler, M. (1974). *The apprenticeship of Duddy Kravitz.* Toronto: McClelland and Stewart.

Rischin, M. (Ed.). (1968). *The American gospel of success: Individualism and beyond.* Chicago: Quadrangle.

Rockhill, K. (1987). Literacy as threat/desire: Longing to be somebody. In J. Gaskel and P. McLaren (Eds.), *Women and education: A Canadian perspective* (pp. 315–333). Calgary, Alberta: Detselig Enterprises.

Rogers, C., & Nelson, L. (1969). *The nature of teaching.* Waltham, MA: Blaisdell Publishing.

Rohter, L. (1986, April 13). The scourge of adult illiteracy. *New York Times,* pp. XII-33–37.

Roth, P. (1959). The conversion of the Jews. In *Goodbye, Columbus and five short stories.* Boston: Houghton Mifflin.

Runcie, J. (1980). *Experiencing social research.* Georgetown, Ontario: Dorsey Press.

Russell, D., & Shrodes, C. (1950). Contributions of research in bibliotherapy to the language arts program. *School Review, 58,* 411–420.

Russell, W. (1942). Shortages in the midst of plenty. *Teachers College Record, 44*(2), 75–83.

Ryan, W. (1976). *Blaming the victim.* New York: Random House.

Salinger, J. D. (1951). *The catcher in the rye.* New York: Bantam Books.

Schied, F. (1993). *Learning in social context: Workers and adult education in nineteenth century Chicago.* DeKalb: Northern Illinois University, LEPS Press.

School principals issue certificates. (1922). *School Life, 8*(1), 71.

Schumacher, S., & McMillan, J. (1993). *Research in Education.* New York: HarperCollins.

Scribner, S. (1988). Literacy in three metaphors. In E. Kintgen, B. Kroll, & M. Rose (Eds.), *Perspectives on literacy* (pp. 71–81). Cardondale and Edwardsville: Southern Illinois University Press.

Shaw, G. B. (1964). *Pygmalion.* New York: Penguin Books. (Original work published 1916).

Shrank, F., & Engels, D. (1981). Bibliotherapy as a counselling adjunct: Research and findings. *Personnel and Guidance Journal, 60,* 143–147.

Shreeve, J. (1994, September). *Smithsonian,* pp. 17–18, 20.

Shrodes, C. (1955). Bibliography. *Reading Teacher, 9,* 24–29.

Silver, H. (1980). *Education and the social condition.* London: Methuen.

Smart, B. (1993). *Postmodernity.* New York: Routledge.

Smith, E. (1977). Foreword. In W. D. Cook, *Adult literacy education in the United States* (pp. 5–6). Newark, DE: International Reading Association.

Smith, G. (1988, December). A success as a teacher and a builder, John Cocoran had a humiliating secret: He couldn't read or write. *People,* pp. 199, 209.

Smith, G. (1990, December). The haunted man. *Reader's Digest,* pp. 158–162.

Smith, L. (1989, January). America's need to read. *Harper's Bazaar,* pp. 70–71.

Soifer, R., Irwin, M., Crumrine, B., Honzaki, E., Simmons, B., & Young, D. (1990). *The complete theory-to-practice handbook of adult literacy: Curriculum design and teaching approaches.* New York: Teachers College Press.

Solarzano, R. W. (1989). *Reducing illiteracy in California: Review of effective practices.* Final Report. (ED 335 526).

Spiegelberg, H. (1960). *The essentials of the phenomenological method.* The Hague, Netherlands: Martinus Nijhoff.

Stampp, K. (1956). *The peculiar institution: Slavery in the Antebellum.* New York: Knopf.

Stanage, S. (1986). Unrestraining liberty: Adult education and the empowerment of persons. *Adult Education Quarterly, 36,* 123–129.

Stanage, S. (1987). *Adult education and phenomenological research: New directions for theory, practice, and research.* Malabar, FL: Krieger.

Stavisky, S. (1954, July). Ignorance cuts production and defense. *Nation's Business, 42,* 23–24.

Stead, R. (1926). *Grain.* New York: George H. Doran.

Stechert, K. (1985, November). Illiteracy in America: The shocking silent crisis. *Better Homes and Gardens,* pp. 27–28.

Steck-Vaughn Company. (1974). *Steps to learning,* Books 1–2; Adult Reader. Austin, TX: Author.

Steck-Vaughn Company. (1987). *Reading for today,* Books 2–5. Austin, TX: National Education Corporation.

Stein, S., & Sperazi, L. (1991, October). *Workplace education and the transformation of the workplace.* Paper presented at the American Association of Adult and Continuing Educators annual conference, Montreal, Canada.

Stevens, E., Jr. (1987). The anatomy of mass literacy in nineteenth-century United States. In R. Arnove & H. Graff (Eds.), *National literacy campaigns: Historical and comparative perspectives.* New York: Plenum Press.

Sticht, T., & Armstrong, W. (1996). *Understanding adult literacy: Insights from 75 years of quantitative data.* El Cajon, CA: Applied Behavioral and Cognitive Sciences, Inc.

Sticht, T., Armstrong, W., Hickey, D., & Caylor, J. (1987). *Cast-off youth: Policy and training methods from the military experience.* New York: Praeger.

Stubblefield, H., & Keane, P. (1989). The history of adult and continuing education. In S. B. Merriam & P. M. Cunningham (Eds.), *Handbook of adult and continuing education* (pp. 26–36). San Francisco: Jossey-Bass.

Stubblefield, H., & Keane, P. (1994). *Adult education in the American experience.* San Francisco: Jossey-Bass.

Stuckey, J. (1991). *The violence of literacy.* Portsmouth, NH: Boynton/Cook.

Studebaker, J. (1940). Now! *School Life, 26*(1), 1.

Sullivan Associates. (1966). *Programmed reading for adults.* Books 5–8. New York: McGraw-Hill.

Thomas, A. (1976). *Adult basic education and literacy activities in Canada.* Toronto: World Literacy of Canada.

Thompson, J. (1980). Adult education and the disadvantaged. In J. Thompson (Ed.), *Adult education for a change* (pp. 83–108). London: Hutchinson.

Thrall, W., Hibbard, A., & Holman, C. (1960). *A handbook to literature.* New York: Odyssey Press.

Townsend, P. (1975). *Sociology and social policy.* New York: Penguin Books.

Turner, R. (1994, May). Round two in Topeka. *Emerge,* pp. 34–42.

Twain, M. (1958). *The Adventures of Huckleberry Finn.* Boston: Houghton Mifflin. (Original work published 1884).

U.S. Congress, Office of Technology Assessment. (1993). *Adult literacy and new technologies: Tools for a lifetime* (Final Report No. OTA-SET-550). Washington, DC: U.S. Government Printing Office.

U.S. Department of Education, Division of Adult Education and Literacy. (1993). *Adult education delivery service trends program year 1990–91.* Washington, DC: Author.

U.S. Department of Education, Division of Adult Education and Literacy. (1995). *Adult education program statistics for fiscal year 1994.* Washington, DC: Author.

U.S. Department of Labor & U.S. Department of Education. (1988). *The bottom line: Basic skills in the workplace.* Washington, DC: Authors.

Uhland, R. L. (1995). *Learning strategy behaviors demonstrated by low-literate adults engaged in self-directed learning.* Unpublished doctoral dissertation, Pennsylvania State University, State College.

UNESCO & UNDP Secretariats. (1976). *The experimental world literacy program: A critical assessment.* Paris: UNESCO Press.

Valentine, T. (1990). What motivates adults to participate in the federal adult basic education program? *Research on Adult Basic Education, 1,* 1–2.

Vallance, E. (1973). Hiding the hidden curriculum. *Curriculum Theory Network, 4*(1), 5–21.

Vannozzi-Knibbe, M. (1990). *A research study in retention.* Unpublished project report. Philadelphia, PA: The Center for Literacy.

Van Tilburg, E., & DuBois, J. (1989, April). *Literacy students' perceptions of successful participation in adult education: A cross-cultural approach through expectancy valence.* Proceedings, 30th Annual Adult Education Research Conference (pp. 308–313). Madison: University of Wisconsin.

Vella, J. (1994). *Learning to listen, learning to teach.* San Francisco: Jossey-Bass.

Verner, C. (1967). *Pole's history of adult schools.* Washington, DC: Adult Education Associates of the United States.

Verner, C. (1973). Illiteracy and poverty. *B.T.S.D. Review, 9*(2), 9–15.

Vroom, V. (1964). *Work and motivation.* New York: Wiley. Washington, DC: Adult Education Associates of the United States.

Wagner, D. (1991). *International Yearbook of Education. Literacy: developing the future,* vol. XLIII. Paris: United Nations Educational, Scientific, and Cultural Organization.

Walker, A. (1982). *The color purple.* Orlando, FL: Harcourt Brace.

Wantuck, M. (1984, June). Can your employees read this? *Nation's Business, 72,* 34–37.

Warner, L. (1980). The myth of bibliotherapy. *School Library Journal, 27,* 107–111.

Weber, T. (1978). *Deep like the rivers: Education in the slave quarter, 1831–1865.* New York: Norton.

Webster's new world dictionary of the American language. (1982). (2nd ed.). New York: Simon & Schuster.

Weisbord, H. (1987). *Productive workplaces: Organizing and managing for dignity, meaning, and community.* San Francisco: Jossey-Bass.

Welch, S. (1990). *A feminist ethic of risk.* Philadelphia: Fortress Press.

Wellborn, S. (1982, May 17). Ahead: A nation of illiterates? *U.S. News & World Report, 92,* pp. 53–56.

Welton, R. (Ed.) (1995). *In defense of the lifeworld: Critical perspectives on adult learning.* Albany: State University of New York Press.

Whipple, C. (1968). The effects of short-term bibliotherapy on the personality and academic achievement of reformatory inmate students. *Dissertation Abstracts-International, 29,* 2214B.

Whitehead, J. (1989). How do we improve research-based professionalism in education? *British Educational Research Journal, 15*(1), 1–17.

Willis, P. (1977). *Learning to labour: Why working class kids take working class jobs.* New York: Columbia University Press.

Winchester, I. (1990). The standard picture of literacy and its critics. *Comparative Education Review, 34,* 21–40.

Witkin, H. A. (1967). A cognitive style approach to cross-cultural research. *International Journal of Psychology, 2*(4), 233–250.

Witkin, H. A., Oitman, P. K., Raskin, E., & Karp, S. A. (1971). *A manual for the embedded figures tests.* Palo Alto, CA: Consulting Psychologist Press.

Wlodkowski, R. (1988). *Enhancing adult motivation to learn.* San Francisco: Jossey-Bass.

Woodward, C. (1964). The birth of Jim Crow. *American Heritage, 15*(3), 52–55, 100–103.

Wyse, L. (1989, September). The way we are. *Good Housekeeping,* p. 308.

Yetman, N. R. (1970). *Voices from slavery.* Austin, TX: Holt, Rinehart and Winston.

Ziegahn, L. (1992). Learning, literacy, and participation: Sorting out priorities. *Adult Education Quarterly, 43*(1), 30–49.

Ziegler, W. (1977). *The future of adult education and learning in the United States.* Syracuse, NY: Educational Policy Research Center, Syracuse University Research Corporation.

Zucaro, B. (1972). The use of bibliotherapy among sixth graders to affect attitude change toward American Negroes. *Dissertation Abstracts International, 33,* 1340A.

Name Index

Subject Index

85–89; history of, 71–89; illiteracy as, 27–28; and morality, 73–74; patriotic purposes of, 83–85; for redistribution of social justice, 81–83; for regulation of slaves and immigrants, 70, 73–79; and social responsibility, 35, 68–69

Societal threat, illiteracy as, 37, 40, 70–73, 91

Stanley and Iris (movie), 26, 57

Stereotypes, 51–62: of learners' attitudes, 174; of natural man, 60–62; of simple African Americans, 58, 59; of simple male American worker, 54–58; of simple southern whites, 58–59; society's need for, 41–42

Students. *See* Learners; Learners, at-risk; Teacher-student matching

Subordinate group regulation: in hidden curricula, 156; as social policy, 70, 73–79

T

Teacher-student matching: and placement, 135–136; and retention, 184–189, 231–232

Textbooks and curricula, 137–159; commercial materials as, 158; content analysis of, 141–155; gender issues in, 144–147; and hidden curricula, 140–141, 156; learner-written, 157; literary fiction in, 198–201; political perspective characteristics in, 139–141; puni-

tive view in, 140, 144; racism in, 147–149; selection of, 156–158; social class issues in, 149–154; sources of, 157–158; teacher objections to, 155–156

U

UNESCO's Experimental World Literacy Program, 17

U.S. News & World Report, 39–40, 70–71, 72

V

Vocational literacy education, 109–110, 111–117; and acquisition of knowledge, 130; and action research, 234; approaches in, 111–112; and employment and income gains, 112–113; text selection in, 157

Volunteerism, 9, 25–26, 27

W

Women: denial of literacy education for, 73; as literacy volunteers, 25–26, 27; sexist images of in curricula, 144–147

Working philosophies, 109–127; as basis for program design and change, 134–135, 184–186; development of, 128–134; ethical dimensions of, 221–223; and student-teacher matching, 135–136

Workplace literacy programs, 79